The Child
and Its Family

Genesis of Behavior

Series Editors: **MICHAEL LEWIS**
*The Infant Laboratory, Institute for the Study of Exceptional Children
Educational Testing Service, Princeton, New Jersey*

and **LEONARD A. ROSENBLUM**
*State University of New York, Downstate Medical Center
Brooklyn, New York*

The Child and Its Family

Edited by

MICHAEL LEWIS

Institute for the Study of Exceptional Children
Educational Testing Service
Princeton, New Jersey

and

LEONARD A. ROSENBLUM

Downstate Medical Center
Brooklyn, New York

PLENUM PRESS · *NEW YORK AND LONDON*

Library of Congress Cataloging in Publication Data

Main entry under title:

The Child and its family.

(Genesis of behavior; v. 2)
Includes index.
1. Child development. 2. Socialization. 3. Family. I. Lewis, Michael, 1937 (Jan. 10)-
II. Rosenblum, Leonard A. III. Series. [DNLM: 1. Infant. 2. Family. 3. Parent-child
relations. 4. Sibling relations. W1 GE275 v. 2/WS105.5.F2 C536]
HQ772.C43   155.4'18   78-27020
ISBN 0-306-40112-6

35,154

Chapter 3, "Conceptualization of Father Influences in the Infancy
Period" by Frank A. Pedersen, Leon J. Yarrow, Barbara J. Anderson,
and Richard L. Cain, Jr., is exempt from the general copyright
for this title. This chapter was prepared under U.S. Government
auspices, and, therefore, is in the public domain.

© 1979 Plenum Press, New York
A Division of Plenum Publishing Corporation
227 West 17th Street, New York, N.Y. 10011

Contributors

HEIDELISE ALS, *Child Development Unit, Children's Hospital Medical Center, Boston, Massachusetts*

BARBARA J. ANDERSON, *National Institute of Child Health and Human Development, Auburn Building, Room 220, Bethesda, Maryland*

T. BERRY BRAZELTON, *Child Development Unit, Children's Hospital Medical Center, Boston, Massachusetts*

JEANNE BROOKS-GUNN, *Infant Laboratory, Institute for the Study of Exceptional Children, Educational Testing Service, Princeton, New Jersey*

RICHARD L. CAIN, JR., *National Institute of Child Health and Human Development, Auburn Building, Room 220, Bethesda, Maryland*

LINDSAY CHASE-LANSDALE, *Department of Psychology, University of Wisconsin, Madison, Wisconsin*

JUDY DUNN, *Medical Research Council Unit on the Development and Integration of Behaviour, University Sub-Department of Animal Behaviour, Madingley, Cambridge, England*

CAROLYN P. EDWARDS, *School of Education, Skinner Hall, University of Massachusetts, Amherst, Massachusetts*

TONI FALBO, *Department of Educational Psychology, University of Texas at Austin, Austin, Texas*

CANDICE FEIRING, *Infant Laboratory, Institute for the Study of Exceptional Children, Educational Testing Service, Princeton, New Jersey*

GORDON G. GALLUP, JR., *Department of Psychology, State University of New York, Albany, New York*

CHARLES GREENBAUM, *Department of Psychology, Duke University, Durham, North Carolina*

JAMES E. JOHNSON, *Psychology Department, University of Wisconsin, Madison, Wisconsin*

CAROL KENDRICK, *Medical Research Council Unit on the Development and Integration of Behaviour, University Sub-Department of Animal Behaviour, Madingley, Cambridge, England*

MICHAEL LAMB, *Department of Psychology, University of Michigan, Ann Arbor, Michigan*

RIVKA LANDAU, *Department of Psychology, Duke University, Durham, North Carolina*

MICHAEL LEWIS, *Infant Laboratory, Institute for the Study of Exceptional Children, Educational Testing Service, Princeton, New Jersey*

EDWARD MUELLER, *Psychology Department, Boston University, Boston, Massachusetts*

ANN McGILLICUDDY-DE LISI, *Educational Testing Service, Princeton, New Jersey*

MARGARET TRESCH OWEN, *Department of Psychology, University of Wisconsin, Madison, Wisconsin*

FRANK PEDERSEN, *National Institute of Child Health and Human Development, Auburn Building, Room 220, Bethesda, Maryland*

EDWARD H. PLIMPTON, *Downstate Medical Center, Department of Psychiatry, Brooklyn, New York*

LEONARD A. ROSENBLUM, *Downstate Medical Center, Department of Psychiatry, Brooklyn, New York*

IRVING SIGEL, *Educational Testing Service, Princeton, New Jersey*

STEVEN SUOMI, *Psychology Department, University of Wisconsin, Madison, Wisconsin*

EDWARD TRONICK, *Child Development Unit, Children's Hospital Medical Center, Boston, Massachusetts*

LEON J. YARROW, *National Institute of Child Health and Human Development, Auburn Building, Room 220, Bethesda, Maryland*

MICHAEL W. YOGMAN, *Child Development Unit, Children's Hospital Medical Center, Boston, Massachusetts*

Preface

How are we to understand the complex forces that shape human behavior? A variety of diverse perspectives, drawing upon studies of human behavioral ontogeny, as well as humanity's evolutionary heritage, seem to provide the best likelihood of success. It is in the attempt to synthesize such potentially disparate approaches to human development into an integrated whole that we undertake this series on the Genesis of Behavior.

In many respects, the incredible burgeoning of research in child development over the last decade or two seems like a thousand lines of inquiry spreading outward in an incoherent starburst of effort. The need exists to provide, on an ongoing basis, an arena of discourse within which the threads of continuity between those diverse lines of research on human development can be woven into a fabric of meaning and understanding. Scientists, scholars, and those who attempt to translate their efforts into the practical realities of the care and guidance of infants and children are the audience that we seek to reach. Each requires the opportunity to see—to the degree that our knowledge in given areas permits—various aspects of development in a coherent, integrated fashion. It is hoped that this series, which will bring together research on infant biology, developing infant capacities, animal models, the impact of social, cultural, and familial forces on development, and the distorted products of such forces under certain circumstances, will serve these important social and scientific needs.

Each volume in this series will deal with a single topic that has broad significance for our understanding of human development. Into its focus on a specific area, each volume will bring both empirical and theoretical perspectives and analysis at the many levels of investigation necessary to a balanced appreciation of the complexity of the problem at hand. Thus, each volume will consider the confluence of the genetic, psychological, and neurophysiological factors that influence the individual infant and the dyadic, familial, and societal contexts within which development occurs. Moreover, each volume will bring together the vantage points provided by studies of human infants and pertinent aspects of animal behavior, with particular emphasis on nonhuman primates.

Just as this series will draw upon the special expertise and viewpoints of workers in many disciplines, it is our hope that the product of these labors will speak to the needs and interests of a diverse audience, including physiologists, ethologists, sociologists, psychologists, pediatricians, obstetricians, and clinicians and scientists in many related fields. As in years past, we hold to our original objectives in this series of volumes to provide both stimulation and guidance to all among us who are concerned with humans, their past, their present, and their future.

The present volume represents an effort at integrating our past attempts to show the broad and complex social nexus into which the eloping organism must adapt. With increasing clarity it has become apparent that the infant enters into the world with the potential to influence and be influenced by a variety of persons and events. It is most of all a social world full of conspecifics, a small segment of which shares the child's gene pool; a larger segment of which will directly influence the child; and finally the largest segment, which forms the background in which these other interactions will take place. The smallest segment we call the family; the larger, friends, teachers, acquaintances, and peers; and the largest segment, the culture.

The current volume is concerned with the immediate social world into which a child is born and within which it develops. The various chapters deal at first with the structure of the total social network within which the infant and its family must function. The impact of societal demands, the role of the family constellation in the emerging socialization and development of the infant are considered from a broad, inclusive perspective. Subsequent chapters deal with the more specific elements of the infant's family, including the separable but inherently coalescing roles of mother, father, and older and younger siblings in providing the major context for the infant's social development. But the social world of the child goes beyond its own family. Hence, other chapters deal with the ingredients of the immediate social world that surrounds the infant and its family, and consider the role of peers and friends. In addition, these chapters consider the developing differentiation of the infant's social responsiveness toward the panoply of social objects with which it comes into contact. Finally, the socialization network of the human child does not appear to be a unique evolutionary emergence. Hence, various chapters deal with the developing social character of nonhuman primates and the role of various members of their kinship and social group in shaping the development of adaptive behavior in their species, and the implication of such material for enhancing our understanding of the social development of the human child.

The chapters in this volume derive from papers presented and discussed at a conference on the social nexus held under the auspices and with the support of the Educational Testing Service in Princeton, New Jersey. The participants in the conference were T. Berry Brazelton, Jeanne Brooks-Gunn, Judy Dunn, Carolyn P. Edwards, Nathan Fox, Toni Falbo, Candice Feiring, Gordon G. Gallup, Jr., Charles Greenbaum, Michael Lamb, Michael Lewis, Edward Mueller, Frank Pedersen, Edward Plimpton, Leonard A. Rosenblum, Irving E. Sigel, Steven Suomi, and Robert Zajonc.

MICHAEL LEWIS
LEONARD A. ROSENBLUM

Contents

Introduction: Issues in the Study of the Social Network

Michael Lewis and Leonard A. Rosenblum

The relevance of social development, in itself and as it affects all other aspects of the child's development, has been amply demonstrated and has been held, at least in its strong form, for many years. The nature of social development and the critical dimensions of the numerous characteristics of those involved have been the subject of considerable debate.

From positions of biology, primacy, and need fulfillment, the mother, as the principal care-giver, holds the central position in the child's social development. Whether it was Sears's translation of psychoanalytic theory into learning theory, or Bowlby's translation into sociobiology, the key to understanding social development traditionally has rested with the articulation of the mother–child relationship. Scientists visiting our planet from another world, and having only our literature to guide them, would have found it strange to have discovered that most homes not only contained a mother with her child but a father, siblings, other kin, and, on occasion, friends. Any count of the number of studies between mother–child, father–child, or other–child would have shown an enormous predominance of mother–child studies.

In the face of this strong *zeitgeist*, a slowly accumulating set of studies looking at the child's relationship with others has begun to appear. Lamb's (1976) book on father–infant relations, Lewis and Rosenblum's books on strangers and peers (1974, 1975), and Lerner and Spanier's book (1978) on the family attest to the realization that other members of the child's social world are important. The study of the important people in the child's life is still incomplete. There are few studies on grandparents and studies of sibling relationships are just

1

beginning to appear. Even the consideration of the child itself as a member of the social world has been lacking until recently (Lewis & Brooks, 1979). Other important social objects in the child's life have not even been considered. As we have stated previously (Lewis & Rosenblum, 1975, pp. 2–3) it is vital to remember "that no single element (social object) is either excluded from social development or provides the singular basis on which it ensues."

Once committed to the view that the child's social development is something more than the mother–child relationship, several important consequences follow: (1) consideration of the various social objects that people the child's world; (2) understanding the relationship between these objects and the needs of the young organism; and (3) from a systems point of view, evolving the structure of this complex nexus and consideration of the measurement difficulties it presents.

SOCIAL OBJECTS

It is clear that the social world of the child is composed of multiple social objects. Lewis and Rosenblum (1975) articulated a schematic array of potential social elements. Both inanimate and animate categories are included within this array, which in the former subsumed space, toys, and objects and in the latter included animals and humans still further divided into more specific categories. Such a potential array of social objects presents two issues: which social objects to study, and the nature of their change over time.

The interest in multiple social objects grows from a restrictive social theory of development as witnessed by the prototypical "mother nursing her child" scene as the basic social unit. In this regard the observation of the child's activities from a cross-cultural position does offer us some basis for a theoretical construct. For example, wash-day in contemporary middle-class America would probably include a mother alone with her child in the kitchen. The only social relationship would be between mother and child. Contrast this with a mother in a pretechnological environment (or, indeed, in a laundromat in this country). Here a number of mothers and children are together and the diversity and nature of the social interactions become quite complex. For example, there are mother–mother, mother–other child, mother–own child, and child–child relationships, all occurring at the same time. Such observations both expand the commitment to multiply determined social development and suggest the social objects for any type of taxonomy.

This discussion is not meant to suggest that any particular number and type of social objects is necessary for proper development. Rather, it is more important for us to view the number and type of social objects with which the child comes into contact and how they influence the child's development. Peers may not be critical for a child's social development but the nature of that development will be quite different depending on whether or not a peer environment exists. Interest should remain focused on the various possible outcomes given a particular set of social objects.

The meaning and importance of social objects are also subject to individual differences, both from an ontogenetic and cultural perspective. The small brown rabbit is considered more humanlike by the very young child than by one of school age. Likewise, the security blanket possesses social-like attributes for the small child that are lost as the child develops. In a similar fashion cultural differences in social objects need to be considered.

The Role of Social Objects

In the study of the child's early social development, besides restricting the nature of those relationships by focusing more or less exclusively on the mother, a careful analysis of the roles or needs of the child–object dyad has not been undertaken. This limitation has had important consequences on the theoretical models that have been considered in that it leads to a restricted view of what infants and children do and with whom they do it.

In any analysis of social development it is necessary, therefore, not only to consider the range of social objects involved, but also the range of needs and roles. Although different social objects may be characterized by particular social functions, it may be the case that social objects and needs are only partially related. Consequently, the identity of the social object does not necessarily define the type or range of its need or role. For example, "mothering" and mother may not be highly related. The particular set of needs or roles is a function of the model of development. We might, for example, study Murray's need system (1938) for such a set, or Wilson's adaptive functions (1975). The task of articulating a set of needs is quite complex, certainly beyond our conceptual abilities at this time. Nonetheless, efforts in this direction should be undertaken and their absence constitutes a serious loss to any theory of development. The most common needs that have been articulated for the young child include protection, care, nurturance, play, and exploration/learning. Certainly, others could be included.

Given these two sets of social objects and needs (elsewhere they have been referred to as functions) a major analytic task is the construction of a matrix having as ordinates the set of objects and needs. Such a matrix should provide information about who does what with the target child and should begin to allow answers to questions regarding the distribution of social objects by need. This matrix is, of course, constrained by a large number of factors such as the age of the target child, the nature of the family structure, and the cultural millieu in which the family lives. Nevertheless, the construction of such a matrix could provide a framework into which the large number of social objects and needs could be placed. Individual, group, and cultural differences in the matrix could be considered in light of various outcome measures and in this way provide insight into the origins of social development.

But the question remains: How shall we approach the systematic measurement of these complex, multiindividual interactive networks, as they relate to the development of an infant? To be sure, an appreciation of the total network of the social stimuli to which the infant is exposed must not obscure the fact that direct influences on the infant's immediate and maturing behavior can derive from any individual in the network. Such *direct effects*, in which the infant is the focus or object of another's behavior, include such interactions as support or punishment, or sibling aggression or playfulness with the child itself. These directed actions may affect the infant's ongoing behavior and shape future behavior in particular directions. Such effects, though often subtle, intermittent, and variable, may be assessed in an information transfer perspective; i.e., in terms of the relative predictability of the infant's behavior given two conditions: (1) the direction toward the infant of a designated social behavior; and (2) that such behaviors derive from particular members of the infant's family or immediate social group. Similarly, long-term effects of the behavior of particular relatives or friends may be sought in terms of time-lagged correlations of behavior of the two participants in the interactions. Whether viewed in terms of reinforcement, cueing, stimulus enhancement, or the releaser of some inborn consummatory behavior and whether it occurs once or many times, the behavior of a partner directed toward the infant changes the pattern of infant behavior in the future. However, because of the complexity of the social factors that actually operate on the developing infant, great caution must be exercised in attempting such longer-term correlations, unless relatively abrupt changes in the behavior of a given partner is correlated across subjects with subsequent behavioral shifts in the infant. Attempting to relate the stable, ongoing behavior of any given member of the network to developing infant behaviors is far too likely to be inextricably confounded with myriad other effects; these include both other types of "direct" effects and those influences that are of a less direct nature.

These latter, *indirect effects* on infant socialization and behavioral development stem from the complex, overlapping network of interaction that make up the infant's social world. Indirect effects are defined by Lewis and Feiring (1978) as follows: "Indirect effects refer to a set of influences on the target person that occur in the absence of one member of a system. . . ." Thus, for example, the changing pattern of mother–father relations, an argument, for example, occurring in the absence of the child, may nonetheless be viewed as the critical event in bringing about changes in the subsequent behavior of either the mother or the father when either is alone with the infant. In a monkey troop, a mother, losing status after a contest with another female of the hierarchy, may dramatically change her own behavior both toward the infant and others, and equally important, others in the group will act differently toward her infant as well. Similarly, the infant's perception of an interaction between two or more members of its family, even though that interaction does not directly involve the infant, may nonetheless influence the latter's subsequent behavior. Consider the following: A second child, three years younger than its sibling, from the age of about three onward, witnesses parental interactions with its sibling regarding school, homework, etc. Such parental behavior is never expressed with the young child as its object. Nevertheless, the impact of those other dyadic and triadic interactions in the family effectively shape the child's own reactions to the school situation. In a general sense, these "observations" by the child of other patterns of interactions within its family may not differ functionally from the other forms of indirect, noninteractive influences on the child: The two-year-old child may well avoid touching a hot radiator, having once viewed a friend or sibling make that mistake. Indeed, because the functional "family" of the young child may include even the family pet, seeing the family cat knock down a vase and its mother's unconcealed rage at the animal can effectively preclude the child's climbing to the tabletop for some time to come.

The student of the family must be alert to another, all-too-common difficulty in examining developmental sequences. This is the so-called "point-of-entry" problem, i.e., where in an ongoing sequence of interactions does measurement begin? In the current instance, if we fail to determine, for example, the interaction of a child with its father just prior to our observed interactions with its mother, we may miss the actual precipitating stimulus to the reactions of the child we now observe. With regard to the role of "indirect-effects" the time-point-of-entry problem is confounded with a "locus-of-entry problem, i.e., interactive events within the network occur outside the observable field of the investigator. Nonetheless, as we noted above, these events may ultimately shape the infant's subsequent relationships with these partners. One is reminded of John Barth's idea of "The Floating Opera." Barth's metaphor regarding our attempts to evolve a coherent view of life suggests that we are like people standing on shore watching an opera being performed on a riverboat but the boat is not anchored and in the midst of the action, it floats out of sight; but the opera goes on. Soon the performance drifts back into view, the players now further along in their dialogues, and we can only speculate about what must have occurred between them while out of our sight, such that we might account for the events we now witness.

It is clear then that the problems of analysis that emerge as we commit ourselves to viewing the child's social development within this complex social network are monumental. At present no palatable technique exists that enables us to characterize the total flux of familial interactions as these change over time. As suggested above, a mere cataloging of a set of dyadic interactive patterns fails to achieve the global overview that is needed. As we build the scaffolding of our network, as we traditionally have done, we first must measure the direct, dyadicly based effects on the infant; however, we then add a level of complexity by assessing the changes in dyadic patterns as a function of the presence of, or particular mode of behavior, of other members of the network. This brings us to the interplay of direct and indirect effects that constantly influence the child's life. Questions thus emerge in the form of, Does the mother's nursing behavior change in the presence of the father?, or, Does the toddler move from the mother more readily when she and father converse, as opposed to times when they remain silent? This conjoined direct and indirect influence can be seen quite dramatically in a situation in which both mother and father scold or praise a child's behavior or perhaps present a conflicting response to the same situation. Here the direct mother–infant and father–infant dyadic effects are amplified or ameliorated by the fact of the joint participation of both parents in the event, and their relationship with each other, as well as the pattern of interaction each has with the child. More temporarily remote, more indirect effects present even further difficulties. It seems likely to us that, at present, dealing with the incredible array of discrete events that takes place in the interactions of all members of the network and attempting to relate these to systematic changes in an infant's behavior are futile. As Hinde has recently suggested (1976), only if we can synthesize large sets of interactions among individuals into broader conceptual categories, can we hope to see order emerge from apparent chaos. Such synthesis can initially derive from many perspectives: supportiveness, dependency, dominance, pleasure-giving, or pleasure-seeking; each are conceptual frameworks that can be used to characterize these relationships and the changes in relationships with those who influence the child. With some handle on assessing these relationships conceptually, we can seek the systematic determination of events that change these patterned interactions and eventually the means through which this functioning network guides the development of a child within it.

REFERENCES

Hinde, R. A. On describing relationships. In *Journal of Child Psychology and Psychiatry*, 1976, *17*, p. 1–19.

Lamb, M. E. (Ed.). *The role of the father in child development*, New York: Wiley, 1976.

Lerner, R. M., & Spanier, G. D. (Eds.). *Contributions of the child to marital quality and family interaction through the life-span*. New York: Academic Press, in press.

Lewis, M., & Brooks, J. *Social cognition and the acquisition of self*. New York: Plenum, 1979.

Lewis, M., & Feiring, C. The child's social world. In R.M. Lerner and G.D. Spanier (Eds.), *Contributions of the child to marital quality and family interaction through the life-span*. New York: Academic Press, in press.

Lewis M., & Rosenblum, L. (Eds.). *The origins of fear: The origins of behavior, Vol. II*. New York: Wiley, 1974.

Lewis, M., & Rosenblum, L. (Eds.). *Friendship and peer relations: The origins of behavior, Vol. IV*. New York: Wiley, 1975.

Murray, H. A. *Explorations in personality*. New York: Oxford University Press, 1938.

Wilson, E. O. *Sociobiology*. Cambridge, Massachusetts: The Belknap Press of Harvard University Press, 1975.

Zajonc, R., & Markus, G. B. The birth order puzzle. Paper presented at a conference, The Social Network of the Developing Infant: Origins of Behavior, Princeton, N.J., December 1977.

The Child's Social Network: Social Object, Social Functions, and Their Relationship

Michael Lewis and Candice Feiring

The infant enters into the world. It is a social world full of conspecifics, a small segment of which shares his gene pool, a larger segment who will influence him, and, finally, the largest segment that forms the background in which these other interactions will take place. The smallest segment we call the family, the larger, his friends, acquaintances, and peers, and the largest segment, the culture. The people who populate the child's world are many and the behavior they direct toward the child varied. In order to explore the child as a member of its social group or network, it is necessary to explore some ideas concerning the social objects and social functions of the child's world.

Social Objects

By referring to social objects as opposed to other objects we intend to make some sort of differentiation between social and nonsocial. From the adult point of view, social objects are basically designated as persons, that is, entities that belong to the class of *Homo sapiens*. The attributes

Michael Lewis and Candice Feiring • Infant Laboratory, Institute for the Study of Exceptional Children, Educational Testing Service, Princeton, New Jersey 08541.

that define social objects beyond a simple species label are usually defined in terms of the similarities that exist between the object and the perceiver. Work on the acquisition of self-recognition (Lewis & Brooks, 1977) strongly suggests that for the infant social objects are different from other objects to the degree that an object is similar to the self or perceiver. Thus, for the developing infant the categories of social and nonsocial are not some static, unchanging dichotomy, but rather change as a function of ontogeny as well as history. The knowing of an object is, as Hamlyn (1974) has pointed out, dependent on the infant's knowledge of its relationship to that object. This position, not unlike that of G. H. Mead (1934), finds further support in the interactional theory of Piaget (1954).

The potential array of social objects that influence the infant and are influenced by him is exceedingly large. We have collected some preliminary data on the number and kinds of social objects present in the three-year-old child's social network. Of 18 children studied thus far, we have found that the subjects in our sample have approximately six friends that they see at least twice a month (with a range of 2–12 friends). In addition to the nuclear-family members, the children come in contact with an average of 9 relatives (with a range of 4–26 relatives), which include grandparents, aunts, uncles, and cousins. It is also interesting to note that many mothers report that the children in our sample come in contact with almost all the people the mother would include as important in her social network, including friends and, to a lesser extent, co-workers, as well as nuclear family and relatives.

How to make sense of a varied and large array of social objects is one of the more important goals of the child since it is to this array that the child must learn to adapt. For some theorists adaptation is sequential; the infant first adapts to its mother, then perhaps its father, and still later other social objects such as siblings, peers, and grandparents. Moreover, these same theorists would argue quite convincingly that the nature of the adaptation to the earlier objects determines the nature of the adaptation to others that follow. Psychoanalytic theory certainly seems to support the notion that poor adjustment with parents has profound implications for subsequent social behavior. Yet, alternative views exist (Lewis, Young, Brooks, & Michelson, 1975; Harlow & Harlow, 1969) that express the idea that the child's relationships to social objects other than the mother, while mutually interdependent, do not have to (1) follow sequentially or (2) be completely determined by the nature of the mother–child relationship. Harlow and Harlow (1969) and Lewis *et al.* (1975) and more recently Mueller & Vandell (1979) have argued for functional independence of at least the mother–infant and infant–peer systems. Mother–infant and infant–peer relationships may occur at the same time and both may appear very early, within the first 12 weeks of life. While not all the evidence is gathered, still that which does exist would lend support for separate systems.

Work with rhesus monkeys (Suomi, this volume) indicates that infants show different developmental shifts in the proportion of behaviors observed in their social relationships with mothers, fathers, peers, and adults. For example, in the period of 6–4 to 21–24 months, a rhesus infant's relationship to its mother changes considerably, while in the same time span, the infant relationship to male peers shows trivial changes. Suomi suggests that although the various social relationships between rhesus infants and other social objects are not totally independent of each other, it does appear that these relationships develop and stabilize at different rates.

Given that the infant must learn to make its way through a large and complex social array, how might it go about constructing its social knowledge? The use of the schematic representation of space presented in Figure 1 may offer one possibility. The construction of the child's social world is possible if we allow for the use of only several dimensions. One basis for the selection of dimensions alluded to earlier is the self. Lewis and Brooks-Gunn (1979), in a series of studies, have demonstrated the presence of some concept similar to self in infants in the last quarter of the first year. Using this notion, the infant has the potential to differentiate not only self from other but to use this "like me" comparison in order to dichotomize its world. It can be argued that for the infant social objects are therefore objects "like me." As the concept of self is altered, the self-comparison is open to change both as a function of the growing cognitive capacity as well as the infant's experiences. Three dimensions—age, familiarity, and gender—are attributes of the self and of the social world that the child acquires early. These three attributes may be used by the young child as a means to differentiate the social array.

Figure 1 presents this three-dimensional space along with the placement of some of the more common social objects in the child's life. As these dimensions become more differentiated the social objects within it become differentiated as well. Thus, as age becomes differentiated (i.e.; larger than a two-category system) one can add grandparents and adolescents, or within the familiarity dimension different degrees of familiar–unfamiliar allow for the placement of strangers, friends, and family.

Whether the infant uses the dimensions referred to above to help create the social array is indeterminant. However, the ability to construct

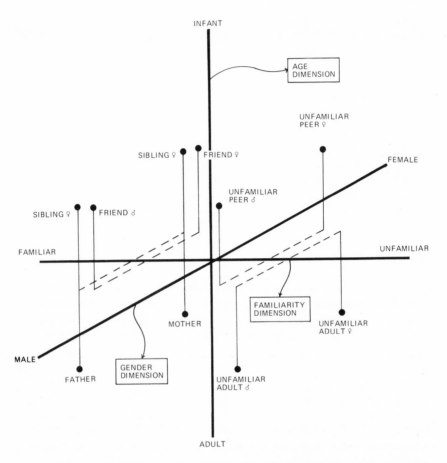

FIG. 1. The dimensions of familiarity–unfamiliarity and adult–infant are continuous while the dimension of male–female is dichotomous (although it is possible that, psychologically speaking, from the young child's point of view sex is more or less a continuous variable, e.g., mothers are more female than five-year-old girls. Siblings and parents have been represented as equally familiar while adult strangers are represented as less familiar than peer strangers. The points given in Figure 4 are merely illustrious of possible location of persons in a child's social world and may vary depending on the child's perception.

such an array from just three dimensions indicates that it may be possible; from a structural point of view it appears to be an interesting possibility that should be further explored.

Over the last decade data have been gathered that could be used to support the early development of gender, age, and familiarity concepts. Bronson (1972) as well as others (Lewis, Goldberg, & Campbell, 1969) have shown that familiarity in the social as well as nonsocial world is a salient dimension of the child's cognitive structures. Moreover, Bronson has demonstrated stranger fear in infants as young as three months, a finding compatible with our own observations of some infants. Money and Ehrhardt's (1972) data on hermaphroditic females supports the notion of early gender identity, and other work (Lewis & Brooks, 1975; Lewis & Weinraub, 1974) has shown infants to be responsive to gender. Responses to age have been shown repeatedly, both to live subjects (Lewis & Brooks, 1974; Brooks & Lewis, 1976a; Greenberg, Hillman, & Grice, 1973) and to pictures (Brooks & Lewis, 1976b). The data are not wanting to argue that the dimension of gender, age, and familiarity are sufficient conditions for the construction of the social array, and that these dimensions are concepts that come into use early in the child's life.

SOCIAL FUNCTIONS

In the study of the infant's early social relationships, besides restricting the nature of those relationships by focusing more or less exclusively on the mother (or father), a careful analysis of the types of function or activities enacted by the social objects has not been undertaken. While it is true that the mother and child have been observed in free-play situations, in separation and reunion, and in the presence or absence of a stranger, these situations, for the most part, have not been analyzed into activities or functions. This limitation has had important consequences on the theoretical models that have been considered, leading to a restricted view of what infants and children do and with whom they do it. The restricted view of function also has affected the study of the number of social objects that the infant interacts with. If only nurturant and protective functions are considered, then the mother as the most important (and only) social object to be studied makes some sense. However, other functions exist as needs in the infant's life, including, for example, play and exploration. This being the case, other social objects more appropriate to the function should be considered. The realization that this is the case, especially for play, has led to a renewal of interest in peer relationships and should result in a continuing study of the origins of friendship and the nature of siblings' interactions (Lewis & Rosenblum, 1975; Dunn & Kendrick, this volume).

In any analysis of the social network, it is necessary not only to consider the range of social objects involved but also the range of functions. While the discussion of social objects was based upon a set of theoretical notions and empirical data, social functions or activities are without such support. While social objects are difficult to define, social functions are considerably harder. The following comments are directed toward such an attempt with the realization that these are halting first attempts.

To start, we would define social functions as those activities that take place within the social network that involve other social objects. Functions that do not need the involvement of other social objects are not social functions. While social functions involve other social objects it remains to be determined whether the presence of another social object is necessary for this distinction. For example, imitation in the absence of the other social object might still be considered a social function. A set of specific social activities would include sexual activity, talking, communication, and play. These are just some of the functions or activities and they involve, first of all, other social objects such as in sexual behavior, talking, or playing.

Social activities or functions have been thought of as having some specific use for the organism's survival or well-being. Talking or communication, for example, or even play, are activities that are usually thought of as facilitating some aspect of development or growth. More specifically, we talk or ask questions in order to obtain information. Recently, Garvey (1977), Lewis and Cherry (1977), and Lewis (1977) have suggested that talking and communication have as a function the act of maintaining social contact. That is, rather than as an information exchange, the more significant function of question-asking may be in its social facilitation rather than in its information-producing capacity. Consider questions asked at conferences and meetings; often these questions have to do with gaining the floor, seeking recognition, or embarrassing the other, rather than information-seeking.

Play behavior can also be argued to have as a primary goal the establishment and maintenance of social relations (Mueller, this volume) rather than what has commonly been thought, the acquisition of skills. It would seem then that one aspect of a function is its social or nonsocial nature. Social functions take place with social objects and may be important because they facilitate and maintain the relationship between these objects. In some sense any activity or function may be considered social. Symbols and words are for Lévi-Strauss (1962) social contracts, the social agreement that words have a common meaning. Even so it may be profitable to make the distinction between social and nonsocial functions or activities.

One of the most important features of social functions is their subjective nature. That is, while it is possible to structurally define a set of functions—some of which we would be more willing to consider social than others—these functions or activities really have a subjective and phenomenological basis. This is less so for social objects. Consider the function called play. It is clear that this activity is a construct that can subsume a large set of diverse activities; fantasy, games, and symbolic representation being just three examples. Moreover, the play of children is work while work when enjoyed has for some adults the quality of play. To illustrate further, consider a dinner-time scene during which a three-year-old son doesn't want to eat his potato that has been taken out of its skin. The father, who has as a goal getting the son to eat his potato (care-giving function), makes up an elaborate fantasy about the magic potato that jumps in and out of its skin (play function). From the father's point of view, he is clearly enjoying the fantasy he has created in order to get his son to eat. However, the son completely ignores his father's attempt at play and reacts to the whole sequence of events with cranky upset. Consequently, from the father's perspective we have observed play, while from the son's perspective, to label the sequence of events as play would clearly be erroneous. In examining social functions it may prove useful to indicate both the form and intention of the behavior (Edwards, personal communication, 1977). For the present example we would note that the intention of the father's behavior involved the care-giving function while the form of the behavior involved the play function. A phenomenological approach to the study of social function may be necessary (Harre & Secord, 1972). Pervin (1975) has made some interesting attempts toward solving this problem by looking at the multiple dimension of a subject's consideration of situations. In this procedure subjects were asked to classify their daily experiences along affect, function, and spatial dimensions, and the results indicated that the subjects' same daily experience could be classified along a variety of dimensions.

In order to specify a set of functions, we could borrow from sets created around adaptive functions (Wilson, 1975), need function (Murray, 1938), or some similar set. That task is beyond the scope of these comments since they themselves required considerable analysis. In any event several large differences in functions are evident even from the beginning of life and must include at least play, protection, nurturance, care-giving, and exploration.

While we do not feel that a list of functions can be adequately realized, the following is an attempt to delineate some of the more important ones:

Protection. This function would include protection from potential sources of danger, including inanimate sources—falling off trees or being burnt in fires—and animate, as in being eaten by a predator or taken by a nonkin.

Care-giving. This function includes feeding, cleaning (at the least), and refers to a set of activities that center around biological needs relating to bodily activities.

Nurturance. This is the function of love, or attachment, as specified by Bowlby (1969) and Ainsworth (1969).

Play. This function refers to activities with no immediately obvious goal that are engaged in for their own sake.

Exploration/learning. This social activity involves the activity of finding out about the environment through either watching others, asking for information, or engaging in information acquisition with others.

The Relationship between Social Objects and Social Functions

Although different social objects may be characterized by particular social functions, it is often the case that social objects, functions, and situations are only partially related (proposition 4, Lewis & Weinraub, 1976). Consequently, the identity of the social object does not necessarily define the type or range of its social functions. For example, "mothering" (a function) and mother (an object) have been considered to be highly related. Some recent work with other social objects would seem to indicate that fathers (Parke & O'Leary, 1975) are more than adequate in performing this function. On the other hand, it could be the case that for some specific functions only a specific social object could fulfill that need. The feeding function, prior to technological advances, required the mother, but even there the use of a wet nurse suggests that a one-to-one relation between object and function may be difficult to demonstrate.

It appears that what is now necessary is the construction of a matrix having as ordinates social objects and social functions. In Figure 2 the vertical dimension labeled $P_1 - P_n$ is the set of social objects and consists of those persons that influence the child. The horizontal dimension labeled from $F_1 - F_m$ consists of the functions that characterize the behaviors that are characteristic of the child's social network. Within each function, there may be several behaviors that comprise the particular category of social function. For example, the function of care-giving may consist of behaviors such as feeding a child (B_{21})*or changing the child's clothes (B_{22}).*

---

* The first subscript indicated the function number and the second the behavior number.

SOCIAL FUNCTIONS

		F_1	F_2	F_3	F_4	F_5	$\ldots F_m$
		PROTECTION B_{11} B_{12} B_{13}	CARE-GIVING B_{21} B_{22} B_{23}	NURTURANCE B_{31} $B_{32} \ldots$	PLAY	EXPLORATION/LEARNING	B_{10}
P_1	SELF		FEEDING, CHANGING	ROCK, KISS			
P_2	MOTHER						
P_3	FATHER						
P_4	PEER						
P_5	SIBLING						
P_6	GRANDPARENT						
P_7	AUNT						
•	•						
•	•						
•	•						
P_n							

SOCIAL OBJECTS

FIG. 2. The relationship between social objects and functions.

The general form of the matrix given in Figure 2 offers the possibility of representing the complete array of social objects and social function that describe the child's network at a given point in time. By examining the horizontal axis of the matrix, one can obtain an idea of what functions characterize a particular social object's position in the child's social network. In some sense the horizontal ordinate describes for each person the content of that person's role in the child's social network. By role, we simply mean the set of functions a person performs when occupying a particular position within a particular social context. By examining the vertical axis of the matrix, one obtains information concerning the extent to which a particular function characterizes a child's social network. The relative amount of time spent in different functions would certainly be expected to influence the child's development. For example, a child whose network was characterized by the function of nurturance would be expected to be different from a child whose network was characterized by the function of protection.

Construction of the child's social matrix provides information about the structure of the child's social world, i.e., information about who does what with the target child. Given the basic matrix of persons and functions, an important question is: how do persons and functions combine; what is the distribution of the social object by social function? In addition to the description of the distribution of object and function in the child's social network, several factors that constrain the structure of the object × function distribution must also be considered. These constraining factors limit the kinds and number of objects and functions represented in the matrix as well as the distribution of functions by social object. For the present, we will discuss four constraints: (1) ontogeny, (2) family structure, (3) situation, and (4) culture, which we view as major factors influencing the nature of the social object × social function matrix.

ONTOGENETIC CONSTRAINTS

From an ontogenetic point of view we would expect the social network matrix to undergo significant and important changes. By examining the matrix at different points in a child's life it should be possible to delineate developmental patterns. Over time we would expect to see changes in the social objects represented as well as in the kinds of social functions that characterize the matrix. For example, Landau (1976) found that the seven-month-old infant was more exposed than the two-month-old infant to play behavior from familiar people. In addition to changes in importance and types of social objects and

| | F_1 CARE-GIVING | | F_2 PLAY | | $...F_m$ |
| | B_{11} | B_{12} | B_{21} | B_{22} | B_{fo} |
	FEEDING, DRESSING		HIDE & SEEK		
P_1 SELF		0		0	
P_2 MOTHER		30		5	
P_3 FATHER		10		10	
P_4 GRAND-MOTHER		5		2	
•					
•					
•					
P_n					
		45		27	

A. SOCIAL NETWORK MATRIX: TARGET CHILD AGE 3 MONTHS

| | F_1 CARE-GIVING | | F_2 PLAY | | $...F_m$ |
| | B_{11} | B_{12} | B_{21} | B_{22} | B_{fo} |
	FEEDING, DRESSING		HIDE & SEEK		
P_1 SELF		10		25	
P_2 MOTHER		5		5	
P_3 FATHER		5		15	
P_4 PEER		1		25	
P_5 TEACHER		5		15	
•					
•					
•					
P_n					

B. SOCIAL NETWORK MATRIX: TARGET CHILD AGE 6 YEARS

FIG. 3. Ontogenetic changes in the social network matrix. The numbers shown in this figure do not represent real data and are for illustrative purposes only.

functions, those behaviors that defined a particular function might also change as well as the distribution of functions by object. For example, consider a matrix that would represent the child's network at three months of age as shown in Figure 3(A). At three months of age we might expect to find the social objects of mother, father, and grandparents exclusively represented by the matrix. Behaviors in the social functions of care-giving and nurturance would be expected to comprise the largest percentage of activity, while play less so. Mother, father, and grandparents, in that order, might be involved in care-giving. However, within the function of play one would expect to see the father (Lamb, 1975) performing this function more than the mother or grandmother. For the sake of contrast consider the child's social network matrix at six years of age in Figure 3(B). As the child gets older the matrix may become more differentiated with the addition of more persons and new functions. In terms of social objects, peers and schoolteachers have most likely been added as social objects of importance to the matrix. In terms of functions, the predominance of care-giving has probably decreased (the child is probably administering many care-giving activities to itself, e.g., feeding, dressing), and other functions have become more important. The amount of time spent in play has probably increased considerably. The distribution of function by object may also alter; for example, the function of play may now be more closely associated with peers than with parents. In addition, those activities that comprise the function of play most likely have undergone change. The child now engages in games of hide-and-seek rather than peek-a-boo.

One can view development and its change by observing the transformation of the matrix structure at three months of age to its structure at six years. Several general points can be made. First, as the child gets older the number of persons he/she has contact with increases along with the number of functions that are operating. With the increase in object and functions the matrix becomes more differentiated and thus more complex in nature. In part, the task of social developmentalists is to describe the changes over time that take place in the object × function matrix. This, of course, requires a study of the behaviors that are subsumed under specific functions and how they are transformed over time (cf. Lewis & Starr, in press), as well as a study of what person and what functions are likely to predominate at specific points in time.

FAMILY STRUCTURE FACTOR

Considering the factor of family structure, we can simply point out the possible differences in a matrix for a child of three years of age who

| | F_1 CARE-GIVING | | F_2 PLAY | | $...F_m$ |
	B_{12}	B_{13}	B_{21}	B_{22}	B_{fo}
P_1 SELF	5		5		
P_2 MOTHER	10		1		
P_3 FATHER	5		5		
P_4 OLDER SISTER	5		3		
P_5 OLDER BROTHER	2		5		
P_6 FRIEND OF OLDER BROTHER	0		1		
P_n					

A. SOCIAL NETWORK MATRIX

FAMILY SIZE = 5

TARGET CHILD AGE 3

| | F_1 CARE-GIVING | | F_2 PLAY | | $...F_m$ |
	$B_{1\prime}$	B_{12}	B_{21}	B_{22}	B_{fo}
P_1 SELF	5		5		
P_2 MOTHER	10		2		
P_3 FATHER	10		14		
•					
•					
•					
P_n					

B. SOCIAL NETWORK MATRIX

FAMILY SIZE = 3

TARGET CHILD AGE 3

FIG. 4. The influence of family structure on the social network matrix. The numbers shown in this figure do not represent real data and are for illustrative purpose only.

is an only child (family size = three) and a child of three years who is a third-born (family size = five), see Figure 4. The first effect of interest is the number of objects available for various functions. The only child has no siblings in the vertical ordinate of the matrix, while the third-born child will have two older siblings in his matrix. In addition, friends of the child's siblings will probably be present in the social array. Family structure will equally affect the matrix of objects and functions when functions that have to do with missing objects are considered. For example, children may be more likely to play with other children, suggesting that the presence, as compared to the absence, of older siblings may provide more opportunities for play. Thus, the function of play may characterize the matrix of a child of a family of five to a greater degree than the matrix of an only child. Another example of how family structure may influence the functions that characterize the child's matrix is suggested by the work of Zajonc & Markus (1977). Small families (e.g., with only one child) may spend more time in the function of information exchange than larger families, thus enhancing the child's early cognitive development. The distribution of function by object will also be affected by family structure. In a family of three the function of care-giving is more than likely performed by the parents while in the family of five care-giving may be taken on by an older sibling as well as the parents. Similarly, a third-born child may spend more time in play with its siblings as compared to its parents, while the only child may have more experience playing with its parents in the absence of sibling companionship. Dunn and Wooding (1977) have reported some interesting data on how family size influences the social functions of play and its distribution among social objects. They have shown that only children received much adult attention that was related to long periods of relatively mature play activity. However, after the birth of a second child a sharp decrease in parental attention to the first child was noted (Dunn & Kendrick, this volume). The older child now tended to spend less time playing with its mother and more time playing with its younger sibling, with the play being characterized by less "mature" activities.

Situational Constraints

Another constraint that operates on the nature of a child's social network matrix is the situation in which interactions take place. For example, a matrix constructed from data taken at a dinner-time situation will most likely limit the social objects to the immediate family members. A dinner-time situation would also constrain the functions that would characterize the matrix. For example, we would expect to see more care-giving than play during a meal-time situation.

While functions as they relate to different objects have not been extensively studied, mothers' behavior toward their children as a function of situation, in which social function has been captured in part, has been examined (Lewis & Freedle, 1973, 1977). In one study the conversational relationship between dyads, 12-week-old infants and their mothers, were examined when the infant was on its mother's lap (presumably when she wished to interact, e.g., play function), and when the infant was in an infant seat (presumably when she wished to do housework and keep her eye on her child, e.g., protective function). Under the former, initiation and responsivity were many times greater than under the latter function, even though the amount of vocalization the mother produced was not different.

CULTURAL CONSTRAINTS

Culture is another factor that will constrain the configuration of the child's social network matrix. To illustrate, consider the matrix of a three-month-old child living on an Israeli kibbutz as compared to the matrix of a three-month-old child in the middle class of the United States (see Figure 5). The numbers and nature of the social objects of the kibbutz child would be different from those of the American child. We would expect to find the *metapelet,* as well as the parents and peers, to be important social objects for the kibbutz child but not the American child. Because of this, one would expect to find the function of caregiving distributed differently among social objects; that is, one would expect the *metapelet* in the matrix of the Israeli child to perform the largest percentage of care-giving as compared to the mother fulfilling this function for the child in the United States. Moreover, because there are more multi-aged children in the Israeli kibbutz than in the American family, there would more likely be more opportunities for different kinds of play. Other examples of high peer interaction and peer care-giving are quite common. In many nonindustrial countries the older female sibling or relative (usually by eight years of age) is in charge of and care for younger children, often siblings still nursing.

SUMMARY

Construction of the social object by social function matrix of the young child provides a framework for a description of the child's social network. The variety of people and activities that comprise this network may alter with age, family structure, situation, and culture. Stipulation of the matrix, or a selected part of the matrix, may provide information

	F_1 CARE-GIVING		F_2 PLAY	$\ldots F_m$
	B_{11}	B_{12}		B_{fo}
	FEEDING, DRESSING			
P_1 SELF	0			
P_2 METAPELET	25		10	
	5		5	
P_3 FATHER	2		2	
P_4 PEER	0		15	
P_6 PEER	0		20	
•				
•				
•				
P_n				

A. SOCIAL MATRIX OF ISRAELI

CHILD AT 3 MONTHS OF AGE

	F_1 CARE-GIVING		F_2 PLAY	$\ldots F_m$
	B_{11}	B_{12}		B_{fo}
	FEEDING, DRESSING			
P_1 SELF	0		0	
P_2 MOTHER	25		10	
P_3 FATHER	10		15	
•				
•				
•				
P_n				

B. SOCIAL MATRIX OF CHILD FROM UNITED

STATES AT 3 MONTHS OF AGE

FIG. 5. The effect of culture on the social network matrix. The numbers shown in this figure do not represent real data and are for illustrative purpose only.

about how objects, functions, and their relationship affect the development of the child. In the past, we have tended to focus on particular cells of the matrix (e.g., object, parent, function care-giving) assuming certain functions and persons were almost synonymous. However, as our theory moves toward a more complete conceptualization of those people and experiences that affect the young child's development, examination of several objects and functions simultaneously will be necessary. To properly construct a model of the child's social world we will need information about the social objects that comprise the child's network, the relationship between these objects, the functions that characterize the child's world and their interrelationships, as well as the relationship between functions and social object. Construction of a matrix or perhaps construction of matrices with age, family structure, situation, and culture as constraints rather than the stipulation of a single cell of a matrix should be our concern (cf. Landau, 1976) if what we intend is a description of the child's social world.

The data are too scant and no psychological theory is broad enough to encompass the total social array of objects and functions that influence the infant's development. A child's social network forms a social environment from and through which pressure is extended to influence the child's behavior and is also a vehicle through which the child exerts influence on others. Thus, a social network can be viewed as a flexibly bounded grouping of persons consisting of a focal person, here the child, everyone the child knows or interacts with, the set of relationships between those persons and the child, and the set of relationships that exist independently of the child. Social networks extend over time and space, and the nature of the persons, roles, activities, values, etc. that characterize the network will influence the child who is a member of this network.

REFERENCES

Ainsworth, M. D. S. Object relations, dependency, and attachment: A theoretical review of the infant–mother relationship. *Child Development*, 1969, 40, 969–1025.

Bowlby, J. *Attachment and loss.* Vol. 1, *Attachment* New York: Basic Books, 1969.

Brooks, J., & Lewis, M. Mirror-image stimulation and self-recognition in infancy. Paper presented at the Society for Research in Child Development meetings, Denver, Colorado, April 1975.

Brooks, J., & Lewis, M. Visual self-recognition in infancy: Contingency and the self–other distinction. Paper presented at the Southeastern Conference on Human Development meetings, Nashville, Tennessee, April 1976(a).

Brooks, J., & Lewis, M. Visual self-recognition in different representational forms. Paper presented at the XXIst International Congress, Paris, July 1976(b).

Bronson, G. W. Infants' reactions to unfamiliar persons and novel objects. *Monographs of the Society for Research in Child Development*, 1972, 47(148).

Dunn, J., & Kendrick, C. Interaction between young siblings in the context of family relationships. In M. Lewis & L. Rosenblum (Eds.), *The child and its family: The genesis of behavior, Vol. II.* New York: Plenum, 1979.

Dunn, J., & Wooding, C. Play in the home and its implications for learning. In B. Tizard & D. Harvey (Eds.), *The biology of play.* London: Heinemann Medical Books, 1977, pp. 45–58.

Garvey, C. The contingent query: A dependent act in conversation. In M. Lewis & L. Rosenblum (Eds.), *Interaction, conversation and the development of language: The origins of behavior* (Vol. 5). New York: John Wiley, 1977.

Greenberg, D. J., Hillman, D., & Grice D. Infant and stranger variables related to stranger anxiety in the first year of life. *Developmental Psychology,* 1973, 9, 207–212.

Hamlyn, D. W. Person-perception and our understanding of others. In T. Mischel (Ed.), *Understanding other persons.* Totowa, N. J.: Rowman & Littlefield, 1974, p. 1–36.

Harlow, H. F., & Harlow, M. K. Age mate or peer affectional system. In P. S. Lehrman, R. A. Hinde, & Shaw (Eds.), *Advances in the Study of Behavior* (Vol. 2). New York: Academic Press, 1969.

Harre, R., & Secord, P. *The explanation of social behavior.* Totowa, N. J.: Rowan & Littlefield, 1972.

Lamb, M. (Ed.). *The role of the father in child development.* New York: John Wiley, 1976.

Landau, R. Extent that the mother represents the social stimulation to which the infant is exposed: Findings from a cross-cultural study. *Developmental Psychology,* 1976.

Lévi-Strauss, C. *The savage mind.* Chicago: University of Chicago Press, 1962.

Lewis, M., Goldberg, S., & Campbell, H. A developmental study of learning within the first three years of life: Response decrement to a redundant signal. *Monographs of the Society for Research in Child Development,* 1969, 34(9, Serial No. 133).

Lewis, M. Socioemotional development in the opening years of life: Considerations for a new curriculum. Invited address for the American Educational Research Association meetings, San Francisco, California, April 1976. *Merrill-Palmer Quarterly,* 1977, 23(4), pp.279–286.

Lewis, M. What is natural? Paper presented at the New York Academy of Sciences, New York, N.Y., October 1976. *The Sciences,* 1977.

Lewis, M., & Brooks-Gunn, J. *Social cognition and the acquisition of self.* New York: Plenum, 1979.

Lewis, M., & Brooks, J. Self, other and fear: Infants' reactions to people. In M. Lewis & L. Rosenblum (Eds.), *The origin of fear: The origins of behavior* (Vol. 2). New York: Wiley, 1974, pp. 195–227.

Lewis, M., & Brooks, J. Infants' social perception: A constructivist view. In L. Cohen & P. Salapatek (Eds.), *Infant perception: From sensation to cognition* (Vol. 2). New York: Academic Press, 1975.

Lewis, M., & Brooks, J. The search for the origins of self: Implications for social behavior and intervention. Paper presented at a Symposium on The Ecology of Care and Education of Children Under Three, Berlin, West Germany, February 1977.

Lewis, M., & Cherry, L. Social behavior and language acquisition. In M. Lewis & L. Rosenblum (Eds.), *Interaction, conversation, and the development of language: The origins of behavior* (Vol. 5). New York: Wiley, 1977.

Lewis, M., & Freedle, R. Mother–infant dyad: The cradle of meaning. In P. Pliner, L. Krames, & T. Alloway (Eds.), *Communication and affect: Language and thought.* New York: Academic Press, 1973.

Lewis, M., & Freedle, R. The mother and infant communication system: The effects of poverty. In H. McGurk (Ed.), *Ecological factors in human development.* Amsterdam, The Netherlands: North-Holland Publishing Company, 1977, pp. 205–215.

Lewis, M., & Rosenblum, L. (Eds.). *Friendship and peer relations: The origins of behavior* (Vol. 4). New York: Wiley, 1975.

Lewis, M., & Starr, M. Developmental continuity. In J. Osofsky (Ed.), *Handbook of infant development.* New York: Wiley, in press.

Lewis, M., & Weinraub, M. Sex of parent × sex of child: Socioemotional development. In R. C. Friedman, R. M. Richart, & R. L. Vande Wiele (Eds.), *Sex differences in behavior.* New York: Wiley, 1974.

Lewis, M., & Weinraub, M. The father's role in the child's social network. In M. Lamb (Ed.), *The role of the father in child development.* New York: Wiley, 1976.

Lewis, M., Young, G., Brooks, J., & Michalson, L. The beginning of friendship. In M. Lewis, & L. Rosenblum (Eds.), *Friendship and peer relations: The origins of behavior* (Vol. 4). New York: Wiley, 1975.

Mead, G. H. *Mind, self, and society.* Chicago: University of Chicago Press, 1934.

Money, J., & Ehrhardt, A. A. *Man & Woman, Boy & Girl.* Baltimore, Maryland: The Johns Hopkins University Press, 1972.

Mueller, E. Toddlers + toys = an autonomous social system. In M. Lewis & L. Rosenblum (Eds.), *The child and its family: The genesis of behavior, Vol. II.* New York: Plenum, 1979.

Mueller, E., & Vandell, D. Infant–infant interaction. In J. Osofsky (Ed.), *Handbook of infant development.* New York: Wiley, 1979.

Murray, H. A. *Explorations in personality.* New York: Oxford University Press, 1938.

Parke, R. D., & O'Leary, S. Father-mother-infant interaction in the newborn period: Some findings, some observations, and some unresolved issues. In K. Reigel & J. Meacham (Eds.), *The developing individual in a changing world. Vol. II. Social and environmental issues.* The Hague: Mouton, 1975.

Pervin, L. Definitions, measurements, and classifications of stimuli, situations, and environments. Research Bulletin 75–23. Princeton, New Jersey: Educational Testing Service, 1975.

Piaget, J. *The construction of reality in the child.* (M. Cook, trans.). New York: Basic Books, 1954 (orig. publ., 1937).

Suomi, S. Differential developments of various social relationships by rhesus monkey infants. In *The child and its family: The genesis of behavior, Vol. II.* New York: Plenum, 1979.

Wilson, E. O. *Sociobiology.* Cambridge, Massachusetts: The Belknap Press of Harvard University Press, 1975.

Zajonc, R., & Markus, G. B. The birth order puzzle. Paper presented at a conference, The Social Network of the Developing Infant: The Origins of Behavior, Princeton, December 1977.

2

The Infant as a Focus for Family Reciprocity

T. Berry Brazelton, Michael W. Yogman,
Heidelise Als, and Edward Tronick

The human infant, from birth onward, exhibits predictable behavioral patterns with an adult conspecific. Within the first few weeks, he establishes differentiated behavioral sets for interaction with objects and with persons (Brazelton, Koslowski, & Main, 1974).

For example, when we analyzed from film his set of behaviors with an object, we saw striking differences by three weeks. His attention with an object is characterized by long (often longer than a minute) periods of rapt attention, followed by abrupt and brief turning away. These brief periods of turning away seemed to be recovery periods— recovery from the cost of his involvement with the object. In fact, all of the infant's behaviors evidenced intense involvement in periods of on-off cycling. When the infant looked, his face, legs, arms, toes, and fingers moved with jerky bursts of movement that swiped out toward the object. When the infant looked away or when the object was moved out of reach space (a conceptual area about 10–12" in front of him), these movements ceased. This cycling of attention and recovery seemed to be a behavioral representation of an endogenous homeostatic mechanism that maintained the balance of his immature cardiorespiratory and other physiological systems.

Quite a different pattern of attention and behavior is seen with adults. With them, in a period of interaction there are repeated cycles

T. Berry Brazelton, Michael W. Yogman, Heidelise Als, and Edward Tronick • Child Development Unit, Children's Hospital Medical Center, Boston, Massachusetts 02115. This section was prepared while the authors were supported by grants from the William T. Grant Foundation, the Carnegie Foundation, and the Robert Wood Johnson Foundation.

(often four times a minute) of attention and disengagement. This cyclical on-off pattern is smooth and rhythmical in normal infants. His movements are smooth and rhythmic rather than the jerky ones seen with an object. The movements of his face, eyes, and mouth build up slowly and smoothly; extremities cycle out toward the adult and return in smooth arcs. The disengagement phase seems to balance the attentional phase. In other words, he is moving smoothly and cyclically in a kind of approach–withdrawal that, when analyzed and plotted on a graph, resembles a homeostatic curve in which the cycles of attention and nonattention are of shorter duration and the buildup and decrease of attention are more gradual than they are with objects. This performance indicates that a very young infant is able to differentiate inanimate as opposed to animate interactants, and we think that he can pattern his attention and behavioral patterns to attend to and respond to their unique qualities. With the object, his goal is its exploration by vision and is an anlage of prehension (Bower, 1970). With an adult, his goal appears to be affective synchrony and he modifies his behavior in response to the feedback he receives within this reciprocal interaction.

For us, this synchrony may represent the condition under which a nurturing adult shapes the newborn infant—both affectively and physiologically. For, as one observes an infant in such affective synchrony, one can see that cognitive and affective information are conveyed by the expressive displays exchanged between both partners in the attention phase, followed by a recovery to basic physiological homeostasis in the withdrawal phase. Thus, the parent learns about his/her infant's immature limits on attention and the necessary recovery phase that balances his investment in such an attentional system. The infant "learns" about himself as he achieves a kind of homeostasis within this context and he learns his own limits for socialization within this system. A caring adult will adjust to these limits and work synchronously within them to transmit information. As the infant's capacity to attend to his environment increases with maturity, he learns how to achieve an optimal state of attention—for both objects and people—and how to capture and control with expressive displays the important persons in his environment within such a mutually regulated feedback system.

We are now using this model of interaction to study families and identify the basic ingredients of a "fit" between mother and baby, and father and baby.

THE RESEARCH MODEL

Our subjects have been mother–infant and father–infant pairs videotaped repeatedly over the first six months of life in our lab as they interact with each other in a face-to-face play situation. We explain to them that we are videotaping their play behavior so as to gain an understanding of the normal development of infant social capabilities, and we make an effort to inform them about our ongoing analyses.

During each session, when alert and calm, the infant is placed in an infant seat situated in a curtained alcove (Figure 1). The mother or father comes from behind the curtain and plays with him for two minutes. She or he then leaves and we continue to record the infant's behavior for 30 seconds while he is alone. The other parent then enters for a second two-minute period of interaction (Brazelton, Tronick, Adamson, Als, & Wise, 1975; Yogman, Dixon, Tronick, Adamson, Als, & Brazelton, 1976).

The videotape is made unobtrusively with two cameras, one focused on the infant and the other on the parent. The camera outputs are fed simultaneously into a special-effects generator that produces a frontal view of the mother or father and the baby. An electronic digital time display is also fed onto the image (Figure 2).

The videotapes are reviewed with several analytic techniques so that we can characterize the type and quality of each interactor's behavior. To aid this review, we have analyzed the tapes with a detailed microbehavioral system. The analysis is done by two trained observers as the videotape runs at one-seventh of normal speed. The behaviors are categorized according to their occurrence during a one-second interval.

To provide the context for discussion of our data, we will analyze a short film of a session—an interaction between a three-month-old male infant and his mother and father.

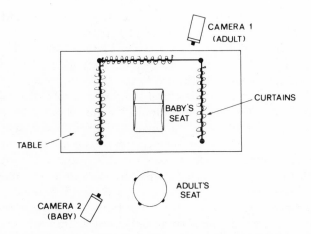

FIG. 1. Schema of laboratory during observations of adult–infant interaction.

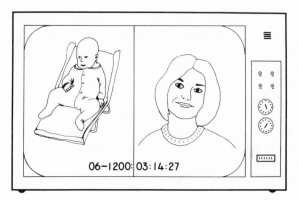

06–1200: 03:14:27

FIG. 2. Schema of TV monitor.

First, we will describe the segment of the infant with his mother. The interaction with mother begins as mother enters smiling and saying "Hi" in a high-pitched voice. The baby responds with an early, but brief smile greeting after a latency of only three seconds. After about 30 seconds, their interaction is characterized by phases of reciprocal vocalizations, each lasting about four to eight seconds and interrupted by shorter three- to four-second pauses. These alternating dialogues constitute a low-keyed verbal game for infant and mother, in which mother talks in a burst–pause manner and the infant vocalizes during the pauses. As mother and baby alternately build to a peak of attentional involvement and then decelerate to repeat the sequence, they illustrate the smoothly modulated rhythmic cycling of mother–infant interaction.

Next, we will describe the episode of this infant with his father. Here, the father enters with a neutral facial expression and begins a narrative vocalization while the infant stills, sits upright, and watches the father intently and quietly. The infant appears "set" to interact. After about six seconds, the infant then greets his father with a wide grin and punctuates this with a large, abrupt movement of his foot. Infant vocalizations are likely to be in the form of laughs, short and intense, followed by long pauses, while father imitates and amplifies his infant's facial expressions. Episodes of mutual play are followed by pauses in which the father becomes less animated, displays more neutral facial expressions, and waits for the infant to reinitiate the play. During the second minute, these episodes of play increase as the father touches the infant with rhythmic tapping patterns. This pattern is seen most clearly at the end of the session when the father walks his fingers up the baby's arms as part of a tapping game. This short burst of tapping is an example of the abrupt shifts that characterize father–infant interaction, in which father and infant alternately accelerate to higher peaks and decelerate to lower valleys than do mother and infant.

We have several kinds of analyses for these tapes. We first analyze them in slow motion (at one-seventh speed) and assign a specific descriptor for each infant and adult behavior during each second of interaction. For this, we follow a manual to describe five behavioral categories for infant and six for mother, Figure 3.

We have come to see that comparing any one behavior of a member of the dyad to one behavior of the other becomes too static to be of any meaning, for each behavior is a part of a cluster of behaviors that interact with a cluster of behaviors from the other member of the dyad. No single behavior can be separated from this cluster and isolated from its sequence without losing its meaning. Furthermore, it is only by using groups of these behaviors that we can convey communicative meaning. Different groups of behaviors can convey equivalent meanings, and substitutability of single behaviors within different clusters makes any analysis complicated. We have come to see that clusters of behaviors, not single behaviors, carry the signals of a communication system from one partner to another.

These behavioral clusters of the individual partners form the structure of the interaction. On the basis of the many descriptions we collected, we arrived at the identification of five dyadic phases (Brazelton et al., 1975; Tronick, Als, & Adamson, 1978). These five phases give us an opportunity to preserve the dyadic meaning of the behavioral clusters in our analysis. Each of the five phases represent a different "dyadic" state of the partner's mutual attentional and affective involvement and subsume the single behaviors in clusters that carry the "intent" of each partner to interact or withdraw (Figure 4).

These dyadic phases are: (1) initiation, (2) mutual orientation, (3) greeting, (4) play-dialogue, and (5) disengagement. *Initiation* may occur when mother brightens and baby-talks to a sober baby, or a baby vocalizes and smiles to a caretaker who has paused too long. *Mutual orientation* may take place with neutral or bright faces, with the caretaker

EXPRESSIVE MODALITIES
SCORED PER SECOND

INFANT	ADULT
FACIAL EXPRESSION	FACIAL EXPRESSION
VOCALIZATION	VOCALIZATION
EYE DIRECTION	EYE DIRECTION
HEAD POSITION	HEAD POSITION
BODY POSITION	BODY POSITION
	SPECIFIC HAND MOVEMENTS

FIG. 3. Expressive modalities scored per second for adult and infant.

talking or the infant making single utterances. *Greetings* occur with smiles and "ooh" faces, and *play-dialogues* with mother talking in a burst–pause pattern and the baby making grunts or continuous vocalizations. *Disengagement* may occur when the caretaker goes from neutral face to sober face, or keeps the neutral face, but starts to talk to the infant in adult conversational terms, or starts looking away from the baby. The phases, defined by clusters of behavior of *both* partners are, therefore, dyadic.

Figure 5 shows the mother–infant and father–infant interaction scored with the "dyadic phase" system. Inspection of this data underscores the similarities in rhythm and levels between the two dyads.

Mother and infant start with a greeting and then after two brief initiations move mainly between mutual orientation and play-dialogue. Father and infant begin with mutual orientation, but enter into a greeting at five seconds, then a brief period of initiation. They also move mainly between mutual orientation and play-dialogue throughout the remainder of the session.

The sequence of dyadic phases resulting from this analysis characterizes the attentional and affective involvement that occurs in a face-to-face interaction. It captures the buildup to greetings and the decelerations to disengagement. In this example, the analysis highlights one of the most striking qualities of successful interactions: the mutual cycling of attention and affectivity. The infant demonstrates his participation in this cycling by alternately attending and then withdrawing either par-

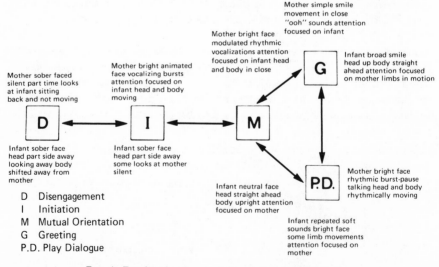

Fig. 4. Dyadic phases scored for adult–infant interaction.

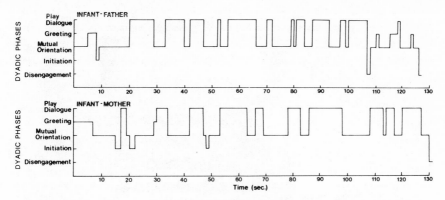

FIG. 5. Dyadic phases during session of 96-day-old infant with mother and father.

tially or completely. The sensitive parent likewise regulates his/her own behaviors so that his/her affectivity cycles along with his/her infant's.

While this system allows one to capture the joint state of infant and adult in a face-to-face interaction, it does not allow one to look at the two partners separately nor at the behavioral ingredients making up a phase.

The quality of each partner's display *relative* to the quality of the other's display is a measure of the match existing between their intentionality and affectivity. When synchronization is achieved, we feel that we are observing a good interaction based on a mutuality of affect and intent. When it is not achieved, there is a dysrhythmia and lack of cyclic buildup of the behaviors into a smooth flow of phases.

In order to preserve the affective message carried in each partner's behavioral display, to assess their relative quality, and to account for the substitutability of single behaviors, we have developed a third kind of data analysis we call *monadic phase analysis* (Tronick, Als, & Brazelton, 1977). We derive these phases from a second-by-second microbehavioral description segmented into individually identified behavioral units called monadic phases. Each monadic phase is made up of a set of substitutable behaviors. They are formed by a clustering of behaviors similar to the dyadic phases, but this analysis maintains the identity of each partner. For both the infant and the adult, we segmented the second-by-second displays into the following monadic phases: Talk, Play, Set, Elicit, Monitor, Avert, and Protest/Avoid. Figure 6 illustrates how the monadic phases are derived from combinations of expressive modalities (Tronick *et al.*, 1977; Als, Tronick, & Brazelton, 1978).

We can use the monadic phase analysis of the two interactions to demonstrate some of the similarities and differences between father–infant

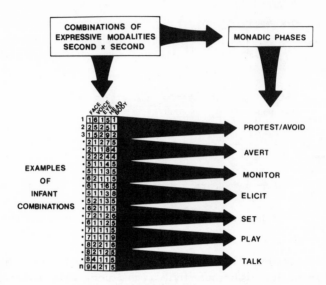

FIG. 6. Derivation of monadic phases.

and mother–infant interactions (Yogman, Dixon, Tronick, Als, & Brazelton, 1977). For each second of interaction, we have translated infant and adult behavior into one of the seven monadic phases just described.

Figure 7 depicts the sequencing of the monadic phases for each of the participants during each second of interaction.

This figure shows the interaction of infant with the father. Infant on the bottom and father on top are presented in mirror image of each other. Each has the neutral axis dotted line at "set," i.e., indicating

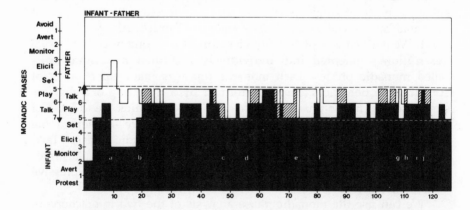

FIG. 7. Monadic phases during session of 96-day-old infant with father (time in seconds on horizontal axis).

readiness to interact. The farther apart the points on the curve are, the more disengaged the partners are. The closer together the points are, the more engaged the partners are. The infant's representational space for the categories Play and Talk has been overlayed with the father's space of Play and Talk, thus graphically indicating the shared quality, the relaxed, joyful mutuality. The figure shows that both father and infant cycle through similar phases shifting from Set to Play and Talk and then to Set again. We see that both father and infant spend more than 90% of the interaction in the phases of Set, Play, and Talk, the three most affectively positive phases.

Furthermore, the graph allows us to focus on the transitions between monadic phases and to see that these transitions are jointly regulated. The small letters "a" through "j" below the graph mark transitions in which both partners move in the same direction within seconds of each other. We can see that father and infant often change monadic phases simultaneously.

Figure 8 shows the similarities between father–infant and

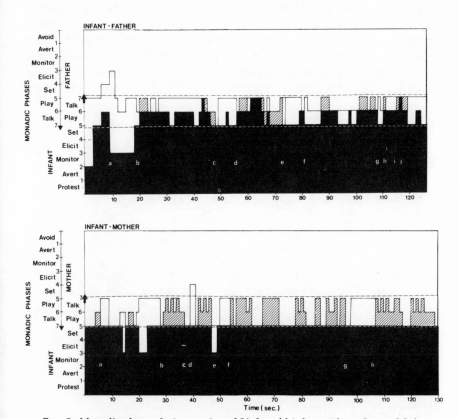

FIG. 8. Monadic phases during session of 96-day-old infant with mother and father.

mother–infant interaction. Mother and infant cycle through similar monadic phases and on several occasions change monadic phases simultaneously as indicated by the small letters "a" through "h" below the graph. With both mothers and fathers, cycling appears to modulate the level of affective involvement of each partner in a homeostatic fashion.

During each second, parent and infant monadic phases may be related in one of three joint states: match, conjoint, or disjoint.

1. First, their phases may be identical and we have called this a *match*.

2. Second, both partners may be in adjacent phases as when the adult is in Play and the infant is in Talk. We have called this *conjoint*.

3. Third, the partners may be more than one phase apart as when the adult is in Elicit and the infant is in Play. We have called this *disjoint*.

Figure 9 shows more clearly the relative proportion of time spent in each of these three joint states during infant interaction with mother and father. The area of the boxes represents the proportion of time spent in each joint state. The arrows between or within the joint states represent the transitions between the joint states for each second of the interaction. One can see that interactions are mostly conjoint with both parents: 56% of the time with mother and 60% of the time with father.

QUALITY AND TRANSITIONS BETWEEN DYADIC STATES

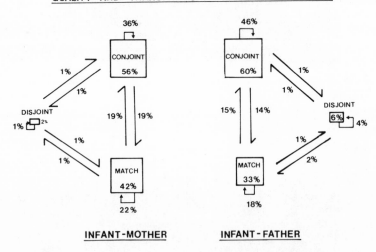

Fig. 9. Amount of time spent in joint states during session of 96-day-old infant with mother and father.

There are also a large proportion of matching states with both parents. Disjoint states are rare, occurring less than 10% of the time. The transitions between joint states demonstrates the way partners achieve this meshing. Most of the second-to-second transitions either remain within conjoint or matched states or a cycle between the two. These data suggest similarities in joint regulation and reciprocity displayed during interactions of infants with mothers and fathers. Similarities exist in the levels of affective involvement of the partners, the simultaneous or nearly simultaneous timing of transitions between monadic phases present during the interactions, and in the quality of joint states as well as in the nature of transitions between joint states.

Now, we would like to discuss some of the differences between father–infant and mother–infant interaction. These differences are demonstrated in the sequencing of monadic phases, and in the temporal structure and behavioral content of the Play and Talk phases (Yogman et al., 1977).

If we focus on the mother–infant pair (see Figure 8), we can see that mother remains in the monadic phase of talk for prolonged periods, while the infant makes multiple brief one-second transitions between the Play and Talk phases. In contrast, we can see that father shifts predominantly between monadic phases Set and Play, while the infant moves between Play and Talk phases, often spending three or more seconds in each and shifting through the phases of Monitor or Set before returning to Talk. Mother seems to provide an envelope for interactive vocal behaviors while father provides a base from which Play can emerge. Furthermore, the mean duration of the interval between episodes of Talk is significantly longer with fathers (8.0 sec) than with mothers (2.8 sec). After infants talk with fathers, they are likely to shift into a lower phase and remain there for a longer time, while with mothers they more quickly return to Talk. The difference in the quality of transitions between monadic phases is characteristic of the more accentuated shifts from peaks of maximal attention to valleys of minimal attention that occur during infant interaction with father. This can be compared with the more gradual and modulated shifts that occur during mother–infant interaction.

Further differences are evident in the temporal structure and specific behavioral content of mutual Talk or mutual Play. These mutual states can be called *interactive games* in the same sense that Stern (1974) has defined them: "A series of episodes of mutual attention in which the adult uses a repeating set of behaviors with only minor variations during each episode of mutual attention."

We looked specifically at verbal games and at tapping games. We classified a game as verbal when both adult and infant were in the monadic phase Talk. We classified a tapping game when the infant was either in monadic phase Play or Talk, while the adult was in the monadic phase Play and touched the infant with a repetitive tapping pattern. Mother and infant spent much more time playing verbal games while father and infant spent more time playing tapping games.

Differences between mother–infant and father–infant interaction can be seen in all of the families we have studied, both in the quality of transitions between phases and in the content of games played. They suggest that, at least for these families, interactions with fathers can be characterized as heightened and playful while the interactions with mothers appeared more smoothly modulated and contained.

Further, this communicative system is so finely tuned that one can not only differentiate among individual pairs, for differences in individual goals, and even for cultural expectations in the parents, but one can see the effect of temperamental variations in the infant on the adult (Brazelton, Koslowski, & Main, 1974). Thus, it serves as an instrument for detecting and assessing the effect on the dyad of such problems as central nervous system defects in the infant, of blindness, of hypothyroidism, to name a few. We can also identify the ingredients when the mother–father–infant triad are failing each other and we are now in the process of looking at high-risk families with this model of interaction.

These analyses help us to see the regularities in parent–infant interaction, the levels of rhythmic reciprocity and the interchangeable behavioral ingredients of the display clusters that make up the interactional give-and-take that characterize adult–infant interaction. The regularities that underlie both parents' responses define the requirements of reciprocity with an immature infant, and probably are limited by his immature capacity to attend to important signals from the adult for long periods interspersed with recovery periods.

The differences between his reactions to mother versus father are stable over time and are registered in predictable behavioral clusters. They seem to define his expectation for reactions from them. These signal to the adult partner that he recognizes him or her and expects a certain pattern of responses in return (which he gets). They also point to the different roles in setting the kind of reciprocity he expects of them (e.g., mother providing an envelope for interactive behaviors, father a base from which Play can emerge). Their stability points to the infant's need for stable, expectable responses to be different from each parent. These will offer him the richness of two stable bases for developing a cognitive and affective expectancy from his world.

That this system is adaptive in holding the important people to him seems obvious to us. He learns necessary inner controls over this psychological system from his parents' control over him within reciprocal

FIG. 10. Dyadic model of interaction.   FIG. 11. Triadic model of interaction.

containment. The parents learn about him, but they also learn about themselves in their nurturing roles as they respond to and interact with the infant's nonverbal cues.

The interlocking feedback of a mutually regulated system seems to be best captured by the concept of cybernetics (Ashby, 1956). Within the concept of cybernetics, the mother–infant and the father–infant dyads (Figure 10) can be depicted, as well as the mother–father–infant triad (Figure 11). Ashby's cybernetic system (1956) provides us with a model to conceptualize the way the baby learns about synchronization as well as differentiation with each partner, and they in turn with him. Each disruption of the system allows for separation, differentiation, and individuation for each member of the triad. With reorganization, the feeling of equilibrium and of resynchronization is achieved by each member. One can visualize the intensity of feedback gratification in a new family as each member of the triad achieves resynchronization after disruption.

As Sander (1977) points out in his paper on the regulation of exchange in the infant–caretaker system, loosely coupled subsystems allow for temporary independence of some subsystems in relation to the larger system. In such stable but flexible systems, perturbations of a subsystem need not seriously affect overall stability. However, when the subsystems are too tightly coupled (as in Figure 12) and inflexible, a perturbation is likely to disturb this overall stability. Such a tightly overcontrolled condition might lead to a more pathologic symbiotic

COPING SYSTEM (FATHER ABSENT
OR OUT OF CONTACT)   FIG. 12. Perturbation of triadic system of interaction.

affective relationship between mother and infant or father and infant in which the work of autonomy and detachment cannot proceed at an optimal rate for the baby to achieve necessary independence.

In a flexible but stable system, subsystem independence is easily managed. A balance of togetherness as well as of separation between an infant and his care-givers allows the infant the opportunity for learning about autonomy within a reciprocal system that provides organization to the infant when he needs it. We have become more and more aware in our research of the necessary homeostatic balances between attention and nonattention, excitement and recovery, and of reciprocity in both togetherness and separateness. The infant learns about others in the attention phase, and about himself as he recovers in the inattentive phase.

Above all, he can learn about more than one other in relation to himself in a triadic system. Thus, the earliest anlage for learning about attachment and detachment are laid down within the envelope of the family. We do not question but that an infant can learn the rules of reciprocity necessary for affective development within a dyad, but the increase in available organization and of richness in a well-balanced triad becomes obvious in such a cybernetic model. Such an interlocking system would allow for a readjustment on the part of any two members when there is a violation or disruption of one. The triad is likely to be more loosely coupled and, thus, more stable. Each member must be sensitive to necessary readjustments and must be able to achieve the homeostasis necessary to reestablish communication within a regulatory feedback system. Thus, each member of a triad must learn about each other partner as an individual, but also about the underlying rules regulating the other dyad. With this concept, one can visualize the power of the regulatory systems of communication as a way of learning about oneself as a partner in a dyad and also as a member of a family.

References

Als, H. Tronick, E., & Brazelton, T.B. Analysis of face-to-face interaction in infant–adult dyads. In M. Lamb, S. Suomi, & G. Stephenson (Eds.), *The study of social interaction: Methodological problems.* Madison: University of Wisconsin Press, 1978, in press.

Ashby, R. *An introduction to cybernetics.* London: Chapman & Hall, 1956.

Bower, T.G.R., Broughton, J.M., & Moore, M.K. Demonstration of intention in the reaching behaviour of neonate humans. *Nature.* 1970, *228*, 679–681.

Brazelton, T.B., Koslowski, B., & Main, M. The origins of reciprocity. In M. Lewis & L. Rosenblum (Eds.), *The effect of the infant on its caregiver.* New York: Wiley, 1974.

Brazelton, T.B., Tronick, E., Adamson, L., Als, H., & Wise, S. Early mother–infant reciprocity. In M.A. Hofer (Ed.), *The parent–infant relationship.* London: Ciba, 1975.

Sander, L.W. The regulation of exchange in the infant–caretaker system and some aspects of the context–content relationship. In M. Lewis & L. Rosenblum (Eds.), *Interaction, conversation and the development of language*. New York: Wiley, 1977, p. 133.

Stern, D.N. The goal and structure of mother–infant play. *Journal of the American Academy of Child Psychiatry*, 1974, *13*, 402.

Tronick, E., Als, H., & Adamson, L. The communicative structure of early face-to-face interactions. In M. Bullowa (Ed.), *Before speech: The beginnings of human communication*. Cambridge, England: Cambridge University Press, 1978, in press.

Tronick, E., Als, H., & Brazelton, T.B. The structure of face-to-face interaction and its developmental functions. Paper presented at the biennial meeting of the Society for Research in Child Development, New Orleans, 1977.

Yogman, M.W., Dixon, S., Tronick, E., Adamson, L., Als, H., & Brazelton, T.B. Development of social interaction with fathers. Paper presented at Eastern Psychological Association, New York, 1976.

Yogman, M.W., Dixon, S., Tronick, E., Als, H., & Brazelton, T.B. The goals and structure of face-to-face interaction between infants and fathers. Paper presented at biennial meeting of the Society for Research in Child Development, New Orleans, 1977.

Conceptualization of Father Influences in the Infancy Period

FRANK A. PEDERSEN, LEON J. YARROW,
BARBARA J. ANDERSON, AND RICHARD L. CAIN, JR.

There is no longer a need to intone the standard opening litany that psychologists have been preoccupied with maternal influences to the exclusion of other social agents. On the contrary, there is now considerable evidence of research interest in father–infant relationships, the paternal role, and distinctive aspects of father–infant interaction. The more serious problem, however, is that there has not been an adequate effort to *conceptualize* paternal influences in the infancy period. To redress this oversight, we will present some theoretical ideas in order to encourage the development of an explanatory network for research on fathers. The central thesis is that father influences must be understood as occurring within the family unit. It is not meaningful to make global generalizations about what fathers do, or what their effects are, without considering the larger family context.

Rudolph Schaffer, in his engaging little volume entitled *Mothering* (Schaffer, 1977), defined four essential components in the mother–infant relationship: (1) the provision of stimulation; (2) a sensitivity to the

FRANK A. PEDERSEN, LEON J. YARROW, BARBARA J. ANDERSON, AND RICHARD L. CAIN, JR. • Social and Behavioral Sciences Branch, National Institute of Child Health and Human Development, Bethesda, Maryland 20014. Dr. Anderson is now affiliated with the Washington School of Medicine, St. Louis, Missouri 63130.

infant's needs and states so that there can be a temporal organization of behavior that is in phase with the infant's receptivity, which Schaffer calls interlocution; (3) the growth of an affectional bond between mother and infant; and (4) a reasonable degree of constancy in the relationship. He concludes the book by dealing with the question, Do babies need mothers? His answer is *no* insofar as one means the biological mother. The mother, says Schaffer, "can be any person of either sex." He says, indeed, that the father can be the mother "if that is the role that he and his wife choose it to be." Obviously, Schaffer is talking about a distinctive psychological relationship, not a relationship that is conferred simply by virtue of gender and biological events.

There is much that is appealing in Schaffer's formulation, but its fundamental problem from the standpoint of understanding early experience in a family context is that it addresses a single, intense dyadic relationship. He allows interchangeability among people who might enter into such a relationship with the infant, but he does not deal with the significant experiences with people other than the one assuming the maternal role. Our point of departure from Schaffer is to assert that there are, indeed, significant experiences associated with the other adult in the nuclear family, the father, and that mothers and fathers are generally not interchangeable objects in relation to the baby. We need to understand the infant's responses to *multiple* adults and how these adults might interact differently with the infant and with each other. A conceptualization of father influences in the infancy period would be incomplete without considering these issues.

Since Schaffer uses the term "mothering" in the most inclusive manner imaginable, it might be well to define the boundaries of our concepts from the outset. The term "mother" will imply a gender and status identity, a female adult who meets to varying degrees the conditions identified by Schaffer. In the same way, a father is a male adult who interacts *similarly* with the infant, even though a mother and father in the same family may bring to their respective relationships with the infant different sensitivities, values, attitudes, and socialization goals. The differences may be partly a product of their own sex role histories as well as many unique experiences that are not sex-typed at all. Moreover, a mother and father have a distinctive relationship with each other that may impinge upon their parenting roles. There is usually an affectional bond between parents and an anticipation that their relationship is an enduring one despite all statistical probabilities to the contrary. There is some system of role organization that identifies areas of behavioral specialization as well as commonality, and they are sexual partners. The latter condition defines their relationship in a more specific way than did Feiring and Taylor (1978) who used the concept of

"Secondary Parent" to apply to both grandparents and husbands. Our picture of the two-parent family is rather conservative and conventional compared to more exotic family organizations that have been described (Eiduson, Cohen, & Alexander, 1973), but it still applies to 80 percent of the United States households with children under 18 years of age (Glick & Norton, 1977).

THE SCOPE OF A THEORY OF FATHER INFLUENCES

Given this type of family structure, there are at least three issues that a theory of father influences must encompass. First of all, it must address the infant's *multiple relationships*. It is important to identify the distinctive experiences that each parent provides, as well as areas in which parents' behaviors are relatively interchangeable. Moreover, we must consider the social comparisons that an infant makes in relating to these two very particular adults. Perhaps one important reason why fathers have been ignored in the infancy period is that, until recently, infants were not conceived of as capable of making the complex discriminations necessary to enter into multiple relationships. Not until the infant's competencies were appreciated could one hypothesize that infants could interact meaningfully in more complex environments than ones containing only the mother.

It is interesting to note in passing that while traditional attachment theory deals with only a single dyadic relationship, there are other theories that involve more explicit social comparisons of adults by the young. Psychoanalytic theory, Whiting's Status Envy Theory, and Parson's Role Theory are all fairly explicit about differential relationships and social comparisons. In each theory, the significance of parents having differential relationships with the child comes to the fore during the identification period. Only recently has there been discussion in the psychoanalytic literature (Burlingham, 1973; Forrest, 1967) about the father's positive contribution to development at an earlier period. Neither Status Envy Theory nor Parson's Role Theory speaks to father influences during infancy. Indeed, in Parson's framework, the fundamental division of parental roles into primarily instrumental for the father and expressive–affective for the mother probably contributes to the *exclusion* of the father from consideration as a nurturing figure in the infancy period.

A second condition that a conceptualization of father influences should meet is that it should be open not only to individual variation but to important secular changes in the culturally shared definition of appropriate parental roles, attitudes, and values regarding child rearing.

As Lois Hoffman (1977) recently pointed out, the roles of women have clearly changed, with the maternal role occupying less and the wage-earner role occupying more of her adult life. Corresponding adjustments are beginning to appear in men's roles in the form of a more active fathering role and perhaps a decreased emphasis on the breadwinner role. Part of the irrelevance of developmental theory to the father's contributions in the infancy period may stem from an image of them as rather remote, which, indeed, may have been the prevalent pattern before the secular changes described by Hoffman occurred. A good theory, however, should be broader than a simple mirror image of the prevailing cultural practices. It should contribute to our understanding of environmental experience for both modal family patterns as well as family roles and behaviors that depart from our current conceptions of conventionality.

Finally, a conceptualization of father influences must recognize the interdependencies that exist among different family subsystems. It has been a "fiction of convenience" to consider the mother–infant dyad as if it exists and functions in isolation from the social influences of the father–infant and husband–wife relationships. It would be a great disservice to study the father–infant relationship as if it too had an identity that existed in total psychological isolation from the mother. The problem with looking at all interactions involving mother, father, and infant in a totally systemic perspective is that it quickly becomes extraordinarily complex. Therefore, it still seems heuristically useful to abstract out certain components of the father's contribution to different family subsystems and consider them conceptually in relative isolation from each other. In doing so, however, we must still not lose sight of the interrelatedness that each family member has with the others.

Conceptually, then, we may distinguish two different effects of the father. The first is *direct* effects, influences of the father upon the infant that are a product of their immediate interactions. Hypotheses of such influences would seem most cogently formulated in terms of distinctive experiences provided by fathers, ways of interacting that are relatively unique to the father–infant relationship. Direct effects, however, need not be restricted to distinctive experiences. The father also could have a reinforcing effect on development through his behaviors that are highly redundant with the mother's behavior.

A second type of influence is *mediated* effects, influences of the mother on the child mediated through the father's relationship with the mother. This is an instance of the more general proposition that different subsystems of the family influence each other. The husband–wife relationship, of which the father is a part, can provide emotional support to the mother. In meeting some of the mother's emotional and affectional needs, there may be an enhancement of the mother's relationship with the infant. Similarly, the mother might be a source of emotional support to the father, which might influence his interactions involving the infant. The point is that a conceptualization of father influences must recognize these multiple and interlocking networks of influence.

DEVELOPING AN EMPIRICAL BASE FOR UNDERSTANDING FATHER INFLUENCES

Until recently, the most frequently employed research design for studying fathers has been an indirect one: the comparison of children reared in father-absent families with ones reared in father-present families. Biller (1974) has summarized this extensive literature. Herzog and Sudia (1973) provided valuable criticism of the technical and methodological limitations of many of these studies. Pedersen (1976) also noted that this emphasis on *outcome*, effects discernible in the child, does not illuminate the psychological processes that are operating. A deficit-oriented approach does not direct attention to the father's actual behavior within the nuclear family. The father-absence research model cannot contribute to knowledge of the father–child relationship any more than did research on the effects of depriving institutional environments enhance our understanding of the normal mother–child relationship.

With the advent of observational studies of fathers, investigations typically have been concerned with identifying *differences* between father–infant and mother–infant interaction. Two strategies have been used: (1) a comparison of mothers and fathers on frequency counts of parental behaviors that were generally observed in home settings; and (2) a comparison of the infant's behaviors with the mother and father, utilizing the presence or absence of differences as a basis for making inferences about the nature of the infant's relationships with each parent. In the latter strategy, which is often utilized in laboratory observations, parental variance is sometimes reduced (at least theoretically) by instructions to avoid social initiations toward the infant.

A summary of a few of the findings will suffice to illustrate generalizations that may be made. Lamb (1977a, 1977b) found that father–infant interaction, as compared to mother–infant interaction, tended to involve physically vigorous, robust exchanges in play during the first year of life. In the second year, fathers also played more physical games while mothers engaged in verbal and vocal play and play with toys. Yogman and his colleagues (Yogman, Dixon, Tronick, Als, & Brazelton, 1977) also identified differences in sensory modalities preferred by mothers and fathers. In a brief structured interactional situation, distinctive tactile patterns were observed as frequent components of father–infant interaction, while soft repetitive and imitative vocalizations were more characteristic of mothers. This same verbal–physical dichotomy was described by Clarke-Stewart (1977) in a study of 15–30-month-old infants and their parents. Fathers' play was relatively more likely to be physical and arousing, while the play of mothers tended to be verbal and didactic.

A reversal of this pattern of modality preferences was reported in the newborn period by Parke and Sawin (1975). When the infant vocalized, fathers responded with an increased vocalization rate; mothers were more likely to react to infant vocalizing with touching than fathers. Parke and Sawin (1977) also report that, compared to the newborn period, by age three months there tends to be some *convergence* in parental behavior; as they share the care and stimulation of the infant, parents seem to adopt some of their partner's behavior.

New findings from our investigation (Pedersen, Anderson, & Cain, 1978) show additional differences between fathers and mothers. During two home observations conducted in the evenings with five-month-old infants, three out of 12 measures significantly distinguished mothers and fathers. Mothers talked more, smiled more, and fed liquids more; measures of play and physical contact, including vigorous tactile–kinesthetic stimulation, failed to differentiate mothers and fathers even though findings (primarily at older ages) would lead to expectations of differences.

While the global descriptive findings of these investigations are probably a useful first step in understanding the behavior of fathers, the results also may be easily misunderstood. Findings of statistically significant differences between groups of subjects often have a history of becoming reified as if to suggest that *all* members of one group are different from the other. It is easy to forget the very great within-group variability and degree of overlap in the distributions of behavioral scores for the groups. Thus, global findings may foster overgeneralizations. Moreover, the only "findings" of interest are usually differences. The absence of differences in the behavior of mothers and fathers has a tendency to be treated as a nonfinding. Yet, virtually every investigation involved more measures for which differences were not found than ones for which there were differences. The fear of a Type II error should not keep us from appreciating the many ways in which fathers and mothers behave similarly with infants.

The descriptive results that we summarized also suffer from a lack of an explanatory network. On the surface it would appear that differences between mothers and fathers are in some mixture a reflection of basic biological differences and a product of the distinctive socialization and acculturation experiences that males and females receive in relation to their parental roles. Neither explanatory hypothesis is easily testable. A situationally oriented explanation, which appeals more to the demand character of spending differing amounts of time with infants, is also possible. Perhaps to a significant degree behavioral differences related to sex of parent are largely the result of the family's decision regarding their degree of specialization in the wage-earner and child-care roles. All of the major investigations of fathers in the infancy period involved samples that predominantly had the traditional division of labor in which men were highly involved in the wage-earner role and women provided the major proportion of child care. The family's decision on this issue greatly influenced *time distributions* in various kinds of social settings. Time distributions may control, to some extent, not only opportunities for interaction but also affect the quality of interaction. Time in or out of the home is often looked at in terms of whether there is "enough" time for fathers to be with infants, but time distributions may have other influences as well.

To examine the larger picture of how mothers and fathers spend time with infants, we asked families to keep a record over a one-week period to tell us how much time was spent in broad spatial boundaries for different combinations of three people: mother, father, and infant. Time in which father and infant were in general proximity of each other—in the home or out on an errand together—and the mother was totally removed from the situation was on the average a half hour a day, while the time that mother and baby were similarly together without the father was approximately six hours. By far the greatest periods of time in which fathers were potentially available to the infant for interaction were times that *included* the mother within the larger spatial boundaries. There are three implications of this simple finding. The first is that the father frequently has a "back-up," as it were, if he is apprehensive or uncertain about his child-care role. This may help explain the degree of specialization that fathers show in *play* with infants, which has been identified by Richards, Dunn, and Antonis (1975) as well as others. If two parents are potentially available, there is the possibility of some negotiation and contracting between husband and wife regarding the content of activities that occur in interaction with the infant. The mother, most often without a potential substitute during her most characteristic time with the baby, does not have the luxury of behavioral specialization that fathers show. A broadening of fathers' behavioral repertoires with infants might be expected if they were merely together more time when the mother was not also available.

The second implication of the nature of the father's time in the home is that it may provide a pull toward *more* time spent in three-person interaction and less in purely dyadic interaction with the infant.

Lower rates of interaction with the infant characteristically occur in three-person settings. Lamb (1977b) reported such a finding for measures of parental verbal behavior, and our own data show this to be the case with several more differentiated measures as well (Pedersen *et al.*, 1978). The reason for the diminution in interactional rates with the infant is because husband–wife communication occurs during these periods, a point that will be returned to later. What this means is that the father/husband frequently divides his behavior between infant and spouse, while the mother during the day has more focused interaction with the infant, even to the point where she may feel deprived of adult interaction by the end of the day. Thus, three-person settings may have a pull toward a systematic dilution of interactional rates in the father–infant relationship, which in some families might be offset by the father's interludes of more intense and arousing interactional bouts of focused play.

A third feature of time distributions, which may modify the previous point, is that fathers experience relatively long periods of time *away* from the baby, but the mother who provides full-time child care does not. This may increase the potency to the infant of behavior emitted by the father because he represents an element of novelty and change in contrast to the extended periods of interaction with the mother that the infant characteristically experiences. Thus, the salience to the infant of the father's behavior may be enhanced even if he showed relatively low frequencies and duration of interaction. Moreover, the father's attraction to the infant might be heightened and the quality of their interaction may be more intense because of the novelty value that the infant has to the father. There is also a methodological point here that should be considered: Home observations of father–infant interaction are most often made in the early evening, which is the father's "prime time" with the baby. The mother, during this interval, may look for some respite from her child-care role, and observational measures may underestimate the quality and rate of her interaction. Her "prime time" may be during the day in a dyadic context. Thus, it may be difficult to identify a single slice of time in which to conduct observations of mothers and fathers that represents a psychologically equivalent experience for both parents.

THE NEED FOR A MORE COMPLEX ANALYTIC MODEL THAT VIEWS FATHERS IN A FAMILY CONTEXT

The research strategy of looking for differences between mothers and fathers in central tendencies has another limitation from the perspective of understanding infant experience in a family context. It seems plausible that infants know little of central tendencies except when they exceed the limits of adaptation, but they know a great deal about interaction with two particular parents. If we take any variable and find that in about half of the families fathers provide more of it and mothers provide less, while in the other half of the sample the reverse pattern holds, then a comparison of means will show no difference. But the patterning of experiences provided by mothers and fathers with respect to the infant in the two groups will be exactly the opposite of each other. Even *with* a significant difference between the means of fathers and mothers on any measure, the overlap in scores is usually great enough so that very different *patterns* of maternal and paternal behavior are likely to occur. We have argued that, at least for certain questions, it is crucial to preserve the family as the unit of analysis since it is within this context that the infant's experiences occur.

To develop an example of this, differential hypotheses will be presented based upon the Schaffer and Emerson (1964) monograph on attachment, recognizing from the outset that the "state of the art" is now much advanced over their original work. They defined attachment by maternal report as crying at separation in a variety of circumstances. Two variables were found to be associated with the formation of attachment relationships: (1) responsiveness to crying; and (2) the provision of stimulation. At a conceptual level, these two parental behaviors would seem to promote respectively in humans the two major developmental trends that Mason (1970) identified in infant monkeys: the contact-seeking filial responses of early infancy—sucking, clinging, and the like—and the exploitative responses that are arousal-increasing, as reflected in vigorous motor play, exploration, and robust social activities. If the human mother and father in the same family were differentially responsive to their infant on Schaffer and Emerson's dimensions, it would be possible to make differential predictions of the nature of the infant's attachment relationships. To keep this simple, we will examine only one variable and use as a dependent variable proximity seeking in a mildly stressful situation, recognizing Bretherton and Ainsworth's (1974) distinction of attachment and affiliative behavior.[1]

In Figure 1, Cell A represents a mother and father who are both highly responsive to crying. An infant from such an environment might show early multiple attachments. Mothers and fathers would be predicted to be equally satisfactory sources of comfort in an anxiety-

---

[1] A similar approach to understanding parental influences in a family context has been examined empirically in research conducted by Jay Belsky at Cornell University (personal communication).

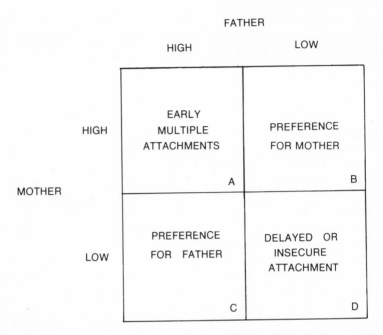

FIG. 1. Hypotheses of variation in maternal and paternal responsiveness to crying as predictors of the infant's proximity seeking. Independent variable: responsiveness to crying. Dependent variable: proximity seeking in a mildly stressful situation.

arousing situation. Simple matters of convenience in the setting should account for any differential responsiveness and attachment preferences. This pattern, indeed, might correspond to many of the middle-class parents included in the sample studied by Spelke, Zelazo, Kagan, and Kotelchuck (1973), who found few differences between infants' reactions to separations from mothers and fathers. Cell B represents a mother high on responsiveness to crying and a father who is low. This pattern, if it occurred in slightly more than half of the sample, would explain Lamb's (1977b) finding of the infant preferring the mother in a mildly stressful situation. It also might explain the failure of Lester, Kotelchuck, Spelke, Sellers, and Klein (1974) to replicate the findings with respect to fathers in a Guatemalan sample that Spelke *et al.* (1973) reported for the United States sample; in Guatemalan culture fathers have more remote relationships with infants. Cell C consists of fathers who are high on responsiveness to crying and mothers who are low. This is similar to a pattern that we have identified in a small group of cesarean-delivered infants. Perhaps because these mothers were somewhat uncomfortable and debilitated in the posthospitalization period, the fathers took over much of the care-giving responsibilities when they were home. When the

infants were five months old, the fathers were observed to be significantly more responsive to fussing and crying than fathers whose infants
were vaginally delivered as well as more responsive than their wives. In
this case the father would be predicted to be the preferred fear-reducing
figure in mildly arousing situations. Cell D might represent the "insecurely attached" infants described by Ainsworth, Bell, and Stayton
(1971) or infants with a delayed attachment, since neither parent is
particularly responsive to the infant's needs for arousal reduction.

A similar formulation may be worked out for Schaffer and Emerson's
other predictor of attachment, providing stimulation, although the more
plausible dependent variable would be the infant's responsiveness to
arousing stimulation. Obviously, all possible combinations of two levels
for two variables with both parents greatly increases the complexity of
the formulation, but the general principle remains the same: the influence of one parent can only be meaningfully evaluated in relation to the
other parent as well. We hypothesize that infants learn expectancies that
certain behaviors will be forthcoming from their parents as responses to
signals, and when a mother and father show differential responsiveness,
the infant will make appropriate social comparisons and seek out the
more responsive parent when choices are available. An analysis that
does not preserve the identity of differences between parents at the level
of an individual family cannot unscramble such potentially important
differential effects.

MEDIATED EFFECTS: THE IMPORTANCE OF THE
HUSBAND–WIFE RELATIONSHIP

In the previous section we have discussed the distinctive experience
provided by fathers to infants, and emphasized that notions of distinc-
tiveness are *comparative* in nature. Thus, any consideration of paternal
behavior must be seen in relation to similar or contrasting experiences
provided by the mother. In this section, we will examine mediated
effects, also called indirect effects by Lewis and Weinraub (1976) and
second-order effects by Bronfenbrenner (1974). Generally speaking, the
problem is one of understanding how the interaction of two people, for
example, mother and infant, may be influenced by a third person, such
as the father. In this example, the questions may be formulated in terms
of whether the father causes the mother to inhibit certain behaviors,
whether the father has an influence that facilitates or increases certain
maternal behavior, or whether the father's influence is one that causes
a distortion or change in the character of the mother's behavior. Just as
the question of distinctive father experiences has tended to ignore the

family as the unit of analysis and concentrate on group comparisons, research addressing mediated or second-order effects has also tended to be global in nature. The simplest formulation of the problem has been to compare rates of behavior in two-person settings with those in three-person settings. The characteristic finding, illustrated in Lamb's research (1977b), is that there is a diminution of rates of verbalizations directed toward the infant in three-person settings. This effect has been accepted as an "ecological reality" that requires no special explanation. As we alluded to earlier, it seems much more meaningful to understand the diminution of interaction with the infant in terms of observable family interactional processes.

We hypothesized that the interactional rates with the infant are influenced by spouse communication, which, of course, is more likely to occur in three-person settings. By means of a time-sampling observational system that described the interaction of all *three* dyadic units within 10-second observation intervals, we obtained interesting descriptive data that allowed more complex analyses than would be possible merely by observing the mother–infant and father–infant interaction. The categories of spouse communication included general verbalizations, verbalizations about the baby, helping or requesting help in the care of the baby, and expressions of positive or negative affect.

The data indicate, first of all, that spouse interactions were highly prevalent when mother, father, and infant were together. Fifty-one percent of the observation units included spouse interactions (scores were derived from two observations an hour in length conducted usually during the evenings). When we compared the rates of behaviors directed toward the baby (separately for mothers and fathers) during units when the parents were communicating with each other to units when the parents were *not* communicating with each other, we were able to observe an interesting synchrony between spouse interaction and infant-directed behavior.

To simplify the reporting of results, we have consolidated the 12 measures of parent–infant interaction into four, more general indexes. They are as follows: (1) *Distance Receptor Stimulation*, which includes any instance of mutual visual regard, talking, or vocalizing to the infant, or smiling; (2) *Near Receptor Stimulation*, including holding, rocking, active touching, or vigorous tactile–kinesthetic stimulation; (3) *Social Play*, including focused social play or play involving toys and physical objects; and (4) *Feeding*, which includes feeding solids or liquids. All measures were proportions, with the denominator being the number of units the parents were observed when they were interacting with each other or when there was no co-occurring spouse interaction. Table 1 indicates the results using analyses of variance.

TABLE 1. Comparisons of Maternal and Paternal Behaviors Directed to Infant During Intervals in Which Spouse Communication Occurred or Not[a]

Variables		Intervals in which spouse communication occurred		Intervals in which no spouse communication occurred		F-ratios		
		Mothers	Fathers	Mothers	Fathers	Sex of parent	Spouse communication condition	Interaction
1. Distance receptor stimulation (4 measures)	M	.22	.21	.43	.32	5.5[b]	143.2[c]	11.6[c]
	SD	.10	.10	.11	.17			
2. Near receptor stimulation (4 measures)	M	.23	.26	.26	.23	.05	.00	3.3
	SD	.18	.16	.18	.15			
3. Play (2 measures)	M	.03	.04	.08	.07	.01	60.3[c]	3.3
	SD	.03	.04	.06	.06			
4. Feeding (2 measures)	M	.12	.09	.12	.06	2.8	3.5	1.7
	SD	.12	.11	.14	.08			

[a]Entries represent the proportion of observation intervals in which a behavior occurred.
[b]$p < .05$.
[c]$p < .01$.
$df = 1/40$ for all comparisons.

The results indicate one significant sex of parent difference, distance receptor stimulation, accounted for by the higher verbalization and smiling rates that mothers showed toward infants. Two measures, distance receptor stimulation and play, had highly significant relationships with the spouse-communication conditions. For these measures there was a decrement during units in which any spouse communication occurred, but there was a marked intensification of interaction with the baby during units when there was no spouse communication. Distance receptor stimulation also showed a significant sex of parent by spouse-communication interaction. While for mothers there was a two-fold increase in rates of distance receptor interaction with the infant when spouse communication did not occur, the rate of increase for fathers was still substantial but only half-again as great. For both distance receptor stimulation and play, parent–infant interaction in three-person settings partake of some of the elements of more intensive dyadic interaction when the spouse unit is not psychologically engaged, but there is a decrement in interaction rates with the infant when husband and wife are in active communication with each other. Thus, the differences in interaction rates between two- and three-person settings that have been reported appear to be largely mediated by the spouse relationship. Near receptor stimulation often involves parental behavior requiring less focused attention, such as holding, rocking, or touching the infant, and this variable does not reflect variation in relation to spouse communication. Similarly, feeding the infant, which by age five months is a highly routinized activity, also is insensitive to the occurrence of spouse communication. An important implication of these findings is that knowledge about interactional processes involving husband and wife contribute to our understanding of the kind of stimulation parents are likely to provide the infant in three-person settings.

The value of observational measures of husband–wife interaction for broader research questions is supported by the approach taken by Robert Weiss and his colleagues (Weiss, Hops, & Patterson, 1973; Wills, Weiss, & Patterson, 1974). They have all but abandoned traditional global indexes of "marital satisfaction" and other self report techniques that are highly subject to response sets or social desirability motives. Methodological critiques show little convergent validity to self-report measures of the marital relationship and meager construct validity to measures of marital satisfaction. Behavioral approaches may provide a more promising access to the spouse relationship.

Other investigations of the husband–wife relationship have tended to rely on self report methodologies. For example, the concept of emotional support provided by the husband for the wife is widely accepted. Barry (1970) has offered the most comprehensive formulation of the importance of emotional support to the mother. His thesis is that emotional support is most important during periods of role transition, and the transition from wife to wife and mother involves a more pervasive role transition than does the counterpart change for fathers.

Among the interesting findings in the literature, Shereshefsky and Yarrow (1973) report that the wife's successful adaptation to pregnancy is associated with the husband's support. Husband support during labor and delivery lessens maternal distress (Anderson & Standley, 1976). Additional evidence for the importance of emotional support to the mother is seen in a retrospective study of postpartum depression, a condition in which maternal effectiveness is at a very low level. Mothers who exhibited depressive symptoms characterized their husbands as particularly cold and distant (Kaplan & Blackman, 1969). Feiring and Taylor (1978) reported that the mother's evaluation that there were positive supportive elements in her relationship with the "Secondary Parent" was associated with her provision of stimulation to the baby and a heightened sensitivity to infant signals. In a study of four-week-old infants that had thorough methodological independence in accessing the husband–wife relationship and the mother–infant interaction, Pedersen (1975) found that the wives whose husbands evaluated them positively in their performance of the mothering role were independently rated as more capable and proficient in managing the feeding process. As a final example of this type of relationship, an unpublished study by Switzky, Vietze, and Switzky (1974) showed that the mother's practice of breast feeding was associated with support and encouragement from the husband, which was less in evidence in families where the mother bottle-fed.

Many other dimensions of the husband–wife relationship merit attention to see whether they impinge on either parent's interaction with the infant. Competition between parents in relation to the infant and conflicting expectations regarding each other's behavior would be predicted to undercut the confidence of an inexperienced parent. Discrepant *perceptions* of the infant's behavior and temperament, which are most likely to occur when the parents have few shared experiences with the baby, may also influence each's interactions with the infant (Pedersen, Anderson, & Cain, 1977).

It is also interesting to speculate whether *fathers* need emotional support to maintain effective parent–infant relationships. Fein (1976) reported that many men feel excluded and "left out" after the birth of a child; they also feel that there are few institutional supports for the paternal role. There has been little research on fathers' needs for support, perhaps because traditional sex-role sterotypes foster the image of men as "strong" and women as "weak" and in greater need of support. Wills *et al.* (1974), in a study that focused on the behavioral components of marital satisfaction and excluded explicit consideration of parental behaviors, suggest that husbands do indeed have needs in the spouse relationship, but they may be somewhat different than the needs of wives. They reported that the husband's discontent in the spouse relationship was associated with his wife's low rates or low quality of instrumental behavior, while the wife's dissatisfaction was associated with low rates of affectional behavior provided by her husband. The mention anecdotally that husbands, moreover, sometimes have difficulty distinguishing instrumental from affectional behavior. When a husband was asked to increase his rate of affectional responses to his wife and the wife reported no change in her observations of her spouse, the husband replied, "I don't know why, I washed her car!" The interesting paradox here, from Parson's perspective, is that the so-called instrumental leader, the husband, desired instrumental performance from the wife, while the expressive leader, the wife, desired expressive and affectional responses from the husband.

Since virtually all socialization research has been formulated in terms of dyadic parent–child units, these complex influences of a third member of the family have rarely been examined. This may be one of the greatest conceptual and methodological challenges to our understanding of early experience in the home environment.

HYPOTHESES REGARDING PATERNAL INFLUENCES ON THE INFANT

Just as we urged caution regarding the value of making global generalizations regarding the behavior of fathers as a homogenous class of parent, as distinguished from mothers, so also it would appear unwise to hypothesize outcomes that are inherent to *all* father–infant relationships. Outcomes must ultimately depend upon the character and unique properties of the relationship, and upon how it meshes with the total family organization. Thus, we would expect few monolithic effects of fathers that would occur universally, independently of variation in paternal behavior and the larger family context of which it is a part. On the other hand, we do not wish to restrict hypotheses to a clinical case level of specificity. Therefore, what we will present are hypotheses of effects on development that, within the nuclear family, have a high likelihood of being relevant to a reasonably wide range of paternal behavior.

The earliest father–infant interactions, particularly those occurring in proximity to the mother, provide a basis for wide range of sensory discriminations that, on the basis of experimental evidence, would appear to be well within the young infant's capacities. Such discriminations include: differences in the visual configurations of the mother's and father's faces; differences in the frequency range, intensity, and modulation of their voices; olfactory differences; differences in the vigor and tempo of physical movements involving the baby's body; and differences in behavior that is responsive to the infant's needs and signals. It is not unusual to observe the young infant apparently make visual comparisons between two people at the time when the baby is transferred from one person to another. At the very least, such opportunities to make relatively simple perceptual discriminations are likely to provide the basis for more complex later discriminations and learning. As a consequence of these discriminations, the father encourages an expansion of the infant's environment and promotes an awareness that interesting and responsive people exist outside of the tight symbiotic unit with the mother. The introduction of another distinctive nurturant and stimulating figure therefore is likely to aid in establishing boundaries between the infant and the outside world, an important step in the individuation process and the subsequent development of autonomy.

A second hypothesis is that the father–infant relationship affects early schema development and, in turn, the infant's cognitive capacities. Paternal interactions introduce other dimensions to the infant's experiences. Differences in the behavioral repertoires of father and mother add to the variety and novelty of the infant's life and increase the richness of the infant's experiences. As a result, the infant may become receptive to a wider range of stimulation and show more differentiated behaviors. Some support for this hypothesis has been reported by Clarke-Stewart (1977); she found that differences in parental stimulation tended to have a positive effect on children's intellectual and social development.

The young infant also appears capable of establishing differential expectancies for mother and father. In an early study based upon maternal report (Pedersen & Robson, 1969), about three-fourths of a sample of middle-class nine-month-old infants were described as showing "greeting behavior" to their fathers upon reunions that followed time out of the home associated with work. These greetings consisted of smiles, vocalizations, bursts of excitement, and efforts to approach the fathers; their most obvious interpretation was that pleasurable interactions were anticipated from the fathers at that time. The expectations appear differential because few mothers reported similiar glee to their own reunions, largely because very few had such predictable absences. Infant excitement with the mother was more typically associated with the initiation of a particular care-giving activity, such as a bath, or a familiar social game. Using highly refined observational technology, Brazelton and his associates (Chapter 2, this volume) suggest that even the much younger infant has differential expectancies during face-to-face interactions with mother and father, and that it can regulate its own behavior to maintain synchrony with either parent. At a later age, evidence of differential expectancies is seen in the syntactic structure used for requests by a two-year-old girl (Lawson, cited in Ervin-Tripp, 1977). She differentiated strongly between her father and mother, using repetition and politeness modifiers more with her father than her mother. The significance of establishing differential expectancies, we believe, is that they equip the child for interaction in a broader social world than that encompassed by the mother. They may assist in the development of early role-taking behavior, which requires that the child "read" the behavior of another and respond within appropriate boundaries.

Lewis and Weinraub (1976) have presented the hypothesis that the infant's development of representational thought is associated with the special relationship provided by the father. Their core idea is that representational thought and language are often used in the service of dealing with objects that are not physically present. Because in so many children's lives it is primarily the father who departs and reappears daily, children learn the label "Daddy" before they learn the label "Mommy." This is apparently so despite more exposure to the Mommy label. To this hypothesis we may add an idea formulated by George Kelly (1955). Kelly maintains that the form a "personal construct," a schema with which a person organizes his or her own behavior in relation to another, the construct must differentiate among *three* people. Simply to make a distinction between two people, such as "me" versus "not-me," does not require a construct, according to Kelly. The construct must subsume two people and differentiate them from a third; otherwise, it is not clear that an abstraction exists, that something more than a concrete discrimination has been made. If the child has a construct of "me" versus "not-me," and "not me" subsumes two people such as mother and father, then the child is on the way to developing the construct system needed for more complex social exchanges. If this formulation is valid, then a three-person (or larger) family might lend itself to the process of developing personal constructs and representational labels.

Another effect of the father is his influence on the infant's attachment to the mother. We know of no investigations that have directly pursued this research question; mother–infant attachment has been investigated only as a purely dyadic process. Yet, as we suggested earlier, the differences between father and mother in appearance and behavior, especially behavior coordinated with the infant's dues, signals, and arousal patterns, provide important discrimination learning opportunities that are necessary for the development of focused relationships. Even if the father were somewhat inept in his behavior and insensitive to the infant, as some stereotypes suggest men with little experience with children are, these very differences could accentuate the infant's awareness of the mother's sensitivity and responsiveness, thus promoting the intenseness of their relationship. The father also may contribute to the development of mother–infant attachment through other indirect routes; his providing care as well as periods of playful interaction can give the mother a respite that is supportive. The affectional relationship between husband and wife and his emotional support to her in the mothering role may enhance her nurturant behavior. The father's involvement in activities that are instrumental to family functioning, whether income production or the performance of household tasks, can also free the mother for a very specialized relationship with the infant if that is how the parents prefer to structure their roles for this period of development.

Several of the effects we described—social discriminatory capacities, differential expectancies, and an expanded repertoire of behavior—are likely to be consolidated in the development of the father–infant attachment relationship. Despite a burgeoning literature on attachment between mother and infant, there is still a paucity of research dealing with the development of attachment to the father. To give one example of a glaring omission, there has not been a single longitudinal investigation reported that spans the preattachment period and the period when a focused father–infant relationship is clearly manifest. We do not know whether there are conditions that promote father–infant attachment as a gradually evolving process or whether there are instances when it shows a significant degree of discontinuity. Moreover, it is not known whether, or under what circumstances, the father–infant attachment relationship is a substitute or a supplementary relationship, or whether it is completely different in a qualitative sense from the infant's characteristic relationship with the mother. Just as Ainsworth, Bell, and Stayton (1971) identified multiple categories for describing mother–infant attachment—albeit in rather evaluative terms—it would seem possible to identify multiple patterns of father–infant attachment in both descriptive and dynamic understandings that recognize the spectrum of variation found in the family today.

In addition to defining types of attachment to the father, we need to understand what this particular relationship means to the infant for subsequent development. It may be that establishing a positive and intense relationship with a person in addition to the mother makes it easier for the infant to extend social ties beyond the immediate family and to establish trusting relationships with others. This speculation is one of several interpretations possible from the finding that infants whose fathers interacted frequently with them cried less when they were left by either father or mother with a stranger in an unfamiliar setting (Kotelchuk, 1976; Spelke *et al.*, 1973). These children may have been able to "use" the stranger, as it were, in a more trusting manner, thereby showing less apprehension in an unfamiliar separation situation. Another hypothesis of consequences of the father–infant attachment relationship is that, insofar as their interaction contained robust, arousing, and activating stimulation, it may promote in the infant greater receptivity to activities involving high rates of stimulus change. This might appear as greater novelty-seeking and exploratory behavior, as well as greater tolerance for the fear-arousing aspects of unfamiliar events. Finally, it is likely that the father– infant attachment relationship is the foundation for the identification process of later childhood. Identification does not arise out of a psychological vacuum; it is likely that many of the precursors of identification begin with earlier interactions and experiences during infancy.

ACKNOWLEDGMENTS

The authors gratefully acknowledge the constructive suggestions provided by Dr. Martha Zaslow. Appreciation is also expressed to Ms. Nancy Gist, who assisted in the research project mentioned in this paper, and to Mrs. Terry Pezza Schmidt and Mrs. Shirley Meeks, who prepared the manuscript.

REFERENCES

Ainsworth, M. D., Bell, S. M., & Stayton, D. J. Individual differences in strange situation behavior of one-year-olds. In H. R. Schaffer (Ed.), *The origins of human social relations.* New York: Academic, 1971.

Anderson, B. J., & Standley, K. A methodology for observation of the child-birth environment. Paper presented at the meeting of the American Psychological Association, Washington, D.C., September, 1976.

Barry, W. A. Marriage research and conflict: An integrative review. *Psychological Bulletin,* 1970, 73, 41–55.

Biller, H. B. *Paternal deprivation.* Lexington, Mass.: D.C. Heath, 1974.

Bretherton, I., & Ainsworth, M. D. Responses of one-year-olds to a stranger in a strange situation. In M. Lewis & L. A. Rosenblum (Eds.), *The origins of fear.* New York: Wiley, 1974.

Bronfenbrenner, U. Developmental research, public policy, and the ecology of childhood. *Child Development*, 1974, *45*, 1–5.

Burlingham, D. The preoedipal infant–father relationship. *Psychoanalytic Study of the Child*, 1973, *28*, 23–47.

Clarke-Stewart, K. A. The father's impact on mother and child. Paper presented at the biennial meeting of the Society for Research in Child Development, New Orleans, La., March, 1977.

Eiduson, B., Cohen, J., & Alexander, J. Alternatives in child rearing in the 1970s. *American Journal of Orthopsychiatry*, 1973, *43*, no. 5, 720–731.

Ervin-Tripp, S. Wait for me, roller skate! In S. Ervin-Tripp & C. Mitchell-Kernan (Eds.), *Child discourse*. New York: Academic Press, 1977.

Fein, R. A. The first weeks of fathering: The importance of choices and supports for new parents. *Birth and the Family Journal*, 1976, *3*(2), 53–58.

Feiring, C., & Taylor, J. The influence of the infant and secondary parent on maternal behavior: Toward a social systems view of infant attachment. Unpublished manuscript, 1978.

Forrest, T. The paternal roots of male character development. *The Psychoanalytic Review* 1967, *54*, 81–99.

Glick, P. C., & Norton, A. J. Marrying, divorcing, and living together in the U. S. today. *Population Bulletin*. 1977, *32*, no. 5, 3–39.

Herzog, E., & Sudia, C. E. Children in fatherless families. In B. M. Caldwell & H. N. Ricciuti (Eds.)., *Review of child development research* (Vol. 3). Chicago: University of Chicago Press, 1973.

Hoffman, L. W. Changes in family roles, socialization, and sex differences. *American Psychologist*, 1977, *32*(8), 644–657.

Kaplan, E. H., & Blackman, L. H. The husband's role in psychiatric illness associated with childbearing. *Psychiatric Quarterly*, 1969, *43*, 396–409.

Kelly, G. A. *The psychology of personal constructs*. New York: Norton, 1955.

Kotelchuck, M. The infant's relationship to the father: Experimental evidence. In M. E. Lamb (Ed.), *The role of the father in child development*. New York: Wiley, 1976.

Lamb, M.E. Father–infant and mother–infant interaction in the first year of life. *Child Development*, 1977-a, *48*, 167–181.

Lamb, M. E. The development of mother–infant and father–infant attachments in the second year of life. *Developmental Psychology*, 1977-b, *13*(6), 637–648.

Lewis, M., & Weinraub, M. The father's role in the child's social network. In M. E. Lamb (Ed.), *The role of the father in child development*. New York: Wiley, 1976.

Lester, B. M., Kotelchuck, M., Spelke, E., Sellers, J. J., & Klein, R. E. Separation protest in Guatemalan infants: Cross-cultural and cognitive findings. *Developmental Psychology*, 1974, *10*, 79–85.

Mason, W. A. Motivational factors in psychosocial development. In W. J. Arnold & M. M. Page (Eds.), *Nebraska symposium on motivation*. Lincoln: University of Nebraska Press, 1970.

Parke, R. D., & Sawin, D. B. Infant characteristics and behavior as elicitors of maternal and paternal responsiveness in the newborn period. Paper presented at the meeting of the Society for Research in Child Development, Denver, Colo., April, 1975.

Parke, R. D., & Sawin, D. B. The family in early infancy: Social interactional and attitudinal analyses. Paper presented at the meeting of the Society for Research in Child Development, New Orleans, La., March, 1977.

Pedersen, F. A. Mother, father and infant as an interactive system. Paper presented at the meeting of the American Psychological Association, Chicago, Ill., September, 1975.

Pedersen, F. A. Does research on children reared in father-absent families yield information on father influences? *The Family Coordinator*, 1976, *25*(4), 459–464.

Pedersen, F. A., Anderson, B. J., & Cain, R. L. An approach to understanding linkages between the parent–infant and spouse relationships. Paper presented at the meeting of the Society for Research in Child Development, New Orleans, La., March, 1977.

Pedersen, F. A., Anderson, B. J., & Cain, R. L. Parent–infant interaction observed in a family context at age 5-months. Manuscript in preparation. Bethesda, Maryland, 1978.

Pedersen, F. A., & Robson, K. S. Father participation in infancy. *American Journal of Orthopsychiatry,* 1969, *39,* 466-472.

Richards, M. P. M., Dunn, J. F., & Antonis, B. Caretaking in the first year of life: The role of fathers' and mothers' social isolation. Unpublished manuscript, University of Cambridge, 1975.

Schaffer, H. R. *Mothering.* Cambridge: Harvard University Press, 1977.

Schaffer, H. R., & Emerson, P. E. The development of social attachments in infancy. *Monographs of the Society for Research in Child Development,* 1964, *29*(3), (Whole No. 94).

Shereshefsky, P. M., & Yarrow, L. J. *Psychological aspects of a first pregnancy and early postnatal adaptation.* New York: Raven Press, 1973.

Spelke, E., Zelazo, P., Kagan, J., & Kotelchuck, M. Father interaction and separation protest. *Developmental Psychology,* 1973, *9,* 83–90.

Switzky, L. T., Vietze, P., & Switzky, H. Attitudinal and demographic predictors of breast-feeding and bottle-feeding behavior in mothers of six-week-old infants. Unpublished manuscript, George Peabody College, Nashville, Tn., 1974.

Weiss, R. L., Hops, H., & Patterson, G. R. A framework for conceptualizing marital conflict, a technology for altering it, some data for evaluating it. In F. W. Clark & L. A. Hanerlynck (Eds.), *Critical issues in research and practice: Proceedings of the Fourth Banff International Conference on Behavior Modification.* Champaign, Ill.: Research Press, 1973.

Wills, T. A., Weiss, R. L., & Patterson, G. R. A behavioral analysis of the determinants of marital satisfaction. *Journal of Consulting and Clinical Psychology,* 1974, *42,* No. 6, 802–811.

Yogman, M. J., Dixon, S., Tronick, E., Als, H., & Brazelton, T. B. The goals and structure of face-to-face interaction between infants and fathers. Paper presented at the meeting of the Society for Research in Child Development, New Orleans, La., March, 1977.

4

The Infant's Exposure to Talk by Familiar People: Mothers, Fathers, and Siblings in Different Environments

Charles W. Greenbaum and Rivka Landau

The caretaker's verbal stimulation of infants has long been considered an important element in the cognitive and emotional growth of the child. A basic problem in this area is the identification of the components of this stimulation that contribute to the child's cognitive and linguistic development (Bruner, 1975). This report will attempt to approach the problem through an examination of the speech to which the infant is exposed by significant others in his environment during his first year of life. We will pay attention to the speech of the infant's father and his sibling as well as that of his mother, and we will take note of possible changes in familiar people's speech during this first year.

It has been demonstrated that infant vocalization is subject to influence by reinforcement or stimulation (Rheingold, Gewirtz, & Ross, 1959; Ramey & Ourth, 1971; Bloom, 1975). Vocalization responses by

CHARLES W. GREENBAUM AND RIVKA LANDAU • Department of Psychology, The Hebrew University of Jerusalem. The authors are grateful to the following organizations that have tendered financial support to this research at various stages: U.S. Office of Education, Bureau of Research, Grant No. C–1–70173084465; Human Development Center, Research and Development Authority, John Dewey School of Education, and Paul Baerwald School of Social Work, all at Hebrew University of Jerusalem; U.S. Joint Distribution Committee; and the Ford Foundation through the Israel Foundation Trustees.

infants and mothers appear to occur with high frequency relative to other responses (Lewis, 1972; Landau, 1976) and to occur in close time proximity to one another (Gewirtz & Gewirtz, 1969; Lewis, 1972; Lewis & Lee-Painter, 1974). Some recent studies (e.g., Snow, 1977) suggest that mother–infant interaction may have a consistent structure. For example, the mother uses a large number of interrogatives; mother and child take turns talking; and the mother's speech takes on a more complex quality at about seven months of age. While these studies provide important insights into the nature of early interaction, they are based on small samples in controlled situations that do not necessarily constitute natural settings for the child or the mother.

A number of studies have reported social-class differences in verbal stimulation of infants by mothers: Pavenstedt (1965); Tulkin and Kagan (1972); Snow, Arlman-Rupp, Hassing, Jobse, Joosten, and Vorster, (1976); and Dunn, Wooding, and Hermann (1977). The middle-class mother is likely to display more speech, and of a more detailed or complex quality, than the lower-class mother. Similar findings are reported for older children's age groups (Bernstein, 1961; Hess & Shipman, 1965; Bee, Van Egeren, Streissguth, Nyman, & Leckie, 1969; Sigel & McGillicudy-De Lisi, this volume), which suggests that a pattern of low frequency and/ or quality of speech by mothers in the presence of children may be established early and continue on into the school-age period. It is a matter of dispute, however, whether such patterns of interaction signif- icantly affect the child's linguistic or cognitive development; some studies argue against the existence of such effects (Labov, 1970; Kagan & Klein, 1973).

Although much of the research on infant–environment interaction involves mothers, there has been a recent surge of interest in fathers and siblings (e.g., see Lamb, 1976a, 1978). Results are uniform in showing that fathers interact with infants less than mothers do, but it is not clear how much of such interaction fathers actually engage in. Some interview studies (Pedersen & Robson, 1969; Newson & Newson, 1974) report relatively high rates of self-reported interaction, of one hour or more. At least one study, however (Lewis & Weinraub, 1974), reports self-reported interaction averaging no more than 15 or 20 minutes a day. In addition to the methodological problems associated with interview studies, it is uncertain from these data whether the parents were reporting on the amount of time they spent in the presence of the child or in interaction with him or her.

The picture yielded by research based on observations of interaction suggests that the amount of father presence and degree of interaction, particularly verbal and vocal interaction, are low, even lower than that which would be expected from the interview studies (Gewirtz & Gewirtz, 1968, 1969; Rebelsky & Hanks, 1971; Friedlander, Jacobs, Davis, & Wetstone, 1972). A considerable range exists, however, and there is a small number of fathers who interact with their children a great deal. The father's interaction with the child is usually of a different nature from that of the mother: he is more likely to engage in social interaction and play than in caretaking activities (Lamb, 1976b, 1977; Rendina & Dickersheid, 1976), and his play may be characterized by rapid cyclical changes (Brazelton, Yogman, Als, & Tronick, this volume). The father is capable of caretaking activities (Parke & Sawin, 1976), however, and despite the relatively low amount of interaction that infants engage in with their fathers, they become attached to their fathers, perhaps as strongly as they do to their mothers (Spelke, Zelazo, Kagan, & Kotelchuk, 1973; Lewis & Weinraub, 1974; Lamb, 1976b, 1977).

With regard to siblings, Dunn and Kendrick (this volume) have shown that infants of eight and fourteen months are capable of sustained, complex, and affective interaction with their older siblings. However, we have very little information from available research on the long-term effects of infant interaction with siblings.

The data-base for any firm conclusions concerning the importance of vocal interaction between the infant and the significant others (mother, father, and sibling) in his social environment is thus small despite some reliable findings. Most of the studies of the infant's interaction with mother, father, and sibling have concentrated on one or, at the most, two of these individuals, making direct assessments of the impact of each of them, as well of their total influence, impossible. In order to understand the social network of the infant (Lewis & Feiring, this volume), observation of his interaction with all familiar people, and particularly all the significant others just mentioned, is needed. There is also a lack of systematic study of infant–environment interaction in societies other than Western, industrialized ones; and of vocal interaction at different time points during the first year.

This report is one of a series from a project in which 96 infants under the age of one year were observed for one full day. Each infant's behavior and that of any person who came into contact with him was recorded by trained observers who coded the behavior according to a detailed scheme that covered social, emotional, and motor behaviors as well as vocal behaviors. Many thousands of responses were thus recorded, constituting a data set from which topics are selected for report. Infants were observed in their natural settings in a cross-sectional design at four age points: two, four, seven, and eleven months. The ages were chosen in order to capture possible transition points in social development. The infant subjects were drawn from five different Israeli child-rearing environments. One environment is represented by the Bedouin of the Negev desert, whose native language is Arabic. The four other environments are Jewish, in which Hebrew is the spoken language: middle-class, lower-class, kibbutz, and residential institution. All but the last of these environments will be termed "home" environments.

Previous reports in this series have shown that the mother provides the bulk of the stimulation provided by people familiar to the child. This was particularly true with respect to some major social and verbal responses, including the speaking of sentences and words (Landau, 1976) in all four home environments studies here. The mother's contribution to total stimulation was somewhat less in the kibbutz, though there, too, she is the most active person. The mother's verbal stimulation in any of the home environments was greater than that of all the caretakers of a child in the institution (Greenbaum & Landau, 1977). Furthermore, the mother's vocal and social behaviors and those of her infant are somewhat different in a short-term "directed" situation in which she is requested to elicit certain responses from her child, from those that she exhibits during the course of an entire day (Landau, 1977). The Landau findings indicate the problems involved in generalizing from studies that examine infant–mother interaction in short-term situations to the nature of such interactions in the long term, and the need for assessing the natural settings in which the infant's behavior takes place.

The first part of this report will describe the rate of speaking of sentences by mothers, fathers, and siblings in the presence of the infant under observation. Sentences constitute the single most frequent verbal category displayed by adults in these environments. Greenbaum and Landau (1977) reported that mothers' rates of speaking sentences and words were generally less in the presence of eleven-month-old infants than in the presence of two-month-olds.

The second part of the report will describe some selected verbal responses made by familiar people interacting with the infant, responses that may reflect characteristic styles of interaction at different age points in the infant's first year. These responses are: asking questions; using baby talk; and calling the child by name.

The vocalization responses selected for study in this project represent a middle road between the detailed examination provided by psycholinguistic studies, and the general term "vocalization" used in many studies of interaction involving the infant. It was our assumption that the molar level of analysis of the responses studied here may shed useful light on the nature of the vocal exchange between infants and others.

Our investigation thus attempted to obtain basic information necessary for the eventual solution of the problems concerning infant

–environment interaction that we raised earlier. We chose the environments studied here for a number of reasons. First, they allow us to
examine variations in the amount and type of stimulation to which they
expose the growing infant. Institutions were assumed to have the least
amount and least variation, while the kibbutz and middle-class were
thought to have the most. The number of caretakers who deal with the
child can also be examined; the largest number of different caretakers
exists in the institution, where the child has no contact with his family.
In the kibbutz the mother's caretaking is shared with a special caretaker
(called a *metapelet*) at the children's house. In the other environments
the mother is the single major caretaker. Finally, the environments also
differed in the degree that their ideologies demanded a division of labor
between mother and father in the caretaker role: the Bedouin are the
most traditional society in this respect. In their society, the mother is
assigned the major responsibility for child care. The kibbutz, on the
other hand, has the most egalitarian ideology. The kibbutz father is
expected to take an active part in the socialization of his child from the
earliest stage.

Thus, evidence that mothers, fathers, or siblings act differently from
each other and similarly to others in the same role in other environments
would provide support for a hypothesis that emphasizes a universal
division of labor concerning child-care roles. Differences among environments, on the other hand, could support hypotheses based on
assumptions that regard the effects of culture on such roles as critical.
We also tried to determine whether age-related patterns exist in the
speech of others to infants, and whether these patterns differ in various
cultures and at different ages of the child. We had particular interest in
the difference between the middle-class environment and the other
environments, less studied previously.

METHOD

A brief description of the subjects, the methods used in observation,
and the environments studied will be presented here. Further details
may be found in earlier publications in this series (Landau, 1976, 1977;
Greenbaum & Landau, 1977).

Subjects and Their Environments

Subjects were 96 infant boys studied by means of a cross-sectional
design at two, four, seven and eleven months of age. Five environments
were studied. Five children were observed at each age level in four of

these environments: middle-class, lower-class, kibbutz, and residential institution; a total of 20 infants was thus sampled from each of these environments. We observed four Bedouin infants at each age, for a total of 16 in that environment.

The behavior of the infant and of all people coming into contact with the child was observed and recorded. This report will concern itself only with the people with whom the child has contact, and not with the behavior of the child. We will present behavior rates of three specific participants in interactions with the child: mother, father, and the sibling; the last could be either male or female. In addition, means of combined behavior measures (to be described below) are presented for the following familiar people (including the three already mentioned): mother, father, older sibling (in home environments), caretaker (in the kibbutz or institution), grandparent, and neighbor child.

All infants in the middle-class, lower-class, and Bedouin samples were members of intact families in which the mother was not working from the birth of the child until after the observation. In the kibbutz, middle-class, and lower-class families, the infant observed was a second-born boy in a family of Western (i.e., not of Middle Eastern or North African) origin. Middle-and lower-class families all lived in apartments of two to three-and-one-half rooms in an urban area. Middle-class parents had at least 12 years of education and were drawn from the managerial, academic, or free professional occupations. Lower-class parents had a maximum of nine years of education and represented merchant, semiskilled, or unskilled occupations.

The Bedouin studied here live in tents or huts arranged in tribal groupings in the Negev (southern) region of Israel. The Bedouin mother is continuously occupied with the care of her infant during his first year of life, and carries him with her wherever she goes. The Bedouin engage in shepherding, some agriculture, and occasional work in nearby towns. Marx (1967) gives an extensive account of the life of Israeli Bedouin.

The collective settlement known as the kibbutz has been described by a number of writers (see Spiro, 1958; Talmon-Garber, 1972). The kibbutz infants studied here were born to second-generation kibbutz parents who had high-school educations. Although the infants live in special children's houses under the care of a *metapelet*, the parents take an active part in the care of the child, particularly during the first half-year (Gewirtz & Gewirtz, 1969; Landau, 1976).

The institutionalized children were selected from two institutions in which children from problem families and children born to unwed mothers were placed. Most of the children were of North African and Middle Eastern origin. The children received excellent nutritional and medical care and adequate clothing. The physical plant was well-kept. Infants were kept in more or less homogeneous age groups, six or seven to a room. A head nurse was in charge of three or four rooms, but most of the infant care was in the hands of student nurses who came and went in the course of a day, and were replaced every few months.

Observation System

The observation system used has much in common with that developed by Gewirtz and Gewirtz (1965, 1969). One important difference is the larger amount of detail devoted to vocalization in the observation system used here. One hundred and eleven infant response categories were noted and 107 for those who came into contact with him. Sixteen of the infant response categories and 24 of the response categories of others consist of vocalization responses. All responses were recorded, and the observer noted whether or not they were directed at the child. This report will deal with all responses, whether or not the child was the target.

The specific verbal responses of familiar others to be reported on in this study are described below. Two reliability indices, based on percentage agreement between two independent observers, appear in parentheses after each category. They are based on a total of approximately eight hundred half-minute units of observation, carried out by pairs of observers from a pool of six. These observations were carried out before and during the collection of data, on infants who were not part of the study sample. The first index to appear in each case shows percent agreement as the result of dividing agreements between two observers by agreements, disagreements, and omissions; the second index ignores omissions.

Sentences (60,82). These are declarative strings of words expressing a thought. One-word utterances were considered in a separate category, not reported on here. Sentences constitute the most frequent category used by others in contact with the child.

Questions (56,79). These are statements of a clearly interrogative nature as judged by word order or pitch.

Baby Talk (55,71). Statements characterized by intonations and inflections similar to those of children but not a direct imitation of a specific response of the child.

Calling the Child by Name (78, 95).

These reliability levels are similar to those obtained for systems of comparable levels of complexity (see Caldwell, 1969; Gewirtz & Gewirtz, 1969; and Lytton, 1973). A large part of the error in observation is due to omissions. Agreement concerning a response is reasonably high once it is detected. This suggests that much of the bias concerning response levels would be in the direction of underestimation.

Six female graduate students, who had trained for six months, served as observers. They noted the behavior of the child and those who came into contact with him sequentially, in spiral notebooks. All behaviors were located in 30-second time units.

Procedure. All infants were observed in their natural habitats for the equivalent of one full day, to be called a behavior day. The observations were held on weekdays, not Sabbaths or holidays. In all environments except the Bedouin, a time-schedule similar to that developed by Gewirtz and Gewirtz (1969) was used. The observation was conducted over two successive half-days. The observation on the first half-day began at about noon and continued until the child went to sleep. The next day the observation began as early as possible in the morning and ended at the same time as the beginning of the previous day's observation. The same observer worked both days. Due to special problems in carrying out the observations among the Bedouin, the observations there were carried out in one day, working from the morning until the late afternoon, using two observers who relieved each other at hourly intervals.

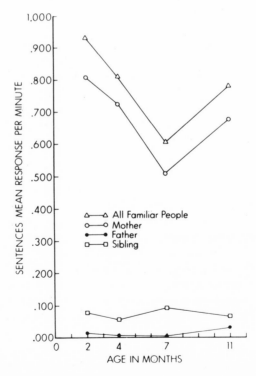

Fig. 1. Mean rate per minute of sentence speaking in presence of infant by all familiar people, mothers, fathers, and siblings, in the middle class, in four age groups.

RESULTS

The vocal responses reported on here were subject to multivariate and univariate analyses of variance using the Miami MANOVA program (Clyde, Cramer, & Sherin, 1966). The basic design used was a factorial consisting of the factors of age (four levels) by environment (five levels), performed separately for all familiar people, mothers, fathers, and siblings.

Vocal stimulation to which the child is exposed: sentence-speaking by mothers, fathers, and siblings. Figures 1 to 5 show the mean rates of speaking of sentences to which children were exposed. These data are presented for mother, father, and sibling separately, and for the total rate summed over all familiar people (including the above three). Each figure shows a different environment. The data for all familiar people, except institutions, were reported by Landau (1976); Greenbaum and Landau (1977) presented the data on sentences spoken by mothers. The results are displayed here for purposes of comparison with fathers and

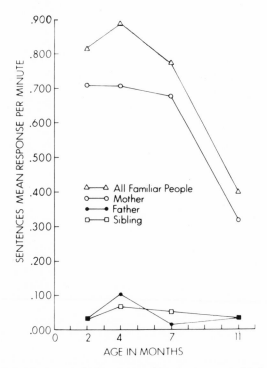

FIG. 2. Mean rate per minute of sentence-speaking in presence of infant by all familiar people, mothers, fathers, and siblings, in the lower class, in four age groups.

siblings. The rates of speaking were determined by dividing the total number of sentences spoken by the total number of minutes in the behavior-day observation. These figures thus reflect the amount of exposure of the child to this stimulation during the time that he was awake. Since mothers, fathers, and siblings were not present in the institutions, Figure 5 shows means for summed data for all familiar people only.

A number of striking results are worth noting in these data. One is the relatively small part played by fathers in providing this type of verbal stimulation; in every subgroup, the mother provides several times more than the father. Siblings provide more stimulation than fathers in most cases. It is thus clear that not only do the mothers provide the bulk of the verbal stimulation to which the child is exposed as reported by Landau (1976), but fathers provide little verbal stimulation, generally less than that of siblings. Within-subject t-tests show that

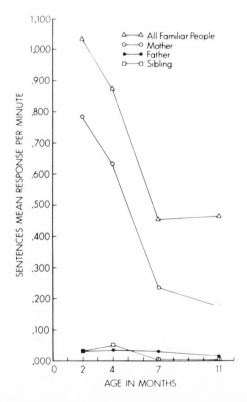

Fig. 3. Mean rate per minute of sentence-speaking in presence of infant by all familiar people, mothers, fathers, and siblings, in the kibbutz, in four age groups.

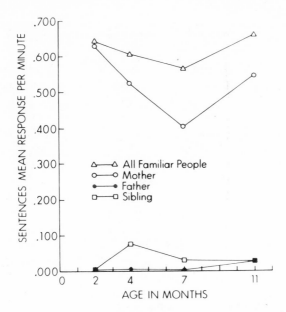

FIG. 4. Mean rate per minute of sentence-speaking in presence of infant by all familiar people, mothers, fathers, and siblings, among the Bedouin, in four age groups.

the differences between mothers and fathers and between mothers and siblings are significant at every age level in every environment; in some comparisons the distributions of sentence-speaking by mothers, as compared with fathers and siblings, do not overlap. The differences between fathers and siblings are not significant.

The total exposure to this kind of verbal stimulation does not increase with age: analysis of variance shows that the effect of age on all familiar people's response is not significant. Previously (Greenbaum &

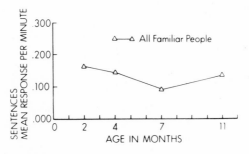

FIG. 5. Mean rate per minute of sentence-speaking in presence of infant by all familiar people in institutions, in four age groups.

Landau, 1977) we showed a drop in mother's vocalization with age. The presence of other people helps to mitigate, but not reverse, this downward trend. This previous report has also shown that despite the fact that the child's exposure to stimulation does not increase with age, his own rate of vocalization increases dramatically: vowels peak at seven months, and consonants and vowel-consonant combinations continue to increase until eleven months (Greenbaum & Landau, 1977).

Institutionalized children studied here are exposed to far less verbal stimulation than children in home environments, as indicated by a significant effect for environment on speaking of sentences, $F(4,76) = 8.35, p < .001$, and between-group comparisons by t-test, which showed that only the difference between the institution and the other environments was significant. The difference is very large in an absolute sense: Home-reared children receive four or five times as much exposure to sentences as institutionalized children. These results augment those reported earlier comparing mothers in home environments with caretakers in institutions (Greenbaum & Landau, 1977): institutionalized infants of the type studied here are deprived, even when familiar people in homes and institutions are considered.

How does the talk to which the infant is exposed change as he grows older? While sentences have been shown to fall off slightly with age, other verbal behaviors, less often used, may develop differently. The data in Figures 6 to 8 show the behavior of all familiar people in their

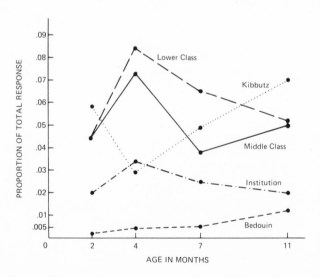

FIG. 6. Familiar people's questions as mean proportions of their total responding, by age and environment.

interaction with each child expressed as proportions of their total behavior. The means of these proportions appear for each subgroup. Proportions are presented here instead of rates because they better reflect the relative effort, compared to other behaviors, which the familiar people invested in these verbal responses. Results for rates are very similar to those presented here.

Figure 6 indicates that the use of questions expressed in phrases in the presence of the infant increases from two to four months in four of the five environments; the effect of age, however, is not significant. Environment does show a significant effect, $F(4,76) = 18.33, p < .001$, indicating that the familiar people in the urban and kibbutz environments use this response much more than do the familiar people in the Bedouin and institution environments.

Figure 7 shows a different course of development for another response category, baby talk. Here, no environment peaks at four months while three environments peak at seven months. The effect of age is significant, $F(3,76) = 2.94, p < .04$; so is the effect of environment, $F(4,76) = 9.02, p < .001$, indicating that institutionalized infants receive far less of this stimulation than do infants in home environments.

A similar pattern is found for the category of calling the child by name (Figure 8). Familiar people in the two urban environments used this response the most when the child was seven months old. The effect of age is significant, $F(3,76) = 2.88, p < .04$.

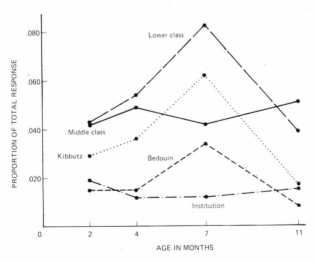

Fig. 7. Familiar people's baby talk as mean proportions of their total responding, by age and environment.

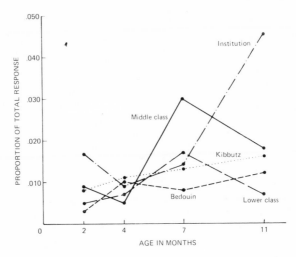

FIG. 8. Familiar people's calling the child by name as mean proportions of their total responding, by age and environment.

While we cannot provide systematic data concerning imitations by familiar people of infant responses because of observer reliability problems with this category, some impressions may be enlightening. Frequencies of imitations appear to be quite low, lower than any of the other verbal responses. Imitations of consonants uttered by the child, however, increase in frequency at seven and eleven months in contrast to the preceding ages.

The indications are that familiar people do change their strategies of speaking in the presence of the child as he grows older: sentences peak at two months, questions at four months, baby talk and calling the child by name at seven months. Sentences remain the most frequent category. Institutionalized infants not only receive a small amount of stimulation, but caretakers do not appear to change their behavior very much as the child grows older, and verbal stimulation forms a low proportion of their total behavior.

DISCUSSION

What part do fathers play in the infant's development? The relatively small part played by fathers in the verbal stimulation of the child, in contrast to the large, even overwhelming part played by mothers, raises the question of the relative importance of the father in the development of the infant. The data from this study appear to be consistent with those of other studies (e.g., Rebelsky & Hanks, 1971; Friedlander, Jacobs, Davis, & Wetstone, 1972; Rendina & Dickerscheid, 1976) that have reported a relatively small degree of vocal interaction between fathers and infants. The present study provided direct comparison with the amount of stimulation provided by mothers, siblings, and the total of all familiar people. It showed similar patterns of low rates of father–infant interaction in four home environments. Egalitarian kibbutz fathers interacted verbally no more than traditional Bedouin fathers. These findings are made more salient when we consider that verbal stimulation accounts for a large proportion (about 30%) of the total stimulation provided the child, that most caretaking activities are the mother's province, and that the mother alone provides about 80% of the total social stimulation of the child (see Landau, 1976).

The results reported here suggest that the fathers' relative inactivity is not necessarily explained by lack of time to spend with the child. In the Bedouin environment the fathers are often around the home a great deal of the time, but not in interaction with the child. Family time in the late afternoon is part of the daily program for every kibbutz family, but here, too, proximity does not necessarily mean interaction, even though fathers in all environments may be seen to engage in intensive bursts of playful activities with their infants. A learning-performance distinction may be helpful here (Lewis & Weinraub, 1976): fathers are capable of caring for and interacting with infants (Parke & Sawin, 1976), but generally they do little of either.

A somewhat different perspective on fatherhood has been presented in the recent research by Pedersen and Robson (1969), Pederson, Yarrow, Anderson, and Cain (this volume), Lewis and Weinraub (1974), Parke and Sawin (1976), Lamb (1976b, 1977), and Brazelton, Yogman, Als, and Tronick (this volume). These studies emphasize the unique role that fathers may play in the development of the infant, especially in the acquisition of attachment responses to the father. These studies also indicate that the mother plays a major role in the caretaking of the child, and the leading role in verbal stimulation. The father engages the infant primarily in play, but he spends relatively little time even on that (Rendina & Dickerscheid, 1976).

It should be remembered that results reported here are based on full-day observations in different environments, and on comparisons among mothers, fathers, siblings, and others within each environment. Taken together with the research we have cited, our results suggest that the demonstrated capabilities of fathers do not receive a great deal of expression in day-to-day life. However, our results have not shown in detail all the distinct avenues of expression, verbal and nonverbal, which may characterize the father (see Lamb, 1976b; Brazelton *et al.*, this volume). A preliminary examination of other data from our project indicates that fathers do not spend a great deal of time playing with their infants. Here, too, fathers' play, though less than the mothers', may be of a different character. We have also not dealt with the possible "indirect" effects of the father's influence (see Pedersen *et al.*, this volume), such as emotional and material support for the mother, which may have an effect on the child.

One hypothesis that suggests itself from the results of the various research studies, including this one, is that the father has little influence on the growing infant, and a particularly small effect on his cognitive development. There is no evidence that father deprivation in the first year of life has any adverse effect on the infant (see Biller, 1971, 1974; Radin, 1976). The interaction that fathers engage in could be compensated for by siblings, relatives, or consistent visitors. In fact, father deprivation *only* in the first year or two of life has not been studied, but some preindustrial societies practice separation of fathers from mothers for long periods after childbirth. In this arrangement, the infant is almost exclusively in the company of the mother and other women. While this practice may have characteristic effects (see Whiting, 1961), it may not necessarily lead to any obvious harm. In fact, enforced separation of fathers from infants is seen in some societies as beneficial.

These results showing similar patterns of verbal interaction between fathers and infants in four environments lead to the tentative conclusion that the pattern of intense mother–infant interaction coupled with low father–infant interaction may be universal. This pattern could reflect an avoidance of verbal interaction on the part of fathers. While there is no evidence that this pattern has a biological base, such a possibility cannot be ruled out; neither can the explanation that fathers learn not to interact verbally with infants. The father's avoidance would complement the active role of the mother at this stage of the child's life, and thus play an important indirect role (Pederson *et al.*, this volume).

All of this does not mean to say that fathers may not be important for other aspects of the child's growth, particularly social–emotional behavior. They may also become important at later stages in the child's life. However, the nature and the timing of the father's contribution to the child's development, while potentially important, remains to be determined.

The fact that older siblings interact with the infant slightly more than the father suggests that the role of the child as "teacher" (Zajonc & Markus, 1975) should be explored and utilized. One suggestion would be for intervention programs to encourage and train siblings to talk to their younger infant brothers and sisters. They may be better at doing this than fathers. The complex interaction of which even young siblings are capable is encouraging in this regard (see Dunn, 1979).

Are there stages in the development of talk to children? There is tentative support for a hypothesis that at least three definable stages exist in the development of talk in the presence of infants. These may be characterized as follows: (The ages indicated here are those that appeared as peaks in our sample, and should be regarded as approximations only).

1. *Two months: Sentences and words.* These elements of ordinary discourse appear to be at their highest level at the age of two months. (See Landau, 1976; Greenbaum & Landau, 1977, for data on frequency of exposure of the infant to speaking of words.) While they decrease in overall usage, sentences and words remain as the two response categories most frequently used by people in the child's environment in his first year.

2. *Four months: Questions.* This category coincides with a high use of vowel sounds and a moderate use of consonants by infants (Greenbaum & Landau, 1977). The use of questions may be seen as an attempt to stimulate talk by the child, at a time when more complex babbling is beginning to make its appearance.

3. *Seven months: Baby talk and calling the child by name.* These categories come into a great deal of use at a time when the child is continuing a high rate of vowel sounds, along with a further moderate increase in consonant sounds. This may be the context in which adults enter into a dialogue with the child "on his own level." The adult may now feel less need to specifically stimulate the child to vocalize by using the interrogative form. The use of the infant's name in the conversation may indicate an implicit assumption by the adult that the child has a growing self-awareness that may be fostered by addressing the child in this manner.

There is a hint in our data, indicated previously, that there may be a fourth stage in adult speech, one characterized by imitations. If this stage exists, it may reflect a recognition by the adult of the more complex nature of the child's vocalizations, and an attempt to engage in specific instruction.

The pattern of adult speech to which the child is exposed is based on selection rules that are not as yet well understood. Adults use a heavy barrage of sentences and words that decreases as the child grows older. As the child's vocal repertoire becomes more varied (see Irwin, 1948) and his vocalization more frequent, questions, followed by baby talk and calling the child by name make their appearance in adult speech. The adult thus selects those responses that appear to be appropriate to the child's developmental level.

The stages described above appear to be most typical of the urban environments, both middle- and lower-class. Adults among the Bedouin and the kibbutzim appear to have somewhat different patterns when examined across age levels, indicating that there may be no "universal" set of stages in adults' talk with infants. Familiar others in the institutions studied here exposed their children to rather low levels of speech, which (except in the case of calling the child by name) did not change much as the child grew older.

These considerations emphasize the need for caution in interpreting any differences in adult speech associated with the child's age as universal "stages." The stages suggested by our data should be seen as tentative hypotheses. This caution should also be applied to other recent studies that posit stages on the basis of observations of the child in short segments of interaction enacted for the observer (e.g., Snow, Arlman-Rupp, Hassing, Jobse, Joosten, & Vorster, 1976; Snow, 1977). These studies report results divergent from ours in some respects. Snow (1977), for example, reports a greater use of interrogatives by mothers than that found here. While such differences may be due to a number of factors, including somewhat different definitions of the category, we suggest that a major element in the discrepancy may be the nature of the situation in which the data are collected. The use of interrogatives may be higher, for example, in short-term situations in which the interaction is videotaped, and where the adult may be trying to elicit as much speech from the child as possible in a short time period. Such behavior may not be typical of the adult's behavior in the course of a day covering many hours of interaction (see Landau, 1977). In brief, any suggestion of stages in adult or child behavior must be qualified by the situation in which the data are collected, and stages that appear in Western middle-class home environments may not be typical of cultures in other areas. We will now briefly turn to a discussion of those "other" environments.

The Adequate Environment: Non-Middle-Class and Non-Western Cultures

In one of the few studies that compare the behavior of parents in Western industrialized societies with those in nonindustrialized societies Kagen and Klein (1973) report that rural Guatamalan parents spend less time with their infants than do middle-class American parents. The present study, however, indicates that the Bedouin child, who also lives in a nonindustrialized society, receives no less verbal stimulation from his environment than does a middle-class Western child. This result emphasizes the need for taking into account specific behaviors on the part of adults in the child's environment, in addition to the time that adults spend in the child's presence. There may be differences in the amount and kind of stimulation provided by parents in preindustrial cultures from that provided by parents in industrial societies. It would be important to determine this directly. The patterns of stimulation provided by familiar others in the Bedouin and kibbutz environment are different from each other and somewhat different from those provided in urban Western home environments. For example, familiar others in Bedouin society appear to talk in the presence of their older infants more than Western familiar others do. Thus, our data strongly indicate that a preindustrial society, far from depriving its children in their first year, may provide a social environment as rich as that of Western environments, though the pattern of stimulation over time may be different.

The studies indicated earlier have reported more verbal stimulation provided by middle-class than lower-class mothers (Pavenstedt, 1965; Tulkin & Kagan, 1972). However, the present report and the previous ones from this project (Landau, 1976, 1977) have found that lower-class parents provide at least as much social and verbal stimulation as middle-class parents. In contrast to the Bedouin, lower-class parents show age patterns similar to the middle class in amount of stimulation. Comparability of the samples used here may provide the answer: both middle- and lower-class families studied here were of the same ethnic group and lived in apartments of similar size. This suggests that neither a relatively small amount of education nor living in a non-Western culture leads to lower levels of stimulation than those provided by the Western middle class. Living in an urban home environment, whether middle- or lower-class, appears to be associated with one kind of age-related pattern of adult stimulation. Other environments may lead to different patterns, but not necessarily lower levels of stimulation.

If these conclusions prove valid, it follows that different cultures and environments, and not only the Western middle-class family, have the potential to provide adequate verbal stimulation for the growing infant. The meaning of "adequate" most probably refers to a quantitative level above that provided the infants in the institutions reported on here. An adequate level of stimulation probably implies a variety of alternative strategies for talking to the growing, and growingly vocal, infant. We suggest that many such strategies are possible, once parents respond to the child above a minimum baseline. The long-term effects of such different patterns of interaction could be subjected to systematic study.

A further implication concerns infants in residential institutions. Clearly, infants in large institutions of the type studied here were exposed to low levels of stimulation in comparison to all the other home environments studied. The effects are potentially disastrous. Assessment of the infant's environment in the institution using methods similar to those used here could serve as the basis for intervention directed at administrative change in the institution and the retraining of caretakers. The goal of such intervention would be to bring the levels of verbal stimulation and the types of contingency relationship in line with those found in normal home environments. It appears that institutions can be homelike and effective in their approach to child care (Tizard & Tizard, 1974).

The infant under the age of one year in a number of different environments grows up in a social network in which the mother is the central figure. Other people, including fathers and siblings, play supporting roles whose importance needs to be assessed. In their interaction with the child, the behavior of familiar others changes in response to growth in the behavior of the child; the child is thus an active agent in his own socialization, and in the socialization of those around him (see Bell, 1968, 1974). We have still to work out the degree of influence that the child and those around him exert on each other. This can best be done by directly studying the contingency relation between the child's response and the behavior of the people with him (see Gewirtz & Gewirtz, 1969; Lewis & Lee-Painter, 1974). The direct observational study of the behavioral interaction between the child and others in different social environments is critical for gaining proper perspective on the effect of the social environment on the growing infant.

ACKNOWLEDGMENTS

We wish to thank the following individuals for their devoted service to the project in performing observations and/or analyzing data: Martha Haddad, Zafrira Yourgroy, Rachel Dotan, Miriam Natan, Shulamith Wishniak, Meira Ben-Dov, Aliza Rosen, Chaim Nissimov, Eliahu Komay, Therese Haddad, Daniella Nahon, Michal Kaplan, Gadi Blum, Aliza Hed, Shalom Zur, Avner Zur, Yisraela Novak, and Nili Yohan. The following institutions gave generously of their time and advice in obtaining subjects for research: Kibbutz Seminary, Oranim; the Ministries of Health and the Interior; Wizo Baby Home, Jerusalem; and Omna Baby Home, Haifa; We are grateful to the families of the children and to individual kibbutzim for allowing us to enter their homes for purposes of observation. This study owes much to discussions with Jacob Gewirtz and Yitzchak Schlesinger.

REFERENCES

Bee, H. L., Van Egeren, L. F., Streissguth, A. P., Nyman, B. A., & Leckie, M. S. Social class differences in maternal teaching strategies and speech patterns. *Developmental Psychology*, 1969, 1, 726–734.

Bell, R. Q. A re-interpretation of the direction of effects in studies of socialization. *Psychological Review*, 1968, .75, 81–95.

Bell, R. Q. Contributions of human infants to caregiving and social interaction. In M. Lewis & L. Rosenblum (Eds.) *The effect of the infant on its caregiver*. New York: Wiley, 1974, pp. 1–20.

Bernstein, B. Social class and linguistic development: A theory of social learning. In A. H. Halsey, J. E. Floud, & C. A. Anderson (Eds.), *Education, economy and society*. New York: Free Press of Glencoe, 1961, pp. 288–314.

Biller, H. B. *Father, child and sex-role*. Lexington, Mass.: Lexington Books, 1971.

Biller, H. B. *Paternal deprivation: Family, school, sexuality and society*. Lexington, Mass.: Lexington Books, 1974.

Bloom, K. Social elicitation of infant vocal behavior. *Journal of Experimental Child Psychology*, 1975, *20*, 51–58.

Brazelton, T. B., Yogman, M., Als, H., & Tronick, E. Mother–father infant interaction. In M. Lewis & L. Rosenblum (Eds.), *The child and its family*. New York: Plenum, 1979.

Bruner, J. The ontogenesis of speech acts. *Journal of Child Language* 1975, *2*, 1–20.

Caldwell, B. M. A new "approach" to behavioral ecology. In J.P. Hill (Ed.), *Minnesota symposia on child psychology* (Vol. 2). Minneapolis: University of Minnesota Press, 1969, 74–109.

Clyde, D. J., Cramer, E. C., & Sherin, R. J. *Multivariate statistical programs*. Coral Gables, Florida: University of Florida, 1966.

Dunn, J., & Kendrick, C. Interaction between young siblings in the context of family relationships. In M. Lewis & L. Rosenblum (Eds.), *The child and its family*. New York: Plenum, 1979.

Dunn, J., Wooding, C., & Hermann, J. Mothers' speech to young children: Variation in context. *Developmental Medicine and Child Neurology*, 1977, *19*, 629–638.

Friedlander, B. Z., Jacobs, A. G., Davis, B. B., & Wetstone, H.S. Time sampling analysis of infants' natural language environments in the home. *Child Development*, 1972, *43*, 730–40.

Gewirtz, H. B., & Gewirtz, J. L. Visiting and caretaking patterns for kibbutz infants. *American Journal of Orthopsychiatry*, 1968, *38*, 427–443.

Gewirtz, H. B., & Gewirtz, J. L. Caretaking settings, background events and behavior differences in four Israeli child-rearing environments: Some preliminary trends. In B. M. Foss (Ed.), *Determinants of infant behavior*, IV. London: Methuen, 1969, pp. 229–252.

Gewirtz, J. L., & Gewirtz, H. B. Stimulus conditions, infant behaviors, and social learning in four Israeli child-rearing environments: A preliminary report illustrating differences between the "only" and the "youngest" child. In B. M. Foss, (Ed.), *Determinants of infant behavior*, III. London: Methuen, 1965, 161–184.

Greenbaum, C. W., & Landau, R. In P. H. Leiderman, S. R. Tulkin, & A. Rosenfeld (Eds.), *Culture and infancy: Variations in the human experience*. New York: Academic Press, 1977, pp. 245–270.

Hess, R. D., & Shipman, V. Early experience and the socialization of cognitive modes in children. *Child Development*, 1965, *36*, 869–886.

Irwin, O. C. Infant speech: Development of vowel sounds. *Journal of Speech and Hearing Disorders*, 1948, *13*, 31–34.

Kagan, J., & Klein, R. E. Cross-cultural perspectives on early development. *American Psychologist*, 1973, *28*, 947–961.

Labov, W. The logic of nonstandard English. In F. Williams (Ed.), *Language and poverty: Perspectives on a theme*. Chicago: Markham, 1970, pp. 153–189.

Lamb, M. E. (Ed.) *The role of the father in child development*. New York: Wiley, 1976a.

Lamb, M. E. Interactions between eight-month old children and their fathers and mothers.

In M. E. Lamb (Ed.), *The role of the father in child development*. New York: Wiley, 1976b, pp. 1–61.

Lamb, M. E. Father–infant and mother–infant interaction in the first year of life. *Child Development*, 1977, *48*, 167–181.

Lamb, M. E. Father–infant relationships: Their nature and importance. *Youth and Society*, 1978, *9*, 277–298.

Landau, R. Extent that the mother represents the social stimulation to which the infant is exposed: Findings from a cross-cultural study. *Developmental Psychology*, 1976, *12*, 399–405.

Landau, R. Spontaneous and elicited smiles and vocalizations of infants in four Israeli environments. *Developmental Psychology*, 1977, *13*, 389–400.

Lewis, M. State as an infant–environment interaction: An analysis of mother–infant behavior as a function of sex. *Merrill-Palmer Quarterly*, 1972, *18*, 95–121 ·

Lewis, M., & Feiring, C. The child's social network. In M. Lewis and L. Rosenblum (Eds.), *The child and its family*. New York: Plenum, 1979.

Lewis, M., & Lee-Painter, S. An interactional approach to the mother–infant dyad. In M. Lewis & L. Rosenblum (Eds.), *The effect of the infant on its caregiver*. New York: Wiley, 1974, 21–48.

Lewis, M., & Weinraub, M. Sex of parent × sex of child; socioemotional development. In R. Richart, R. Friedman, & R. Vande Wiele (Eds.), *Sex differences in behavior*. New York: Wiley, 1974, pp. 165–190.

Lewis, M., & Weinraub, M. The father's role in the child's social network. In M. E. Lamb (Eds.), *The role of the father in child development*. New York: Wiley, 1976, pp. 157–184.

Lytton, H. Three approaches to the study of parent–child interaction: Ethological, interview, and experimental. *Journal of Child Psychology and Psychiatry*, 1973, *14*, 1–17.

Marx, E. *Bedouin of the Negev*. Manchester, England. Manchester University Press, 1967.

Newson, J., & Newson, E. Cultural aspects of childrearing in the English-speaking world. In M. P. M. Richards, (Ed.), *The integration of a child into a social world*. London: Cambridge University Press, 1974, pp. 53–82.

Parke, R., & Sawin, D. B The father's role in infancy: A re-evaluation. *The Family Coordinator*, 1976, *25*, 365–371.

Pavenstedt, E. A comparison of the child-rearing environment of upper-lower and very low-lower class families. *American Journal of Orthopsychiatry*, 1965, *35*, 89–98.

Pedersen, F. A., & Robson, K.S. Father participation in infancy. *American Journal of Orthopsychiatry*, 1969, *39*, 466–472.

Pedersen, F., Yarrow, L., Anderson, B., & Cain, C. Conceptualization of father influences in the infancy period. In M. Lewis & L. Rosenblum (Eds.) *The child and its family*. New York: Plenum, 1979.

Radin, N. The role of the father in cognitive, academic and intellectual achievement. In M. Lamb (Ed.), *The role of the father in child development*. New York: Wiley, 1976, pp. 237–276.

Ramey, C., & Ourth, L.L. Delayed reinforcement and vocalization rates of infants. *Child Development*, 1971, *42*, 291–298.

Rebelsky, F. & Hanks, C. Father verbal interaction with infants in the first three months of life. *Child Developmert*, 1971, *42*, 63-668.

Rendina, I., & Dickerscheid, J. D. Father involvement with first-born infants. *The Family Coordinator*, 1976, *25*, 373–378.

Rheingold, H., Gewirtz, J. L., & Ross, H. Social conditioning of vocalizations in the infant. *Journal of Comparative and Physiological Psychology*, 1959, *52*, 68–73.

Sigel, I., & McGillicuddy-De Lisi, A. The impact of the family on chidren's cognitive development. In M. Lewis & L. Rosenblum (Eds.), *The child and its family*. New York: Plenum, 1979.

Snow, C. E. The development of conversation between mothers and babies. *Journal of Child Language*, 1977, *4*, 1–22.

Snow, C.E., Arlman-Rupp, A., Hassing, Y., Jobse, L., Joosten, J., & Vorster, J. Mothers' speech in three social classes. *Journal of Psycholinguistic Research*, 1978, *5*, 1–20.

Spelke, E., Zelazo, P., Kagan, J., & Kotelchuk, M. Father interaction and separation protest. *Developmental Psychology*, 1973, *9*, 83–90.

Spiro, M. *Children of the kibbutz*. Cambridge, Mass.: Harvard University Press, 1958.

Talmon-Garber, Y. *Family and community in the kibbutz*. Camridge, Mass.: Harvard University Press, 1972.

Tizard, J. & Tizard, B. The institution as an environment for development. In M. P. M. Richards (Ed.), *The integration of a child into a social world*. Cambridge, England: Cambridge University Press, 1974, pp. 137–152.

Tulkin, S., & Kagan, J. Mother–child interaction: Social class differences in the first year of life. *Child Development*, 1972, *43*, 31–42.

Whiting, J. W. M. Socialization process and personality. In F. L. K. Hsu (Ed.), *Psychological anthropology*. New York: Dorsey, 1961, 360–365.

Zajonc, R., & Markus, G. Birth order and intellectual development. *Psychological Review*, 1975, *82*, 74–88.

5

The Family as a System of Mutual Influences: Parental Beliefs, Distancing Behaviors, and Children's Representational Thinking

ANN V. MCGILLICUDDY-DE LISI, IRVING E. SIGEL, AND JAMES E. JOHNSON

INTRODUCTION

Two major research approaches have been used in investigations of the relationship between family environment and the development of cognitive ability in children. One line of research has related family constellation variables, such as spacing and number of children, to intellectual outcomes, while the second line of research has related measurements of the family environment to intellectual outcomes. An instance of the former type of research is the confluence model (Zajonc & Markus, 1975). Within this model, each additional child in the family is viewed as "diluting" the intellectual environment of the home to a degree depending on the spacing between siblings. The focus of this

ANN V. MCGILLICUDDY-DE LISI AND IRVING E. SIGEL • Educational Testing Service, Princeton, New Jersey 08541. JAMES E. JOHNSON • Department of Psychology, University of Wisconsin, Madison, Wisconsin. This research was supported in part by NICHD Grant RO1 H10 686-01.

approach is to predict differences in patterns of family configuration effects found for large samples, rather than to explicate specific interaction patterns in the home environment that could produce such findings.

A second research approach has focused on providing detailed descriptions of patterns and processes in the home environment that relate to children's cognitive performance rather than on status or population variables *per se*. Results of these studies indicate that there is a large degree of variability in parental practices and that specific practices are related to individual variation in children's level of cognitive functioning (Bing, 1963; Bee, Van Egeren, Streissguth, Nyman, & Leckie, 1969; Brophy, 1970; Cicirelli, 1976; Hess & Shipman, 1965; Jones, 1972; Radin, 1974). Based on such findings, it has been argued that there is a need to investigate specific and observable behavior patterns in families that vary with respect to demographic population and status variables (cf. Freeberg & Payne, 1967; Leichter, 1974). Data reported by researchers responding to this need indicate that interaction patterns between family members do vary with characteristics such as SES and number of children (Lewis & Feiring, this volume; Walberg & Marjoribanks, 1976), suggesting that specific measurement of family environments that vary with respect to family configuration will increase our understanding of its role in the socialization of competence.

There have been many attempts to relate hypothetical constructs (such as parental attitudes or values) that are known to vary with family size or SES, to differential childrearing practices or to child outcomes. Few reliable relationships have been found (Becker & Krug, 1965). Perhaps a new approach, rather than the traditional focus on specific caretaking functions or parental styles, e.g., warmth–cold, authoritarian–democratic, will reveal a more salient set of hypothetical constructs that serve as mediators between core inner states and parental behaviors that affect children's development. Our position is that the mediators that are salient for us in understanding family dynamics are parental belief systems, existing with permeable boundaries, and therefore with the potential for change as information provided by a changing family configuration is assimilated to that system.

CONCEPTUALIZATION OF A BELIEF SYSTEM

A basic premise of our research with families is that parent belief systems (constructs) about children in general and about optimal childrearing techniques contribute significantly to parental teaching and managerial strategies that affect the child's level of cognitive functioning. This premise is derived in part from the work of George Kelly, who has created a system known as Constructive Alternativism (Kelly, 1955, 1963), and in part from our own work applying distancing theory to family interactions (McGillicuddy-De Lisi & Sigel, 1977; Sigel, 1971). Kelly proposes that each individual formulates her/his own constructs and views the world through these constructs. We propose that parents actively construct belief systems about children on the basis of their own experiences. The beliefs, or constructs, are used to categorize events and guide parents' behavior with respect to the child, just as Kelly's personal constructs are seen as the directing source of behaviors in interacting with any other person. Thus, the parents' construction of their own children and of child development processes in general are taken to be a source of parental child-rearing practices.

A Definition of Beliefs: The Constructivist Position

The importance of parental belief systems and conceptualizations about the child in relation to parental practices seems obvious. What the parent believes about the cognitive capabilities of the child is likely to be a major influence on parental practices. Furthermore, parental beliefs about the cognitive growth of the child cannot be construed in isolation; rather, beliefs are constructed by the parent and are in part dependent on information obtained from interactions with each child in the family unit and are influenced by cultural, subcultural, and educational factors (Sigel & Cocking, 1977).

Within such a framework, constructs of social and physical reality can serve to maintain a coherent perspective of the world. However, since individuals live in an environment that produces both confirmation and disconfirmation of existing systems, each individual is continually faced with a challenge to these world views. Inherent in this experience are the seeds of change. Change, however, does not come about just by our exposure to that world, but rather by the quality of our engagement in that world and the nature of previously evolved constructions. Although, on the one hand, our experiences may confirm our constructions regardless of the particular content of that experience, they also have the potential, at least, for disconfirmation. When this occurs, possibly as a result of experience with increased numbers of children or with changes in the child due to development, the entire system of beliefs (constructs) may be altered in order to accommodate new information or discrepant constructs that have evolved on the basis of such experiences.

It must be noted that a belief system differs from attitudes and from attribution systems. It is not an attitude since it is not limited to a single object nor is it defined as a predisposition to act (a classical definition of attitude). A belief system does have some aspects in common with attribution, but they are not identical, since attribution tends to emphasize inferences of cause–effect and "deals with the rules the average individual uses in attempting to infer the causes of observed behavior" (Kelley, 1972, p. 42).

In our view, inferring causes of another's behavior is but one set of mediators that influence behavior. Attributions may be seen as dependent on a belief system that is defined as an organization of constructs of the social, physical, and interpersonal environment. Similarly, attitudes or values are applications of a belief system to a particular class of events or singular outcomes. Belief systems, or constructions, are viewed as more complex and systematized bases for behavior and are closely tied to cognitive processes rather than to affective or personality factors.

In addition, different belief systems may generate similar attitudes toward some phenomenon or class of events and vice versa, or specific attitudes can be linked to particular beliefs. Perhaps an example of some parental beliefs and their relation to attitudes will help clarify the contention that beliefs are a more fundamental construct of a mediator between inner states and behaviors. We have found in our investigations that the constructs referred to by parents fall into patterns that resemble theoretical positions espoused by various educators and psychologists addressing processes of development. Although parents do not present such views in the psychological jargon of the literature, some parents have espoused views that form a maturational model, others resemble a Skinnerian approach, some propose an input–output information-processing model, others a constructivist position, or a Freudian framework, etc. We shall present summaries of constructs referred to by two parents who differed in their belief systems and yet indicated similar negative attitudes toward punishment. These parents proposed different ways to handle a situation in which a four-year-old was misbehaving, although they gave almost identical evaluations of the negative consequences of punishment. We maintain that both the parental behavior and the attitude are directly related to the broader cognitive belief system about child development, but that the parent's behavior is better understood through knowledge of the beliefs than knowledge of the attitude.

Throughout the portion of the parent interview that focuses on child-development beliefs, Mr. X referred to an input–output information-processing or computer model. (Interestingly, Mr. X's occupation involves computer programming and he drew many analogies from his work to child development.) This parent espoused the view that the four-year-old child can learn almost anything, although some limits were maintained, as long as the parent "formatted the input" appropriately. Essentially, the process of development was construed as one of data gathering and the programming of such information was largely the responsibility of the parent or educator. Within such a framework, punishment was viewed as a useless and detrimental factor by Mr. X, providing the child with no rationale for appropriate behavior and failing to point out causal links. In the hypothetical situation of the parent interview in which a child was throwing blocks about the room, Mr. X proposed that the optimal response of the parent was to explain to the child that each of his/her behaviors had a consequence on the physical environment. If the child continued to throw blocks, a new tactic of explanation was espoused in which cause and effect (throwing objects → breaking a valuable object) was clearly demonstrated. At no point should punishment be used because the child could not learn cause-and-effect relationships in the physical world in this manner, and would not understand the reason behind prohibitions on such behavior.

Mrs. Y had a similar negative attitude toward punishment, but for quite different reasons. Her responses indicated a view that the four-year-old child was largely deficient in thinking or rational processes and that maturation must take its course before the child can draw inferences concerning cause and effect. The environment, and thus, any parental attempts to teach the child were clearly seen as extraneous variables and development as largely a waiting process, determined by factors intrinsic to the child's makeup. Since, in her view, the four-year-old is totally incapable of understanding her point of view in the matter of damage to the living room, punishment is totally inappropriate. At no point should punishment be used, even when the throwing behavior persists, because the child cannot understand the cause-and-effect relationship of throwing and breakage, and cannot understand the reasons behind prohibitions on such behavior. It should be noted that such an attitude is almost identical to that of Mr. X. Yet, her predicted response to the situation is quite different from Mr. X's. She proposes that another toy be suggested to the child, and if that fails, the parent should actively engage the child in some other activity. In this manner, no damage is done, the child is happy, and only when the child is older will she/he know that throwing objects could lead to breaking something in the room.

We purposely chose two belief systems that are extremely different from one another in order to point out that two similar attitudes can be consistent with two very different belief systems concerning developmental states/processes, and that these belief systems manifest themselves in very different parental strategies despite the concordance of these two individuals' attitudes toward punishment. Few researchers have investigated parental beliefs about the child's cognitive status. A great deal of additional research is needed in this area. For example, many questions about the parent's understanding of the child's intellectual abilities, and the relationship of such understanding to parental behavior and the development of the child remain unanswered.

Changes in Beliefs and Practices with Family Constellation

The formulation of adult cognitive organization, emerging through the course of interactions with objects, people, and events, leads directly to a nonrecursive path model of family influence.[1] Since parental belief systems are subject to modification as a result of new or discrepant experiences, the behavior and abilities of each child in the family have potential impact on these beliefs as the child behaviors are incorporated in the existing parental belief system. When this occurs, parental behaviors may alter so as to be consistent with these changes in beliefs. As parental practices change, so would their impact on the child, and additional feedback from each child in the family must be dealt with in the context of the belief system continuously being constructed by the parent. Thus, within the limited environment of the home, parent affects child and child affects parent (see Figure 1). Similar dynamics also occur between the two parents and interact with each child in the family. Such a model clearly implicates family structure variables such as number of children, ordinal position and sex of the target child, and spacing between children. That is, parents of multiple-child families are likely to have modified their beliefs with regard to the second child as a result of experience with the firstborn. Consider, for example, a parent who was upset by an unwillingness to share in the firstborn's early years. This parent may construe the child as selfish. But if the second-born child manifests similar behavior at the same age and the parent perceives that the first-born has "outgrown" the nonsharing behavior, that parent's beliefs about the source of such behavior may be altered to one of "it's only a stage" and parental actions will be different toward the second-born. Feedback to the parent in the form of the second-born's behavior could lead to confirmation or disconfirmation of such beliefs, affecting the parent's subsequent behavior with all the children in the family.

This conceptual approach to family development is hardly new; an excellent presentation of this perspective is provided by Hill (1973). Models of families as systems in which individuals in the family unit

---

[1] It should be noted that the mathematical definition of "nonrecursive" differs from the usual meaning of the term. With respect to theoretical causal models, nonrecursiveness refers to reciprocal causation and/or feedback.

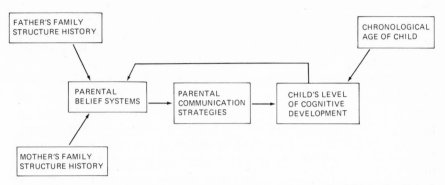

Fig. 1. Proposed model of mutual parent–child influences in a single-child family. (Actual tests of such models will include separate tests for mother's and father's influence, and the relationship between mother's and father's beliefs and communication strategies.)

function in relation to one another have, however, been applied most often by family therapists (cf. Bowen, 1972, 1974; Haley, 1964) and have been seldom subjected to empirical verification with families of a normal developing child. It is because of this need and orientation that we elected to study the family as a system of mutual influences in order to evaluate social factors influencing the cognitive development of young children. Our interest is in the way parental influences are transmitted as well as changed. Research focusing on the mutual influences of members of a family unit must, however, include consideration of family variables such as size and ordinal position of the target child.

In our family research project, we have included three groups of families, which vary with respect to the number and spacing of children: (1) 40 families with an only child aged 3½–4½ years, (2) 40 families of three children with the middle child aged 3½–4½ years and less than three years spacing between children, and (3) 40 families of three children with the middle child aged 3½–4½ years, but with more than three years spacing between children. One-half of the families in each group were characterized as middle class and one-half as lower class, based on parents' education, income, and occupational status.

Ontogenesis of Representational Thinking in the Family Setting

According to the "distancing hypothesis," the acquisition of representational competence is in part a function of particular psychosocial behaviors and events that separate the child from the environment in a cognitive sense (Sigel & Cocking, 1977). Distancing behaviors can be operationalized to include those classes of behavior that "demand" the child to reconstruct past events, to employ his imagination in dealing with objects, events, and people, to plan and to anticipate future actions (with particular attention being paid to articulation of such intentions), and finally, to attend to the transformation of phenomena. Distancing behaviors make a demand on the child to infer from the observable present; and, in the course of making such inferences, the child has to present to himself the outcomes or reconstructions of previous events.

The representational thinking processes of children are influenced by particular environmental demands—in this instance, family interactions. Representational thinking in young children can be related to specific parental behaviors such as teaching styles as well as parental beliefs about the cognitive capabilities of the young child. The utilization of distancing behaviors by the parent can be viewed as a function of parental beliefs about children; moreover, with increasing experience it is possible that there will be a change in the utilization of distancing behaviors by parents. On the assumption that the cognitive environment the parents provide through distancing behaviors will vary as a function of educational level, belief systems, and perspectives of child's capability, it is important to examine the relationship between such conceptual systems and parental teaching strategies in the context of family size and child spacing.

The application of the distancing framework to parent–child relations has been made with an attempt to bring out its significance and the potential for evaluating and understanding the role of the family in the development of representational thinking. What follows is a brief description of some of the measurement instruments devised for testing our model of the family as a social network and some preliminary tests of the constructs comprising the model.

Toward Testing the Model

Our research findings to date are in many cases consistent with our expectations. However, since our research project is ongoing and our data base is incomplete at this time, the findings must be considered preliminary. Most of this section will focus on parental responses to certain portions of a Communication Belief Questionnaire and Interview (CBQI) that deal with four areas: (1) communication strategy preferences and rationales, (2) beliefs about the child's abilities and developmental processes, (3) family structure beliefs, and (4) sources and changes in beliefs. In addition, current findings pertaining to assessment of children's representational thinking, parent–child observations, and the relation between child assessment and observational data will be briefly discussed.

Before presenting some preliminary results based upon the CBQI, it is appropriate to provide some data in support of the reliability and validity of the parent belief instrument. These results are based on a detailed analysis of the responses of two samples of parents not included in our study currently in progress.

Forty-eight parents of children enrolled in the Child Care Research Center at the Educational Testing Service and 21 parents enrolled in an adult education course at a nearby university were interviewed twice with a six-week interval between testing sessions. Product moment correlations were computed separately for the ranks given to each of the five response options at Time 1 and Time 2. These coefficients ranged from .70 to .93 (p's < .01). High correlations (above .80) were uniformly obtained for communication strategies parents liked best and least. Lower correlations (between .64 and .80) were obtained for those options that were ranked somewhere in the middle, usually normative or direct authoritative statements. Thus, parents' communication preferences, as assessed with CBQI, were relatively stable over this period of time. Split half correlations for the 12 situations of the CBQI yielded internal consistency estimates ranging from .53 to .69 for each of the five types of preferred options. Given that the content of the 12 situations was purposely varied to focus on teaching versus management/discipline issues, and that these correlations are significant at the .01 level, there is ample evidence that the CBQI items tap a single dimension, viz., communication strategy preferences. In addition to these estimates of stability and internal consistency, coder reliability was also indicated by the high percentage of agreement between two scorers who independently coded the interview responses of 30 of the parents tested. Agreement between the two scorers ranged from 87–92%.

The 21 students enrolled in the adult education course served as judges for an investigation of the content validity of the five different types of response options contained in each of the 12 situations. Their judgment of the representativeness of 60 samples demonstrated agreement with ours that ranged from 60 to 85% for each of the five types of options.

Relating interview responses to parent behaviors provides a good test of the predictive and concurrent validity of the instrument. Using an observation schedule (Parent–Child Interaction Observation Schedule, Sigel, Flaugher, & Johnson, 1977), parents' use of distancing and management behaviors on two different tasks in a laboratory situation were coded and then related to the interview responses. The 48 preschool program parents were divided into two groups based on their interview scores for preferring distancing strategies. Those parents who scored above the median were grouped as "high preference" and those below were grouped as "low preference." Videotapes of these parents interacting with their child on a structured teaching task (paper-folding) and on a semistructured story-telling task were available. For each task, parents were classified as either high or low "distancers" by an independent rater. A contingency analysis indicated a significant relationship between interview scores for preferring distancing and distancing behavior in the structured teaching task [$\chi^2(1) = 5.72; p < .05$].

A frequent criticism of parental interviews is that responses are influenced by social desirability factors. In order to determine the relation between parental responses to the CBQI and possible contamination of social desirability factors, parents were also administered the Social Desirability Scale (Crowne & Marlowe, 1964). The short form of the Parent Attitude Research Inventory (PARI, Cross & Kawash, 1968) was also administered in order to ensure that the CBQI did in fact assess a dimension different from parental attitudes. Evidence for the discriminant validity of the interview is available from these data. A factor analytic procedure was used involving rankings obtained from parents on the CBQI, social desirability scores, and PARI scores. The results indicate that social desirability and PARI scores load on factors separate from the CBQI. In effect, parental beliefs, as assessed by the CBQI, form their own set of factors. Given confidence in the instrument based on these analyses, it is appropriate to present some preliminary results from it that are consistent with our expectations.

With regard to our conceptualization of the function of parental beliefs and distancing behaviors, it is necessary first to obtain some evidence of the variability of the parental beliefs and practices relative to distancing. Further, a positive relation between parental beliefs and parental practices and between actual distancing behaviors and child outcomes should be indicated before proceeding further into an investigation of the family system operating at some level within the distancing framework. The data presented in this paper will therefore focus on accomplishing these objectives, i.e., provide an indication of the significance of parental beliefs and practices relative to distancing within the family context.

Parents' Preferred Teaching and Management Strategies

Parents' preferences for distancing strategies were obtained and analyzed using the CBQI for 30 families included in the research design. Ten of these families had an only child and were categorized as low education and low income; 10 families were middle-class with an only child; and 10 families were middle-class three-child families with fewer than three-years' spacing between children. It was therefore possible to investigate variability in distancing preferences for sex of parent, family size, and social class.

The format of the CBQI required parents to rank five strategy options from best (#1) to worst (#5) as a means of handling each of the 12 situations. Thus, the lower the sum of ranks for the 12 situations, the more the parent valued that type of response. Analysis of parents' responses indicates that ranked preference for distancing behaviors may vary with family size, social class, and sex of parent.

Comparison of the rankings given by middle-class and lower-class single-child families indicates that the middle-class parents preferred distancing options slightly more than the lower-class parents (mean sum of ranks = 28.05 and 31.20, respectively).

Distancing strategies seem to be the preferred communication strategy more for parents of an only child than for parents of three-child families. Middle-class single-child families gave the distancing option a total rank of 28.05 across the 12 situations (possible range = 12–60 with the lower number reflecting a stronger preference for distancing), while middle-class parents of three children gave it a mean rank of 32.50. Parents of three children preferred authoritative explanations more than Socratic or nondirective approaches. Hence, family size may play a role in preferences for certain child-rearing communication strategies. Such findings may be related to the fact that distancing behaviors are time-consuming as compared to more direct approaches, and parents with more children may simply be operating under more situational and time constraints on a day-to-day basis.

In addition, mothers tended to prefer the Socratic-type distancing strategy more than fathers, who preferred directive and authoritative statements more than mothers. Across all three groups, mothers gave a mean rank of 28.27 to the distancing option, and the mean rank for fathers was 32.90 across all 12 situations $[t(58) = 2.22; p < .05]$. Within each of three groups tested, each group of mothers consistently ranked the distancing option higher than the fathers did. The largest discrepancy between mothers' and fathers' preferences for this option occurred in the middle-class single-child families. The mean rank for mothers across 12 situations was 24.60, compared to 31.50 for fathers $[t(18) = 2.86; p < .05]$.

Child Assessment Data

Findings related to the child assessments on a total of seven physical and social cognitive tasks are based on a summary score that was derived for each child across seven assessment measures. For a present sample of 24 children who have been assessed and coded, (1) scores for single children did not differ from the scores for the middle child of a multiple-child family (means = 96.51 and 90.42, for "singles" and "multiples," respectively, and (2) female children scored somewhat better than male children on the assessment measures (means = 105.21 and 84.84, for females and males, respectively).

Observational Data

An analysis of the frequency of distancing behaviors was conducted separately for each of the two observation tasks and then distancing scores for each task were compared with one another:

1. Paper-folding task (structured teaching task): Chi-square tests indicate that parents of single-child families may utilize distancing behaviors more frequently than parents of multiple-child families ($p <$ .05).

2. Story-telling task (semistructured task): Chi-square tests indicate that parents of multiple-child families may distance more frequently on this type of task than parents of single-child families. In addition, distancing strategies were evidenced more frequently by mothers than by fathers on this task (p's < .05).

3. Comparison of structured and semistructured tasks: The use of distancing strategies was more frequent for the semistructured story-telling tasks than for the structured paper-folding task ($p < .001$).

Observation Scores

A contingency analysis between parental endorsement of distancing as a preferential strategy and parental behavior during the paper-folding task indicated a relation between distancing as a preferred response to the CBQI and actual frequency of distancing behaviors on the paper-folding task [$\chi^2(1) = 5.32, p < .05$].

Relation between Parental-Observation Scores and Child-Assessment Scores

A contingency analysis between the distancing-behavior scores for mothers during the story task and the composite scores for children on the seven assessment tasks indicated a relation between maternal practices and the problem-solving competence of their children (rank order correlation = .53). Mothers who incorporate more distancing strategies into the story-telling situation tended to have children who performed better, overall, on the assessment tasks.

DISCUSSION

The results presented above are, to be sure, preliminary but they are encouraging. That we have created an instrument that has demonstrated appropriate confidence levels for reliability and content validity is but one basis for our optimism. A second is the predictive validity that parental distancing behaviors were related to children's levels of performance on representational tasks, despite the global scores that were used at this level of analysis.

The results indicating that fathers and mothers differ in preferences and distancing strategies are relevant to our concern for studying the family as a unit. Such results suggest that the child is subject to differential treatment from the two parents. This set of findings lends support to plans for evaluating the relative contribution of each parent. Further, parental preferences for distancing strategies may be related to size of family, thus implicating family-structure factors in the system of influences impacting parent and child.

At this point, we need to identify the role of belief systems. Parental preferences for distancing strategies seem to be related to parental behaviors in certain types of teaching tasks. In effect, we have identified a potentially systematic relationship between parental preferences for teaching and management strategies and their actual distancing behaviors that influence children's cognitive functioning. However, distancing behaviors, like other parental practices, are seen as outcomes of parental belief systems, which may be influenced by feedback from the child's behavior. To date, our data support the impact of distancing behaviors. What remains to be shown is how parental beliefs and practices function in reciprocal relation to child behavior and development occurring within the family context.

One of the main advantages of our particular "distancing framework" approach to operationalizing variables for purposes of testing the model given in Figure 1 is the reduction of the fragmentation that often besets research dealing with so many variables. The integration yielded by applying a common theoretical framework to the instrument development makes possible fairly direct analyses among and across parent belief and practice measures as well as analyses with child assessments. Hence, we are able to examine process (i.e., styles of communication, beliefs, etc.) in relation to structure (i.e., family size, density, etc.) in building a causal (i.e., path) model of the family environment and the socialization of competence (cf. Leichter, 1974; Walberg & Marjoribanks, 1976).

The conceptual model we are testing posits, among other things, that family processes affect child outcomes and, moreover, that processes are mediated by personal beliefs and the interaction of beliefs with situations. The beliefs themselves and the translation of beliefs into practices are constrained by the ecology of the family, hence the significance of family structure. For example, we are studying how consistency of beliefs and practices may vary as a function of family size/density and SES. Size, density, and social class may limit the time and energy parents have to devote to "quality" interactions with their children. An additional positive feature of the model of the family is that we are considering mutual influences between parents and children (cf. Bell, 1968), while prior research on the socialization of competence has usually been unidirectional (e.g., Bing, 1963; Brophy, 1970; Hess & Shipman, 1965).

Researchers relating to the Zajonc and Markus (1975) confluence model of the effects of the two family-structure variables of size and spacing on the child's intelligence have suggested various possible mediators to account for this effect. For example, Marjoribanks and Walberg (1975) propose that differences in the amount of parental attention may be one explanation for these effects. On the other hand, researchers have also pointed out that the Zajonc and Markus model deals with families on the population level, not on an individual basis (Grotevant, Scarr, & Weinberg, 1977; Scarr & Weinberg, in press). When the genetic variance within a given family is known (i.e., parental IQ), the effects due to family-structure variables are seen to diminish tremendously in importance. Parental IQ may account for 25 times as much of the variance in children's IQ as the combination of family size, birth order, and child-spacing (Scarr & Weinberg, 1978).

We are also testing individual families in an attempt to identify specific family-environment variables that have impact on the child's development, but we hope to provide data bearing on the role of the processes and patterns of the family *environment* as opposed to *parental* intelligence, although these two factors are assumed to be related. Unfortunately our research does not have parent IQ scores.

Another limitation of our model, in addition to a lack of genetics information, is that it represents *horizontal* but not *vertical* time. In other words, the model is a static reflection of the family network at the particular time of testing. A more complete causal model of the family environment and the socialization of competence would have to deal with the family system in transition over time, requiring longitudinal research methods.

References

Becker, W. C., & Krug, R. S. The parent attitude research instrument: A research review. *Child Development*, 1965, *36*, 329–365.

Bee, H. L., Van Egeren, L. F., Streissguth, A. P., Nyman, B. A., & Leckie, M. S. Social class differences in maternal teaching strategies and speech patterns. *Development Psychology*, 1969, *1*, 726–734.

Bell, R. Q. A reinterpretation of the direction of effects in studies of socialization. *Psychological Review*, 1968, *75*, 81–95.

Bing, E. Effect of child rearing practices on development of differential cognitive abilities. *Child Development*, 1963, *34*, 631–648.

Bowen, M. Family therapy and family group therapy. In H. I. Kaplan & B. J. Sadock (Eds.), *Group treatment of mental illness* (Vol. 12). New York: E. P. Dutton, 1972, p. 213.

Bowen, M. Alcholism as viewed through family systems theory and family psychotherapy. *Annals of the New York Academy of Sciences*, 1974, *233*, 115–122.

Brophy, J. E. Mothers as teachers of their own preschool children: The influence of socioeconomic status and task structure on teaching specificity. *Child Development* 1970, *41*, 79–94.

Cicirelli, V. G. Mother–child and sibling–sibling interactions on a problem-solving task. *Child Development*, 1976, *47*, 588–596.

Cross, H. J., & Kawash, G. F. A short form PARI to assess authoritarian attitudes toward childrearing. *Psychological Reports*, 1968, *23*, 91–98.

Crowne, D., & Marlowe, D. *The approval motive*. New York: Wiley, 1964.

Freeberg, N. E., & Payne, D. T. Parental influence on cognitive development in early childhood: A review. *Child Development*, 1967, *38*, 65–87.

Grotevant, H. D., Scarr, S., & Weinberg, R. A. Intellectual development in family constellations with adopted and natural children: A test of the Zajonc and Markus model. *Child Development*, 1977, *48*, 1699–1703.

Haley, J. Research on family patterns: An instrument measurement. *Family Processes*, 1964, *3*, 41–76.

Hess, R. D., & Shipman, V. C. Early experience and the socialization of cognitive modes in children. *Child Development*, 1965, *36*, 869–886.

Hill, R. Modern systems theory and the family: A confrontation. *Social Science Information*, 1973, *10*, 7–26.

Jones, P. Home environment and the development of verbal ability. *Child Development*, 1972, *43*, 1081–1087.

Kelley, H. H. Causal schemata and the attribution process. In E. E. Jones, D. E. Kanouse, H. H. Kelley, R. E. Nisbett, S. Valins, & B. Weiner (Eds.), *Attribution: Perceiving the causes of behavior*. Morristown, N.J.: General Learning Press, 1972.

Kelly, G. A. *The psychology of personal constructs* (Vols. 1 and 2). New York: Norton, 1955.

Kelly, G. A. *A theory of personality*. New York: Norton, 1963.

Leichter, H. *Family as educator*. New York: Teachers College Press, 1974.

Lewis, M., & Feiring, C. The child's social network: Social object, social functions, and their relationship. In M. Lewis & L. A. Rosenblum (Eds.), *The child and its family* (Vol. 2). New York: Plenum, 1979.

Marjoribanks, E., & Walberg, H. Mental abilities: Sibling constellation and social class correlates. *British Journal of Clinical and Social Psychology*, 1975, *14*, 109–116.

McGillicuddy-De Lisi, A., & Sigel, I. The effects of spacing and birth order on problem solving competence of preschool children (Progress Report, Grant RO1 H10686-01, NICHHD). Princeton, N.J.: Educational Testing Service, July 1977.

Radin, N. Observed maternal behavior with four-year-old boys and girls in lower-class families. *Child Development*, 1974, *45*, 1126–1131.

Scarr, S., & Weinberg, R. A. Intellectual similarities within families of both adopted and biological children. *Science*, in press.

Sigel, I. E. Language of the disadvantaged: The distancing hypothesis. In C. S. Lavetelli (Ed.), *Language training in early childhood education*. Urbana, Ill.: University of Illinois Press, 1971.

Sigel, I. E., & Cocking, R. R. Cognition and Communication: A dialectic paradigm for development. In M. Lewis & L. A. Rosenblum (Eds.), *Interaction, conversation, and the development of language: The origins of behavior* (Vol. V). New York: Wiley, 1977.

Sigel, I., Flaugher, J., & Johnson, J. *Parent–child interactions observational manual*. Princeton, N.J.: Educational Testing Service, 1977.

Walberg, H. J., & Marjoribanks, K. Family environment and cognitive development: Twelve analytic models. *Review of Educational Research*, 1976, *46*, 527–551.

Zajonc, R. B., & Markus, G. B. Birth order and intellectual development. *Psychological Review*, 1975, *82*, 74–88.

6

Self-Recognition in Chimpanzees and Man: A Developmental and Comparative Perspective

GORDON G. GALLUP, JR.

The concept of self has not only been held to be uniquely human, but essential to the beginnings of effective social and intellectual functioning in the growing child. While the self has been and continues to be a pivotal concept in many areas of psychology, surprisingly little attention has been paid to the development of an individual's capacity to conceive of himself. Rather than tracking the emergence of self-conception, most work has been directed at trying to determine the factors that influence the content of one's self-concept and/or how we evaluate ourselves (Wylie, 1974). In this chapter I will describe a technique that can be used to assess self-awareness in animals and man, and review the recent work on self-recognition in human infants. The status of the self-concept and the significance of self-recognition will also be briefly examined.

ANIMAL STUDIES

Mirrors

Mirrors provide a means of assessing the presence of self-awareness. Surprisingly, however, many organisms react to themselves in mirrors

GORDON G. GALLUP, JR. • Department of Psychology, State University of New York, Albany, New York 12222.

as if they were seeing other animals, and engage in a variety of species-typical social responses directed toward the reflection (e.g., aggressive behaviors, sexual postures, greeting gestures, etc.). In other words, a mirror seems to function, at least initially, as a social stimulus. Mirrors also have incentive properties for many species, and animals can be taught to engage in a variety of instrumental responses reinforced by nothing more than brief visual access to their own reflection (see Gallup, 1968, 1975). Some animals even appear to show a peculiar preference for viewing mirrors instead of other animals (Gallup, 1975).

The most interesting aspect of mirrors, and probably the most obvious for humans, is that they provide information about the self. Mirrors enable visually capable organisms to see themselves as they are seen by others. In front of a mirror an animal is an audience to its own behavior. Yet, many animals seem incapable of recognizing the dualism inherent in such stimulation, and even after prolonged exposure fail to discover the relationship between their behavior and the reflection of that behavior in a mirror.

Aside from the fact that most of us undoubtably are given explicit verbal instructions by our parents about the identity of the reflection, the ability to recognize one's own image would seem to be partly a function of prolonged exposure to mirrors. Infants and adult humans who have never seen mirrors before react just like animals, and initially respond to the reflection as if confronted with another person (Amsterdam, 1972; von Senden, 1960). Maybe if animals were given the same opportunity for extended self-inspection, they might also come to recognize themselves in mirrors.

Self-Recognition in Primates

To test this conjecture, in the original study (Gallup, 1970) I gave a number of preadolescent chimpanzees individual exposure to mirrors for ten days. In all instances their initial reaction to the mirror was as though they were seeing another chimpanzee, and for the first few days they engaged in a variety of social gestures while watching the reflection. After about three days, however, the tendency to treat the reflection as a companion was replaced by the emergence of a self-directed orientation. Rather than respond to the mirror as such, after about the third day the chimpanzees began to use the mirror to respond to themselves. They seemed to try to use the reflection to gain visual access to and experiment with otherwise inaccessible information about themselves, such as grooming parts of the body that had not been seen before, making faces at the reflection, inspecting the insides of their mouths, etc.

Although it appeared as though the chimpanzees had correctly identified the identity of the reflection, I was concerned that other behavioral scientists might not be persuaded by my simple observations. In an attempt to clarify and objectify these impressions, an unobtrusive and more rigorous test of self-recognition was instituted. Following the last day of mirror exposure, each chimpanzee was anesthetized and the mirror was removed. After the chimpanzee was unconscious, I painted the uppermost portion of an eyebrow ridge and the top half of the opposite ear with a bright red, odorless, nonirritating alcohol-soluble dye. The animal was then placed back into its cage and allowed to recover in the absence of the mirror.

The significance of this technique is threefold. First, the chimpanzees had no way of knowing about the application of the marks since the procedure was accomplished under deep anesthesia. Second, the dye was carefully selected because of its lack of tactile and olfactory properties. Finally, the marks were carefully placed at predetermined points on the chimpanzee's face so that it would be impossible for the dye to be seen without a mirror.

Following recovery, all subjects were observed to determine the number of times any marked portion of the skin was touched in the absence of the mirror. The mirror was then reintroduced as an explicit test of self-recognition. Upon seeing themselves in the mirror there was a dramatic increase in mark-directed responses, or attempts to touch marked areas on themselves while watching the reflection (see Figure 1).

There was also an abrupt increase in viewing time on the test of self-recognition. Something about the presence of the red marks greatly enhanced their visual attention to the reflection. Finally, in addition to mark-directed responses, there were a number of noteworthy attempts to visually examine and smell the fingers that had been used to touch marked parts of the face, even though the dye was indelible.

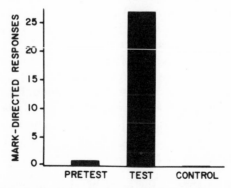

Fig. 1. Number of mark-directed responses made by experimental chimpanzees before being exposed to the mirror, and by experimental and control chimpanzees during the test of self-recognition (Gallup, 1970).

In a further attempt to eliminate any doubt about the source of these reactions, several additional chimpanzees that had never seen themselves in mirrors were anesthetized and marked. When given access to the mirror for the first time, there were no mark-directed responses whatsoever (see Figure 1), patterns of self-directed behavior were completely absent, and the dye was ostensibly ignored. Throughout the test their orientation to the mirror was unmistakably social rather than self-directed. They all responded to the reflection as if confronted with another chimpanzee.

A prevailing view of self-concept formation in humans is that it only develops out of a social milieu and as such is dependent upon interaction with others. In keeping with this general idea, we found in another study (Gallup, McClure, Hill, & Bundy, 1971) that chimpanzees reared in social isolation seemed incapable of recognizing themselves in mirrors. We also have preliminary evidence that remedial social experience, accomplished by housing isolates together in the same cage, is sufficient to provide for the emergence of at least suggestive signs of self-recognition (Hill, Bundy, Gallup, & McClure, 1970).

The existence of self-recognition in chimpanzees has now been replicated several times by a number of investigators (Gallup *et al.*, 1971; Hill *et al.*, 1970; Lethmate & Dücker, 1973), and extended by Lethmate and Dücker to include orangutans. With the exception of man and the great apes, however, attempts to demonstrate self-recognition in all other primates have uniformly failed even after extended exposure to mirrors (see Gallup, 1977). Among primates, the great apes seem to be the only ones with the capacity to extract this more abstract information from mirrors.

Although monkeys can learn to use mirrors to manipulate objects (Brown, McDowell, & Robinson, 1965), they appear incapable of learning to sufficiently integrate features of their own reflection in order to use mirrors to respond to themselves. Again, it is not that they cannot learn to respond to mirrored cues. When looking at the reflection of a human or a bit of food, they can detect the inherent dualism as it pertains to objects other than themselves and, after adequate experience, do respond appropriately by turning away from the mirror to gain more direct access to the object of the reflection (Tinklepaugh, 1928). It would appear, therefore, that monkeys and other animals lack an essential cognitive category for processing mirrored information about themselves.

SELF-RECOGNITION IN MAN

Much like chimpanzees, the available data strongly suggest that in man self-recognition is learned. For example, people born with visual defects, who later undergo operations that provide for normal sight, initially respond to mirrors as if confronted with other people and often react to mirror space as though it were real (von Senden, 1960). At about six months of age infants begin showing other-directed behaviors as well, and are notorious for responding to mirrors as playmates (e.g., Amsterdam, 1972; Gesell & Ames, 1947; Schulman & Kaplowitz, 1977).

Developmental Data

Much of the recent research on humans and mirrors has been aimed at trying to identify what point in ontogeny this ability develops. To date dozens of studies have been published, but until recently none provided an unequivocal demonstration of self-recognition. In a review of the literature several years ago (Gallup, 1975), it was argued that we had better experimental evidence of self-recognition in chimpanzees than man. Fortunately, that has now changed.

Most early investigators were satisfied with intuitive and anthropomorphic data (e.g., Darwin, 1877; Preyer, 1893), and estimates of the onset of self-recognition included such precocial figures as six months of age (Dixon, 1957). Shirley (1933) and Gesell and Thompson (1934), however, questioned whether self-recognition occurred at all in children up to 56 weeks old. Stone and Church (1968) contend that most children recognize themselves in mirrors at about 10 months, but present no evidence to support this claim. Stutsman (1931) found that over 60% of two-year-olds correctly label themselves upon seeing their reflection.

The first definitive study with children was reported by Amsterdam (1972). Unaware of my initial work with chimpanzees, she independently devised a similar procedure. She attempted to assess self-recognition in children of different ages by applying a spot of rouge to the side of each child's nose, and then noted whether the nose was touched when subjects were exposed to a mirror. Evidence of self-recognition, based on touching the nose in front of the mirror, emerged in 65% of the subjects between 20 and 24 months of age. Apparently unaware of either my work or Amsterdam's study, Dickie and Strader (1974) attempted to measure self-recognition in infants 6, 12, and 18 months of age by applying a piece of red tape to the subject's cheek. Only two out of 18 subjects touched the tape while watching themselves in mirrors. Papousek and Papousek (1974) describe a technique using videotape that they feel may be useful in examing self-recognition in infants, but fail to demonstrate how videotape might be used to provide definitive evidence of self-recognition.

Recent Studies with Infants

Using a quasi-distorting mirror and a regular mirror, Schulman and Kaplowitz (1977) tested children aged 1 to 24 months for self-recognition. Their procedure was similar to Amsterdam's (1972) study, and also involved marking the nose with rouge. They found that social behavior in response to the reflection began to appear between 7 to 12 months of age and declined by 19 to 24 months. Children between 7 and 18 months were the most likely to respond to the mirror as though seeing another child. Unlike Amsterdam, however, their criterion of self-recognition was based on the child's ability to say either his name, "me," or point to himself while watching the reflection. None of the infants aged 13–18 months showed any of these behaviors, but 11% evidenced mark-directed behavior. Among the 19–24-month-olds, 62% showed mark-directed responses and 52% correctly labeled the reflection. The lack of correspondence, particularly at 13–18 months, between labeling the reflection and mark-directed behaviors reinforces reservations about whether labeling can be taken as definitive evidence of self-recognition.

Brooks-Gunn and Lewis (1975) improved upon the marking and testing procedure used by Amsterdam to assess self-recognition. First, they included an unmarked condition to control for the incidence of spontaneous behaviors directed toward facial areas targeted for later marking. Next, their procedure for applying the marks was more subtle, even though the nose was the only facial feature that was marked. Each mother was carefully instructed to wipe her child's nose with rouge, but to tell the child that she was wiping his face because it was dirty. All mothers were cautioned against mentioning the nose or the rouge. On the test of self-recognition, children ranging in age from 9 to 12 months of age failed to show any mark-directed behavior, whereas 18% of the 15-months-olds, 25% of the 18-month-olds, 69% of the 21-month-olds, and 75% of the 24-month-olds touched their noses in the presence of the mirror. In terms of the developmental trend these data compare favorable with Amsterdam's (1972) results, but indicate the emergence of self-recognition at a slightly earlier age.

Paralleling my findings with chimpanzees, Brooks-Gunn and Lewis also found that the number of times infants looked at themselves in the mirror increased dramatically after rouge application. It is interesting, however, that this increase was noted in all age groups. It is also curious that a number of infants touched their own image in the mirror when they saw themselves with marks on their faces. Older infants were actually more likely to do this than younger ones, which tends to compromise an interpretation of self-recognition based on mark-directed behavior. If the child clearly recognized himself in the mirror, it is not apparent why he would attempt to touch the image. If you recognize yourself, then ostensibly the image is not the source of the marks. It would be important to know whether these attempts preceded successful mark-directed behaviors in the case of the older children.

In another study, Lewis and Brooks-Gunn (1979) examined the effects of immediate and delayed videotape playback in infants ranging from 9 to 24 months of age. As a control condition infants were also shown the videotape of another child of the same sex and age. From a comparative point of view the results were most intriguing. Just like rhesus monkeys that favor viewing other monkeys over mirrors (Gallup & McClure, 1971), the infants preferred looking at the tape of the other child. Also paralleling the reactions of chimpanzees to mirrors (e.g., Gallup, 1975), infants between 18 and 24 months of age tended to imitate and make faces at the screen under self-videotape playback conditions. The authors conclude that infants are capable of differentiating "between contingent and noncontingent representations of the self and between noncontingent representations of self and other" (p. 14).

More recently, Lewis (1977) and his associates have attempted to use videotape in a different way to assess self-recognition in infants. In an ingenious experiment Lewis videotaped a baby while someone approached quietly from behind. Babies were shown their own tapes as well as those of other infants with someone coming up from behind. Infants as young as 12 months were more likely to turn around under conditions in which they were seeing themselves on the screen. The use of this technique overcomes certain maturationally dependent perceptual-motor problems involved in infants being able to effectively execute mark-directed responding at an early age. With appropriate underwater adaptations, one intriguing spin-off of this work would be to use videotape in conjunction with visual probes to assess self-recognition in porpoises and whales (see Gallup, in press).

On the basis of his data, Lewis argues that object permanence is a necessary condition for self-recognition, and that between 9 and 12 months of age children begin developing a sense of self.

Another study with humans was conducted by Flannery (1976), where she attempted to assess self-recognition in autistic children aged 5.5 to 11.4 years. Since anesthetization would be both impractical and unsafe, at my suggestion Flannery used an alternative means of applying marks to the children's faces. All autistic children were blindfolded, ostensibly for a "pin the tail on the donkey" game. For normal control subjects, with a mean age of two years, clean facial tissue was used to play "peek-a-boo" and the child's face was marked while the tissue covered his eyes. Six out of seven autistic children, and four out of 10 control infants showed self-recognition as measured by significant increases in mark-directed responses upon being exposed to their mirror image. The fact that practically all of the autistic children evidenced self-recognition contrasts sharply with many theoretical views of autism and faulty self-conception. These findings also differ from those on adult schizophrenics, who appear in many instances to have lost the capacity to correctly identify themselves in mirrors.

Based on Piaget's notions of sensorimotor development, Bertenthal and Fischer (1978) have attempted to assess a hypothetical series of precursors to self-recognition in infants. Unlike Lewis (1977), they feel that object permanence is not directly related to self-recognition. They reasoned that self-recognition does not suddenly emerge, but rather must follow some predictable cognitive-developmental sequence. They seem, however, to have confused self-recognition as an act with self-conception as a process. It would be more precise to say that a child's sense of self emerges gradually. My observations of chimpanzees in front of mirrors (Gallup, 1975) suggest that the phenomenon of self-recognition occurs quite rapidly.

Although Bertenthal and Fischer present an intuitively attractive rationale for several stages that ought to antedate self-recognition, an examination of their procedures shows that in all instances these merely assessed the infant's ability to learn to interpret mirror space and respond appropriately by using the reflection to gain access to objects in the background. With the exception of the test of self-recognition, which was accomplished by applying a spot of rouge to the nose, their dependent variables simply measured perceptual-motor capacities involved in learning to respond to mirrored cues. While this ability is undoubtably a necessary condition for self-recognition, it is not sufficient, as evidenced by the fact that monkeys can learn to respond appropriately to mirrored cues but seem incapable of recognizing themselves. Thus, it seems difficult to accept their claim that positive performance at *any* stage prior to mark-directed behavior represents a form of self-recognition. Bertenthal and Fischer report that 13 of 48 children of various ages touched their noses following the application of rouge on the test of self-recognition, but their data are presented in such a way as to obscure the ages of these children, and render meaningful comparisons with the results of other studies difficult. Bertenthal and Fischer conclude that although infants may be capable of self-recognition prior to two years of age, the development of a "true" concept of self only occurs much later. It would be interesting to know just what the authors mean in an operational sense by a true self-concept.

Mental Retardation

While most recent data show that normal infants begin to show evidence of self-recognition at about one and one-half to two years of age, some mentally retarded children, adolescents, and even profoundly retarded adults seem incapable of recognizing themselves in mirrors. Shentoub, Soulairac, and Rustin (1954) exposed 15 mentally retarded children (MA = .75–3.33), ranging in age from four to nineteen years, to mirrors but found no evidence of self-recognition. Brooks-Gunn (1977) has also failed to find evidence of self-recognition in several children afflicted with Down's syndrome.

Pechacek, Bell, Cleland, Baum, and Boyle (1973) tested self-recognition in severely retarded adults. In the first experiment, they employed a dye marker that was used to apply a red mark to the forehead of patients while they were sleeping. In the second study subjects were tested for their ability to select their own snapshot from among three photographs. Both experiments failed to reveal any evidence of self-recognition.

In a more recent experiment, Harris (1977) attempted to replicate the Pechacek *et al.* findings with some additional modifications. In the Harris study a green mark was used to preclude confusion with medication often applied to forehead cuts, and each subject was given 13 consecutive days of mirror training. After the first week, subjects were provided with a triple-mirror display similar to those available in clothing stores. However, none of the profoundly retarded adults touched the forehead marks during testing, and only one subject out of 16 chose his own photograph on 50% of the trials.

Apparently, the capacity for self-recognition requires a level of intellectual functioning that exceeds that of some adult humans.

Schizophrenia

There are numerous reports that schizophrenia may be associated with the loss of self-recognition (Faure, 1956; Frenkel, 1964; Traub & Orbach, 1964; Wittreich, 1959). When confronted with themselves in a mirror, it is not uncommon for schizophrenics to react by talking to the mirror or laughing at the reflection, and in general act as if they were in the presence of another person. Using a mirror that could be adjusted to provide varying degrees of distortion, there is also evidence for systematic differences in the accuracy of self-perception between schizophrenics and normals (Orbach, Traub, & Olson, 1966; Traub & Orbach, 1964). When asked to adjust the mirror so as to achieve an undistorted image of themselves, many patients seemed to have forgotten what they looked like and would either look directly at their bodies or urgently ask to see themselves in an undistorted mirror before proceeding.

In addition, some schizophrenics show a peculiar tendency to spend inordinate amounts of time in front of mirrors, and prolonged mirror gazing has been associated with the onset of schizophrenia (Abély, 1930; Delmas, 1929; Ostancow, 1934). It is curious to note in light of this tendency that isolation-reared rhesus monkeys show a preference for viewing mirrors (Gallup & McClure, 1971), and comparably reared chimpanzees also spend unusually large amounts of time watching their own reflections (Gallup et al., 1971). Like some schizophrenics, as I have already noted, chimpanzees raised in social isolation seem incapable of recognizing themselves in mirrors.

PROBLEMS WITH RECENT STUDIES

A problem with most attempts to adapt the marking procedure to human infants is that in the absence of anesthetization it is usually less than unobtrusive. In experiments employing facial marks, for some reason the nose has been chosen as the target area in the majority of instances (e.g., Amsterdam, 1972; Bertenthal & Fischer, 1978; Brooks-Gunn & Lewis, 1975; Schulman & Kaplowitz, 1977). This is a questionable tactic. Of all the human facial features, the nose is the least suited for unobtrusive marking since it is the most readily accessible to visual inspection without a mirror. If the child can see the mark independent of his reflection, touching the mark in the presence of a mirror becomes uninterpretable. Although monkeys fail to show self-recognition, as evidenced by the absence of mark-directed behaviors following unobtrusive marking, they will almost immediately attempt to remove dye and paint from body parts that can be seen without a mirror.

By applying the mark (which in most instances has been rouge) to the child while he is awake, there is the very real possibility that he may also respond to tactile cues associated with the marking procedure and not the reflection of those marks in the mirror. This problem is even more serious when pieces of tape are applied to the face (e.g., Dickie & Strader, 1974). The use of distraction (e.g., Brooks-Gunn & Lewis, 1975; Flannery, 1976), or waiting until subjects are asleep before applying the marks (Pechacek et al., 1973) helps to reduce this problem. But even with distraction it is essential that records be kept of the number of times facial areas targeted for marking are touched prior to the application of marks.

The near universal choice of rouge as the marking substance is also a potential problem since some kinds of rouge are scented.

Finally, Bertenthal and Fischer (1978) and Schulman and Kaplowitz (1977) can be criticized for including a naming task as another test of self-recognition. Simply because a child can respond with his own name when asked "Who's that?" in front of a mirror, hardly constitutes a test of anything other than verbal behavior and associative learning. Many infants are probably held in front of mirrors while parents and others repeat the child's name over and over. Mere labeling of the reflection need not imply self-recognition (see Gallup, 1975).

Given all of these shortcomings, which are unequally distributed across studies, there is surprising consistency in the data concerning the onset of self-recognition in infants at between 18 and 24 months of age. The impressive work of Lewis and Brooks-Gunn (1979) with videotape represents a potentially powerful technique, and suggests that the beginnings of self-conception may in fact begin to emerge as early as one year. Since only preliminary data have been reported so far (Lewis, 1977), it will be interesting to see how this line of research develops in the future.

CONCEPTUAL ISSUES

The Origin of Self

An early and influential attempt to explain the ontogeny of self-conception was based on the assumption that man's sense of self required social interaction with others (Cooley, 1912). This "looking glass" theory of self held not only that the self-concept was an interpersonal phenomenon, but that reflected appraisals, in terms of the positive and negative reactions we get from others, determine how we see and evaluate ourselves.

George Herbert Mead (1934) elaborated on this view of self as an interpersonal entity. Many people have asserted that the infant's awareness of self depends on body differentiation and experience of various contingencies between action and outcome (Lewis & Brooks-Gunn, 1979; Wylie, 1968). According to Mead, however, one's awareness of his own body and bodily activities fails to provide a sufficient basis for self-conception. Mere body awareness and body differentiation is not enough. In order for the self to emerge as an object of conscious inspection, in Mead's theory it requires the opportunity to examine one's self from another's point of view. Figuratively speaking, in order to conceive of yourself you need the opportunity to see yourself as you are seen by others. Thus, Mead saw consciousness of self as being somehow different from consciousness of other objects and events in the environment. Only by adopting another's point of view is it possible to achieve a sense of self-awareness.

More recently, Duval and Wicklund (1972) have proposed a distinction between subjective and objective self-awareness. Duval and Wicklund criticize Mead's theory on the grounds that knowledge of another person's point of view presumes that the child already has his own differentiated point of view, which begs the question of self as defined by the emergence of a unique perspective. In their view consciousness is a unitary state, which has bidirectional properties in that it can be selectively focused on self or on environmental events. Subjective self-awareness is a state in which attention is directed toward something other than self. But the mere capacity to direct attention implies a monitoring of bodily activities and sensory feedback, thus the designation "subjective self-awareness." In objective self-awareness attention is self-focused. Like both Mead and Cooley, Duval and Wicklund feel that objective self-awareness is dependent on early social experience. However, they see objective self-awareness as being related to the maturational stages of development identified by Piaget. Specifically, they argue that the child's sense of absolutism, or belief that his own point of view is universal and shared by others precludes self-consciousness. The growing child only develops the capacity for objective self-awareness when he realizes that other people have attitudes, values, and intentions that differ from his own. Not until he reaches the point at which he becomes aware of himself as a limited and bounded object that is differentiated from others, does objective self-awareness become possible.

Finally, Duval and Wicklund propose that their account of self assumes only that (1) the child is capable of judging when two objects are different, and (2) is confronted with explicit instances in which his point of view differs from others.

The research with chimpanzees is compatible with all of these theories in showing that the opportunity for early social interaction is an important precondition for self-recognition (Gallup *et al.*, 1971; Hill *et al.*, 1970). One must have knowledge of others in order to have knowledge of self. However, none of the theories explain the difference between the great apes and lesser primates in the capacity for self-recognition. Although Duval and Wicklund present an intriguing account of self-conception, it is difficult to reconcile their position with the data on other primates. While apparently incapable of self-recognition, monkeys are clearly capable of making many fine and complex discriminations, and as a result of conflict and repeated agonistic encounters with other monkeys are confronted with many explicit instances of intentions and motivations that are at odds with their own. Why then do monkeys fail to develop a sufficiently unique and differentiated perspective to recognize themselves in mirrors? Clearly, self-recognition requires more than the mere capacity to make simple discriminations. Just what it is about social interaction that provides for a sense of self has yet to be identified. Perhaps the self is as much an organismic variable as an experiential one. The monkey's inability to recognize himself in a mirror may be due to the absence of a sufficiently well-integrated self-concept (Gallup, 1977).

Another Species' Point of View

If explicit self-awareness is related to social interaction, then some intriguing possibilities arise. Carl Jung (1958), for example, argued that a truly objective view of man would only be possible if we were able to see ourselves from another species' perspective. However, if the present analysis of self-conception is correct and the opportunity to examine oneself was restricted to another species' point of view, this ought to profoundly distort one's concept of self. It is reported, for example, that when Washoe, who was reared with humans, was first confronted with other chimpanzees she referred to them in sign language as "black bugs" (Linden, 1974). As another illustration, it is well-known that being reared in social isolation can have adverse effects on primate sexual behavior (e.g., Mason, 1960). It is less well-known, however, that human-reared chimpanzees are actually more impaired sexually than those reared in complete and abject social isolation (Rogers & Davenport, 1969). Why? Maybe it is because they think they are human.

Then there is the informal experiment conducted with another home-reared chimpanzee named Vicki (Hayes & Nissen, 1971). Among other things, Vicki was taught to sort stacks of snapshots into a human and an animal pile. One day, without Vicki's knowledge, her own photograph was placed in the stack, and when she came to her picture, without hesitation she picked it up and placed it on the human pile. It seems to me that there are at least two ways to interpret this behavior (Gallup, 1977). First, man may not be the only one to appreciate the similarities between chimpanzees and men. The other is that maybe Vicki thought she was human.

Quite in keeping with these results, Temerlin (1975) recently reported that as a consequence of rearing a chimpanzee in his home, his son began to develop doubts about his own species identity! What constitutes a "social object" may be much more fluid than many people realize. The imprinting literature makes it clear that affiliation tendencies are often tied to early social experiences. For you and me and the rest of the great apes, the content of our individual identity may be similarly subject to social influences. It would appear, therefore, that the presence or absence of social interaction somehow determines whether or not you have a self-concept, while the quality and nature of those interactions determine the content of the concept.

Self-Perception and Species Identity

While the behavioral or functional consequences of imprinting may be pretty much the same for most animals, the data on self-recognition can be used to argue that the cognitive consequences of imprinting may be quite restricted (see Gallup, in press).

Contrary to the stance that many people have taken in the literature (e.g., Gottlieb, 1971), affiliation tendencies are far from being isomorphic with species identity. Species identity implies a sense of belonging or membership, while species-specific affiliation patterns, following responses, and attachment behaviors may merely reflect the operation of primitive familiarity effects and genetic predispositions.

An explicit sense of species identity would have to involve the cognitive capacity to equate oneself with other organisms, or the intellectual equivalent of thinking "I am one of them." But to be able to think "I am one of them" presupposes a sense of "I." If a visually capable animal cannot identify himself in a mirror, how could he possibly be expected to identify himself as being a member of some particular class of organisms? I submit that species identify and individual identity may not be mutually exclusive, and that without a concept of self, the designation "species identity" is a misnomer.

The Concept of Self

Among some philosophers it has been fashionable to question the legitimacy of the self-concept on the grounds that it poses a logical impossibility. For instance, as a working definition Johnstone (1970) proposes that "consciousness is ... isomorphic with the act of referring to something by pointing to it" (p. 105). And, by analogy, Ryle (1970) claims that the index finger "cannot be the object at which it itself is pointing" (p. 245). In other words, in the case of self-perception how can the subject and object be one and the same? How can the self be aware of itself?

One way to address this question is to pose a question, namely, "Can you conceive of yourself?" Only if the answer to this question is "No" is the philosopher's position supported. But then, it seems to me that this would be more of a comment on your mentality than on the status of the self-concept.

In practice the distinction between subject and object is only a problem for self-perception in a temporal sense. Thinking about yourself is always after the fact, or at least displaced from the fact. Self-awareness is not equivalent to being conscious of consciousness. But just because you cannot think about yourself thinking about yourself does not make self-conception any less real. As Epstein (1973) points out, "there can be no argument but that the subjective feeling state of having a self is an important empirical phenomenon that warrants study in its own right" (p. 405). While the concept of self may superficially seem untenable, the sense of self is real.

Mirrors represent one way out of the philosopher's dilemma. Whereas one might object on logical grounds to the notion of a subject that can be an object to itself, it turns out that subject and object are always the same in the case of mirror confrontation. In front of a mirror the index finger can indeed be the object at which it itself is pointing. It is important to note, however, that this realization is only possible for an organism with a sense of self.

It would be easy to contrive of another and to my mind more compelling instance in which subject and object are the same. Assume for the moment that your scalp was locally anesthetized, and while you were fully awake your skull was surgically removed. If I then directed your attention to a tilted mirror placed strategically overhead, it would literally be the case that your brain would be seeing your brain! There is certainly no infinite regress here, nor is there any contradiction.

Epstein (1973) proposes another view of self that provides still another alternative way out of the philosopher's dilemma. He argues that the self-concept may not be a concept at all, but rather a theory. One's sense of self, in other words, is really a theory of self. Out of his varied experiences, the individual formulates a set of tacit principles and expectations that coalesce into a theory about himself. This theory in turn serves as a conceptual tool for purposes of planning, integrating, and organizing additional experiences. Epstein argues that this solves the problem of self as both subject and object because "theories influence, as well as are influenced by the acquisition of data" (p. 415).

One might object to self-recognition as a legitimate means of operationalizing the sense of self (i.e., in order to correctly infer the identity of the reflection you have to have an identity of your own) because of circularity. In order to define self-awareness independent of the behavior (self-recognition) it is supposed to explain, we need other empirical anchor points. Fortunately, as a result of the recent attempts to teach chimpanzees various forms of symbolic communication, such evidence is readily at hand in the chimpanzee's and man's capacity to use personal pronouns and refer to themselves (e.g., Gardner & Gardner, 1971). While words such as "I" and "me" are not isomorphic with self-conception, they certainly presuppose a sense of self. In fact, self-conception and the capacity to symbolize oneself may be a necessary precondition for the development and elaboration of language (see Terrace & Bever, 1976).

Another question occasionally raised in this context is the issue of a visual sense of self as possibly distinct from an olfactory or auditory self. According to this view, animals other than the great apes and man, while lacking a visual self may have a sense of self in terms of some other modality. I think this is an artificial distinction. One's sense of self is not modality-specific. Self-awareness does not disappear when you close your eyes or cover your ears. When you think about yourself you do not necessarily conjure up a visual image. The self is a multi-modal phenomenon, and as such presupposes considerable intermodal equivalence. One clue as to the difference between great apes and monkeys is that until recently cross-modal perception has proven difficult to demonstrate in monkeys (e.g., Ettlinger, 1967) but chimpanzees and orangutans are quite capable of learning to match-to-sample across different modalities (Davenport & Rogers, 1970).

Significance of Self-Conception

Self-recognition should not be misconstrued as being the same as self-conception. Self-recognition refers specifically to an organism's capacity to correctly identify itself in a mirror. Whereas self-recognition can be used to infer self-conception, self-conception implies much more than mere recognition. Self-recognition simply addresses the issue of self-awareness, but in no way reflects on the content of one's self-concept.

In its most basic form the concept of self is equivalent to an identity. In order to conceive of yourself it requires a sense of identity. By identity I mean a sense of continuity over time and space. I persist over time and space, therefore I exist. Memory constitutes one form of continuity over time and space. But, by itself memory neither presupposes or necessarily provides for such a sense. One of the unique features of mirrors is that the identity of the observer and his reflection in a mirror are necessarily one and the same. Therefore, the capacity to correctly infer the identity of the image presupposes an already existent identity on the part of the organism making that inference (Gallup, 1977). Without an identity of your own, the source and significance of the reflection would forever remain unknown.

For example, as far as chimpanzees and orangutans are concerned, I do not think their sense of self in any way emerges out of experience with a mirror. Rather, a mirror simply represents a means of mapping what the chimpanzee already knows, and provides him with a new and more explicit dimension of knowing about himself, in the sense that he now has an opportunity to see himself as he is seen by other chimpanzees.

Naturally we are a long way away from being able to specify a neurological basis for the sense of self. However, self-recognition may represent an emergent phenomenon that only occurs once a species acquires a certain number of cortical neurons with sufficiently complex interconnections. Alternatively, one could view this issue from the standpoint of a threshold model. Different organisms may very well have differing degrees of self-awareness, but only with an explicit sense of identity does self-recognition become possible. The threshold for self-recognition may be quite high compared to other forms of self-conception. It is also possible that self-recognition may be an indirect consequence of selection for other cognitive skills, and as such would represent a correlated trait (e.g., as already noted, self-awareness may be a precondition for language).

It is intriguing to note that while the development of an individual identity in great apes probably requires social interaction with others, the object of that interaction need not involve others of the same species. For example, many home-reared chimpanzees show clear signs of self-recognition in response to mirrors but an active avoidance, or even disdain for members of their own species (e.g., Temerlin, 1975). Thus, the existence of self-awareness in chimpanzees does not appear to depend on a particular or even an accurate species identity. The self is an open system, experientially based and in terms of content free from biological predispositions. For this reason, it is possible that self-awareness (E. O. Wilson notwithstanding) has the capacity to emancipate organisms, intellectually at least, from some of the otherwise deterministic and unrelenting forces of evolution (Slobodkin, 1977).

The presence of an individual identity represents a conceptual leap of sorts. As Lewis and Brooks-Gunn (1979) point out, effective social functioning in humans requires that the infant learn that he is separate and distinct from others. Once you can conceive of yourself, then you can begin to think about yourself. Once you can become the object of your own attention, you can begin to contemplate your own existence. If you contemplate your own existence, then it is a fairly simple and maybe even logical next step to begin contemplating your nonexistence. Ultimately, organisms capable of contemplating their own existence may find themselves in the rather precarious position of being able, at least in principle, to take steps to modify that existence.

REFERENCES

Abély, P. Le signe du miroir dans les psychoses et plus spécialement dans la démence précoce. *Annales Médico-Psychologiques*, 1930, *88*, 28–36.

Amsterdam, B. Mirror self-image reactions before age two. *Developmental Psychobiology*, 1972, *5*, 297–305.

Bertenthal, B. I., & Fischer, K. W. The development of self-recognition in the infant. *Developmental Psychology*, 1978, *14*, 44–50.

Brooks-Gunn, J. Personal communication. December 3, 1977.

Brooks-Gunn, J., & Lewis, M. Mirror-image stimulation and self-recognition in infancy. Paper presented at the meeting of the Society for Research in Child Development, Denver, April 1975.

Brown, W. L., McDowell, A. A., & Robinson, E. M. Discrimination learning of mirrored cues by rhesus monkeys. *Journal of Genetic Psychology*, 1965, *106*, 123–128.

Cooley, C. H. *Human nature and the social order*. New York: Charles Scribner's Sons, 1912.

Darwin, C. R. A biographical sketch of an infant. *Mind*, 1877, *2*, 285–294.

Davenport, R. K., & Rogers, C. M. Intermodal equivalence of stimuli in apes. *Science*, 1970, *168*, 279–280.

Delmas, F. A. Le signe du miroir dans la démence précoce. *Annales Médico-Psychologiques*, 1929, *87*, 227–233.

Dickie, J. R., & Strader, W. H. Development of mirror image responses in infancy. *The Journal of Psychology*, 1974, *88*, 333–337.

Dixon, J. C. Development of self-recognition. *Journal of Genetic Psychology*, 1957, *91*, 251–256.

Duval, S., & Wicklund, R. A. *A theory of objective self awareness*. New York: Academic Press, 1972.

Epstein, S. The self-concept revisited, or a theory of a theory. *American Psychologist*, 1973, *28*, 404–416.

Ettlinger, G. Analysis of cross-modal effects and their relationship to language. In F. L. Darley & C. H. Millikan (Eds.), *Brain mechanisms underlying speech and language*. New York: Grune & Stratton, 1967.

Raure, H. L'investissement délirant de l'image de soi. *Evolution Psychiatrique*, 1956, *3*, 545–577.

Flannery, C. N. Self-recognition and stimulus complexity preference in autistic children. Unpublished masters thesis, University of New Orleans, 1976.

Frenkel, R. E. Psychotherapeutic reconstruction of the traumatic amnesic period by the mirror image projective technique. *Journal of Existentialism*, 1964, *17*, 77–96.

Gallup, G. G., Jr. Mirror-image stimulation. *Psychological Bulletin*, 1968, *70*, 782–793.

Gallup, G. G., Jr. Chimpanzees: Self-recognition. *Science*, 1970, *167*, 86–87.

Gallup, G. G., Jr. Towards an operational definition of self-awareness. In R. H. Tuttle (Ed.), *Socio-ecology and psychology of primates*. The Hague, Netherlands: Mouton, 1975.

Gallup, G. G., Jr. Self-recognition in primates: A comparative approach to the bidirectional properties of consciousness. *American Psychologist*, 1977, *32*, 329–338.

Gallup, G. G., Jr. Chimpanzees, self-awareness, and species identity. In M. A. Roy (Ed.), *Species identification: A phylogenetic evaluation*. New York: Garland, in press.

Gallup, G. G., Jr., & McClure, M. K. Preference for mirror-image stimulation in differentially reared rhesus monkeys. *Journal of Comparative and Physiological Psychology*, 1971, *75*, 403–407.

Gallup, G. G., Jr., McClure, M. K., Hill, S. D., & Bundy, R. A. Capacity for self-recognition in differentially reared chimpanzees. *The Psychological Record*, 1971, *21*, 69–74.

Gardner, B. J., & Gardner, R. A. Two-way communication with an infant chimpanzee. In A. M. Schrier & F. Stollnitz (Eds.), *Behavior of nonhuman primates* (Vol. 4). New York: Academic Press, 1971.

Gesell, A., & Ames, L. B. The infant's reaction to his mirror image. *Journal of Genetic Psychology*, 1947, *70*, 141–154.

Gesell, A., & Thompson, H. *Infant behavior; its genesis and growth*. New York: McGraw-Hill, 1934.

Gottlieb, G. *Development of species identification in birds*. Chicago: The University of Chicago Press, 1971.

Harris, L. P. Self-recognition among institutionalized profoundly retarded males: A replication. *Bulletin of the Psychonomic Society*, 1977, *9*, 43–44.

Hayes, K. J., & Nissen, C. H. Higher mental functions in a home-reared chimpanzee. In A. M. Schrier & F. Stollnitz (Eds.), *Behavior of nonhuman primates* (Vol. 3). New York: Academic Press, 1971.

Hill, S. D., Bundy, R. A., Gallup, G. G., Jr., & McClure, M. K. Responsiveness of young nursery-reared chimpanzees to mirrors. *Proceedings of the Louisiana Academy of Sciences*, 1970, *33*, 77–82.

Johnstone, H. W., Jr. *The problem of the self.* University Park: Pennsylvania State University Press, 1970.

Jung, C. G. *The undiscovered self.* Boston: Little, Brown, 1958.

Lethmate, J., & Dücker, G. Untersuchungen zum Selbsterkennen im Spiegel bei Orangutans und einigen anderen Affenarten. *Zeitschrift für Tierpsychologie*, 1973, *33*, 248–269.

Lewis, M. The busy, purposeful world of a baby. *Psychology Today*, 1977, *10* (9), 53–54, 56.

Lewis, M., & Brooks-Gunn, J. *Social cognition and the acquisition of self.* New York: Plenum, 1979.

Linden, E. *Apes, men, and language.* New York: Penguin, 1974.

Mason, W. A. The effects of social restriction on the behavior of rhesus monkeys: I. Free social behavior. *Journal of Comparative and Physiological Psychology*, 1960, *53*, 582–589.

Mead, G. H. *Mind, self and society: From the standpoint of a social behaviorist.* Chicago: University of Chicago Press, 1934.

Orbach, J., Traub, A. C., & Olson, R. Psychophysical studies of body-image: II. Normative data on the adjustable body-distorting mirror. *Archives of General Psychiatry*, 1966, *14*, 41–47.

Ostancow, P. Le signe du miroir dans la démence précoce. *Annales Médico-Psychologiques*, 1934, *92*, 787–790.

Papousek, H., & Papousek, M. Mirror image and self-recognition in young human infants: I. A new method of experimental analysis. *Developmental Psychobiology*, 1974, *7*, 149–157.

Pechacek, T. F., Bell, K. F., Cleland, C. C., Baum, C., & Boyle, M. Self-recognition in profoundly retarded males. *Bulletin of the Psychonomic Society*, 1973, *1*, 328–330.

Preyer, W. *Mind of the child. Volume II. Development of the intellect.* New York: Appleton, 1893.

Rogers, C. M., & Davenport, R. K. Effects of restricted rearing on sexual behavior of chimpanzees. *Developmental Psychology*, 1969, *1*, 200–204.

Ryle, G. Self-knowledge. In H. Morick (Ed.), *Introduction to the philosophy of mind.* Glenview, Illinois: Scott, Foresman, 1970.

Schulman, A. H., & Kaplowitz, C. Mirror-image response during the first two years of life. *Developmental Psychobiology*, 1977, *10*, 133–142.

Shentoub, S. A., Soulairac, A., & Rustin, E. Comportement de l'enfant arriéré devant le miroir. *Enfance*, 1954, *7*, 333–340.

Shirley, M. M. *The first two years. Volume II. Intellectual development.* Minneapolis: University of Minnesota Press, 1933.

Slobodkin, L. B. Evolution is no help. *World Archaeology*, 1977, *8*, 332–343.

Stone, L. J., & Church, J. *Childhood and adolescence.* 2nd Ed. New York: Random House, 1968.

Stutsman, R. *Mental measurement of preschool children.* Yonkers: World Book, 1931.

Temerlin, M. K. *Lucy: Growing up human.* Palo Alto, Calif.: Science & Behavior Books, 1975.

Terrace, H. S., & Bever, T. G. What might be learned from studying language in the chimpanzee? The importance of symbolizing oneself. *Annals of the New York Academy of Sciences*, 1976, *280*, 579–588.

Tinklepaugh, O. L. An experimental study of representative factors in monkeys. *Journal of Comparative Psychology*, 1928, *8*, 197–236.

Traub, A. C., & Orbach, J. Psychophysical studies of body-image: I. The adjustable body-distorting mirror. *Archives of General Psychiatry*, 1964, *11*, 53–66.

von Senden, M. *Space and sight: The perception of space and shape in the congenitally blind before and after operation*. Glencoe, Ill.: Free Press, 1960.

Wittreich, W. Visual perception and personality. *Scientific American*, 1959, *200*, 56–60.

Wylie, R. C. The present status of self theory. In E. F. Borgatta & W. W. Lambert (Eds.), *Handbook of personality theory and research*. Chicago: Rand McNally, 1968.

Wylie, R. C. *The self-concept*. Volume 1. Revised edition. Lincoln: University of Nebraska Press, 1974.

7

Only Children, Stereotypes, and Research

Toni Falbo

Only children are people who grow up without siblings. About 13% of completed American families contain an only child (U.S. Bureau of Census, 1970). Besides being rare, only children are widely considered to be undesirable. In 1950 and again in 1972, Blake (1974) conducted a survey of a representative sample of the American public to determine whether being an only child was considered to be an advantage or disadvantage. Seventy-six percent in 1950 and 80% in 1972 chose "disadvantage" in describing only children.

One of the reasons for this negative view of only children is that only children are stereotyped to be selfish, lonely, and maladjusted (Thompson, 1974). Thompson asked college students to check trait adjectives that they thought were characteristic of only children. The resultant composite description was predominantly negative. Only children were conceived to be "generally maladjusted, self-centered and self-willed, attention seeking and dependent on others, temperamental and anxious, generally unhappy and unlikeable, and yet somewhat more autonomous than a child with two siblings" (Thompson, 1974, pp. 95–96).

Given this view of the only child, it is not surprising that one of the major reasons cited for having a second child is to prevent the first from becoming an only (Solomon, Clare, & Westoff, 1956).

Taken together, this evidence suggests the existence of a popular

Toni Falbo • Department of Educational Psychology, University of Texas at Austin, Austin, Texas 78172.

assumption about child development. That is, the presence of siblings is assumed to be essential for the development of a healthy personality.

Before examining the empirical validity of this assumption and the only child stereotype, we will present recent research on the cognitive bases of stereotypes. This section will demonstrate how stereotypes in general obtain their content and how they perpetuate themselves in the face of scant empirical support. This information will be useful in evaluating the research literature on only children.

STEREOTYPES

Basically, a stereotype is "a set of characteristics which is assumed to fit a category of people" (Hastorf, Schneider, & Polefka, 1970, p. 46). According to Hastorf et al. (1970), stereotyping is an example of basic human thought processes designed to reduce the amount of information we process. In general, this reduction prevents us from being over-whelmed by environmental stimuli. By perceiving individuals as mere instances of a category, we reduce the amount of information processing we need to do.

There is more to stereotypes than simple information reduction, however. Specific cognitive tendencies influence the content of stereo-types. One such tendency concerns the impact of extreme cases on the impressions formed about a group. Another tendency involves the erroneous pairing of infrequent characteristics with infrequently occur-ring groups. Research demonstrating these tendencies is described below.

Rothbart (1977) investigated the effect of extreme cases by including a limited number of extreme cases within a series of descriptive sentences about members of a group. In two separate studies, Rothbart considered both extreme physical (height) and social (crime) character-istics. In both studies, Rothbart found that after the presentation of the descriptive sentences, subjects overestimated the proportion of extreme cases present in the group and that extreme cases had more impact on the overall impressions formed of these groups than their actual fre-quency would justify.

The second cognitive tendency that influences the content of ster-eotypes concerns the tendency to pair rare behaviors with rare groups. Hamilton and Gifford (1976) presented subjects with lists of behaviors attributed to individual members of one of two groups. Many more descriptions were given of one group (called the frequently occurring group) than the other group (called the infrequently occurring group). The rareness of the behaviors was manipulated by varying the relative frequency of desirable versus undesirable behaviors attributed to group members. Hamilton and Gifford found that even though the ratio of desirable to undesirable behaviors was the same for the infrequently and frequently occurring groups, subjects were more likely to overestimate the extent to which rare behaviors were performed by the infrequent group than the frequent group. Further, the overall subjects' impressions of the infrequently occurring group was more affected by the rare behaviors than their impressions of the frequently occurring group. Finally, Hamilton and Gifford found this tendency, regardless of whether the rare behaviors were desirable or undesirable.

Hamilton and Gifford's results have relevance to the content of stereotypes about minority groups. Because there are fewer minority than majority members (by definition), minority groups are the conceptual analog of the infrequently occurring group. The implication of the cognitive tendency demonstrated by Hamilton and Gifford is that members of the majority would be more likely to remember rare behaviors as being performed by minority than majority group members. Furthermore, since in real life negative behavior is rarer than positive behavior (Kanouse & Hanson, 1971), majority groups would be more likely to develop stereotypes of minorities that are predominantly negative in content. Thus, because of basic tendencies we have in processing information, the content of our stereotypes about minority groups is disproportionately loaded with extreme and negative characteristics.

Additional research in the area of social cognition has also established some of the ways stereotypes perpetuate themselves. Both Hamilton (1977) and Rothbart (1977) demonstrated that subjects remember evidence that confirms or is consistent with stereotypes more than evidence that is irrelevant to the stereotype.

The significance of these cognitive tendencies becomes even more apparent when we consider that stereotypes guide behavior. Recent research by Snyder and his colleagues has shown that if we expect an individual to behave in ways consistent with stereotypes, we behave toward that person in ways that anticipate stereotype-consistent behavior. According to Snyder, Tanke, and Berscheid (1977), these anticipatory behaviors can actually elicit the expected behavior in others. Two studies demonstrating this behavioral chain reaction will be presented.

Snyder et al. (1977) used the stereotype of physical attractiveness to demonstrate the self-fulfilling nature of stereotypes. A popular expectation about physically attractive people is that they have more sociable personality traits than less attractive people (Berscheid & Walster, 1974). Snyder et al. presented each male subject (all undergraduates) with a photograph of an unknown, young woman and told them that they would engage in a "getting acquainted" phone conversation with her. Actually, the photograph was not of the woman to whom they spoke, but of a woman whose photograph had previously been rated as very attractive or unattractive. The young women who did talk to the men were a haphazard assortment of college undergraduates who had no expectations about the physical appearance of their male caller.

The phone conversations were tape-recorded and rated by students who were ignorant of the purposes of the study and the appearance of the callers. Preconversation ratings made by the male callers indicated that men who thought they would be talking to an attractive woman expected her to be more sociable, poised, etc., than men expecting a conversation with an unattractive woman. Interestingly enough, the student judges rated the conversations of women expected to be attractive as more sociable, poised, sexually warm, and outgoing than the conversations of women thought to be unattractive. Therefore, the results support the conclusion that the men's expectations were fulfilled in the women's behavior.

But how did this happen? Snyder et al. reported that the judges rated the conversation of male speakers who expected their partners to be attractive as more sociable, warm, outgoing, etc., than the conversation of men who thought they were talking to unattractive women. The judges also rated the conversations of the "expect attractive" men as more confident, animated, and comfortable than the conversations of the "expect unattractive" men. Thus, the men who thought they were talking to an attractive woman behaved in a way that elicited the expected behavior from the women.

In another study, Snyder and Swann (1978) demonstrated that behavior that is induced by the expectations of others outlasts the specific interaction that elicited it. Snyder and Swann led one player of a two-person game to believe that the other player (called the target) was a hostile person. The game allowed for the selection of moves of varying degrees of hostility. The results indicated that the player who expected the target to be hostile selected more hostile moves, thereby eliciting hostile behavior from the target player. This essentially repeats the self-fulfilling prophecy finding of the Snyder et al. (1977) study. However, Snyder and Swann took this finding one step further. After playing the game, the target person was given the opportunity to play the game again, this time with someone who had no expectations about the target. The target was allowed to make the first move. Snyder and Swann reported that the target chose to begin playing at the level of hostility developed in the first game. The new player, of course, responded in kind, and so on. What began as the behavioral fulfillment of someone else's expectations persevered into an interaction with another person, thus becoming the basis for the new person's impressions.[1]

In summary, recent research in cognitive social psychology indicates that stereotypes not only perpetuate themselves in our memory but they also create their own empirical confirmation.

You may be wondering what possible relevance this has for only children. Recall that only children are rare and that the stereotype of the only child contains traits that are predominantly negative and extreme. Further, the stereotype literature explains how the only-child stereotype could be perpetuated not only in the minds of others, but in their behavior toward only children, and therefore, in the behavior of only children. The next section of this chapter is a review of the literature on only children. This review is designed to examine the empirical validity of popular conceptions of only children and to demonstrate that assumptions about the necessity of siblings frequently affect research on only children.

ONLY CHILDREN

This literature review will be limited to four areas: interpersonal behavior, mental health, intelligence, and sex roles.

Interpersonal Behavior. One of the chief concerns about only children is that because they do not have siblings, they lack proper social skills. In a recent study of only children (Falbo, 1978a), I decided to use the stereotype of the only child as a basis for generating hypotheses about the interpersonal behavior of only children. Specifically, I was concerned with whether only children were less cooperative, less affiliative, and more autonomous than others.

I used a simple two-play prisoner's dilemma game to measure preferences for making cooperative versus competitive moves. Presumably, the absence of siblings would result in only children not learning how to cooperate with others. Strangely enough, the results supported the reverse of this hypothesis. Rather than choosing the most competitive move (i.e., moves that take advantage of the other player), only children were more likely than all others to choose cooperative moves in response to a cooperative move. This result was explained in terms of sibling rivalry. That is, the results suggest that growing up with siblings enhances interpersonal competitiveness rather than cooperativeness.

---

[1] A word of caution: the perseveration occurred only if the target was led to believe that his behavior during the first game was indicative of his true personality. Targets who were told that their behavior was situationally induced did not exhibit perseveration.

I also compared only children to others in terms of their affiliativeness. On the basis of the stereotype, one would predict that only children would be more likely to be loners than others. Affiliativeness was measured in three ways. First, the subjects were asked to estimate the number of friends and close friends they had. Second, they were asked to rate their comfort during a group discussion in which they participated. Third, they were to list the clubs they belonged to and the leadership positions they held in these organizations.

The results partially supported the prediction. Only children cited fewer friends than others but an equivalent number of close friends. They belonged to fewer clubs, but were more likely to be leaders in the clubs they joined. Finally, only children reported feeling as comfortable and received peer ratings that were as positive as those received by other participants in the group discussion.

These results suggested that only children are less affiliative than others. Other research evidence also supports this conclusion. Using projective techniques, Conners (1963) found that only children demonstrated less affiliation deprivation than people from two-child families. In addition, he found that only children scored higher on both the wanted and expressed sections of an affection scale than did nononly borns. Overall, Conners (1963) interpreted these findings as supporting the hypothesis that only children suffer less affection deprivation than children with siblings and that this results in their lowered need for affiliation. Consistent with results, Rosenfeld (1966) compared the need for affiliation scores of first and only borns and found firstborns to have significantly higher needs for affiliation than only borns.

Perhaps one of the reasons only children are less interested in affiliating with others is that other people are less interested in affiliating with them. Unfortunately, there are only two published studies that focus on this question and their results are contradictory. The most recent study was conducted by Miller and Maruyama (1976). They found, in a study of sociometric choices within the classroom, that later borns were selected more frequently as playmates and someone to sit close to than first or only borns. Furthermore, this birth-order difference was found regardless of family size or socioeconomic status. Miller and Maruyama suggested that because only and firstborns do not have older siblings, they acquire more autocratic, less interactive interpersonal styles and that this has negative consequences for peer popularity.

Contradictory conclusions about only children were drawn by Sells and Roff (1963). They obtained likeability ratings from same-sex, grade-school classmates and found that only and youngest borns received the highest ratings. A possible reconciliation of these discrepant findings lies in their different measures of peer popularity. Likeability ratings do not necessarily measure the same aspects of peer acceptance as playmate and seating selections. It may be that last borns acquire a more compliant disposition than only borns, thus making last-borns better choices for someone to play with or sit next to in class. However, this does not necessarily mean that only borns are less well liked generally or socially unskilled.

The conclusion that only children are more likely than others to take leadership positions also has some support in the literature. An experimental study of firemen found that both first and only borns (Smith & Goodchilds, 1963) were more likely to take leadership positions in large work groups than later borns. A study of middle managers found that both only and firstborns attained higher earnings and received more career advancements over a six-year period than did later borns (Berger & Ivancevich, 1973). However, there is some contradictory evidence. Farley, Smart, and Brittain (1974) found that firstborns were more likely to be officers in any branch of the military than were only, second, or third borns.

Finally, I tested the hypothesis that only children are more autonomous than others. To do this, I measured autonomy as the amount of discrepancy between the group decision regarding the rank ordering of equipment and the postgroup, private decision made by participants in the NASA game (Pfeiffer & Jones, 1969). Essentially, this measure indicates the extent to which group norms influence an individual's private decision making. The results were in the expected direction. The personal decisions of only children were much more discrepant from the group's than were the decisions of people who had grown up with siblings.

Thus, the results of this study partially supported the stereotype (only children were more autonomous) and partially refuted it (only children were more cooperative). Further, only children appear to seek out less affiliation with others, and take more leadership roles, but it is not clear whether only children are more or less popular than others.

Mental Health. In general, on a variety of mental health indices, no differences have been found between only and nononly children (Burke, 1969; Dyer, 1945; Howe & Madgett, 1975). In fact, there is some evidence that only children are underrepresented among psychiatric or other clinical clients (Blatz & Bott, 1927; Corfield, 1968; Kurth & Schmidt, 1964; Tuckman & Regan, 1967). However, there is recent evidence that only children are more likely to be diagnosed as psychologically disturbed than others (Belmont, 1977). These mental health ratings were made by psychiatrists during a Dutch military preinduction examination. As in the United States, the examination was done for the purpose of screening out individuals with health problems that would make them undesirable military inductees. During the health exam, ratings of the individual's psychological stability were made. If the young man received an unfit rating in psychological stability, further diagnostic categories were specified by consultant psychiatrists who interviewed the young men.

It is unknown what information about the young men was available to the interviewing psychiatrists (Belmont, 1977b). It is entirely possible that the psychiatrists were given information about their background as part of the relevant information on which they should base their diagnosis. Belmont, Wittes, and Stein (1976) report that only children received the most diagnoses of personality disorder (composed mainly of "immature personality"), but the only child frequencies were statistically indistinguishable from those given to last borns. Furthermore, this pattern of results was found only in the nonmanual class. For the manual class, only children were not significantly different from first or last borns of two- to four-child families. Nonetheless, only children were more likely than any other group to receive a diagnosis of "Neurosis" in both manual and nonmanual classes.

These results are questionable on two grounds. First and foremost, it is possible that the psychiatrists obtained information about the inductees' family and used this information to guide their diagnoses. If so, these results are another example of the self-fulfilling nature of expectations. Second, it is not clear why the absence of siblings should lead to the development of an immature personality in the nonmanual, but not the manual class. If the presence of siblings is the critical factor, why should social class alter the results?

Other research on the mental health of only children indicates that only children are more likely than others to be referred for clinical help (Hough, 1932; Ko & Sun, 1965), and to repeat visits to the clinic (Howe & Madgett, 1975). In all three of these studies, the investigators offer as an *ad hoc* explanation for their results the presumed overprotectiveness of only-child parents. While this explanation is plausible, it is also possible that the stereotype of the only child leads professionals to be more likely to send only children for clinical help.

To investigate this possibility, Mary Rowen and I included in a larger study of stereotypes the label "only child" to examine the effects of this label on an observer's evaluation of the child's behavior. We asked 73 psychology undergraduates to pretend that, as part of a teacher training program, they went to a high school to observe students. The undergraduates read descriptions of four events that occurred in the high school and after reading each event they were given a description of the person primarily involved in the event. One of the four events had been previously rated as consistent with the only child stereotype and two of the four fictional high school students were presented as only children (one male; one female). The pairing of character with event was systematically varied. Only the results relevant to the only-child stereotype will be reported here.

One of the hypotheses of the study was that if a behavior consistent with the only-child stereotype is attributed to an only child, it would be rated as more of a problem than if it were attributed to a nononly child. We based this prediction on the Kahneman and Tversky (1973) finding that observers regard behavior consistent with stereotypes as more reliable and valid information about the person than behavior inconsistent or irrelevant to stereotypes. Given that the content of the only-child stereotype is predominantly negative, we reasoned that attributing a behavior consistent with the stereotype to an only child would enhance the observer's belief that the behavior is a problem and therefore should receive attention.

The results supported our hypothesis. When subjects were presented with an only child doing something consistent with the only-child stereotype, they were more likely to say that: (1) the behavior should be reported to the student's parents, $F(1,67) = 4.57$, $p < .04$; (2) the behavior is a problem, $F(1,67) = 6.75$, $p < .01$; and (3) the event should be brought to the attention of the school psychologist, $F(1,67) = 3.93$, $p < .05$, than if the identical behavior was attributed to a nononly child.

Thus, an alternative explanation for the high referral and repeat rate of only children is that behavior consistent with the only-child stereotype, when performed by an only child, results in an enhancement of the evaluation that this child's behavior is a problem and should receive attention.

Intelligence. There are three large-scale studies of intelligence (Belmont & Marolla, 1973; Breland, 1974; Claudy, 1976) that support the conclusion that family size (the number of children in family) is inversely related to intelligence. On the basis of this relationship, one would expect only children to have the highest IQ of all. Unfortunately, among young adults, only children fall short of this, scoring lower than both first and second borns of a two-child family. To account for this descrepancy, Zajonc and Markus (1975) incorporated a sibling tutoring factor into a model (called the confluence model) that accounts for the relationship between IQ and family size. Zajonc and Markus (1975) argued that since only children do not have a younger sibling to tutor, they fail to develop to their full intellectual potential.

Unfortunately, there is no evidence that tutoring a younger child results in a temporary or even permanent intelligence gain for either tutor or tutee. This lack of evidence is caused by a failure on the part of researchers to consider intelligence as potentially altered by the tutoring experience. Research in the area of cross-age tutoring has been limited to the acquisition of social skills and academic content (Allen, 1976). Unfortunately, it is unlikely that much empirical support for the sibling tutoring factor will be found because the Zajonc and Markus (1975) confluence model does not describe individual data points well. Grotevant, Scarr, and Weinberg (1977) found that the model accounted for about 2% of the variance, when actual rather than aggregate IQ data was considered. A more complete critique of the sibling tutoring factor can be found in Falbo (1978b).

Note that Zajonc and Markus's explanation for the IQ discrepancy of only children is consistent with the popular assumption that the presence of siblings is essential for healthy development. Perhaps the lack of support for the existence of a sibling tutoring effect in intelligence was compensated by the fact that it was consistent with popular beliefs about child development. At any rate, because the addition of the sibling tutoring factor made the data simulated by the confluence model almost identical to aggregate data, Zajonc and Markus (1975) did not consider alternate explanations for the intelligence discrepancy of only children. I did (Falbo, 1978b). Furthermore, the alternate explanation I proposed has substantial empirical support and it is even consistent with the basic framework of the confluence model.

Father absence is more common among one-child than multichild families (U.S. Bureau of Census, 1970). According to the confluence model, the absence of a parent has deleterious effects on the child's intelligence. By plugging in values generated by the confluence model, I found that the higher incidence of father-absence among one-child families accounted for 25% of the IQ discrepancy of only children (Falbo, 1978b).

Sex Role. Investigations of the origins of sex-role identification have frequently indicated that the sex-role behavior of parents is determinative of the sex-role behavior of their offspring (Hetherington, 1967; Lynn, 1969; Vogel, Broverman, Broverman, Clarkson, & Rosenkrantz, 1970). Other investigators have expanded this familial influence on the development of sex-role identification to include the birth order and sex composition of the siblings.

Since only children have no siblings, and are more likely to have just one parent, what can we expect about their sex-role identification? Relevant studies are few, but the sparsity of information has not discouraged Sutton-Smith and Rosenberg (1970) from concluding, "There are other data to show that the only boy is more feminine than other males, and the only girls more masculine; moreover, that the deviation in these opposite-sex directions leaves them with a greater tendency toward sex deviations consonant with tendencies" (p. 153).

Sutton-Smith and Rosenberg (1970) cited four references in support of this statement (Gundlach & Reiss, 1967; Heilbrun & Fromme, 1965; Hooker, 1931; Rosenberg & Sutton-Smith, 1964). An examination of these studies, however, indicates that they provide little or no support for the Sutton-Smith and Rosenberg statement. In three of the four studies cited, no measure of sexual deviancy was included in the research. These three studies contained various measures of conformity to American sex-role norms. Hooker's (1931) research concerned teacher ratings of the classroom behavior of elementary-school students. Among other findings, Hooker reported that teachers rated only children as more likely to "show signs of being sissies or tomboys" (p. 126). Since no information is provided by Hooker (1931) to indicate whether the teachers were blind to the number of siblings the students had, it is impossible to determine if the only child stereotype contaminated the results. In the Rosenberg and Sutton-Smith (1964) study, the only-child boys and not the girls demonstrated an unusual sex-role pattern. These boys ($N = 12$) scored high on both masculinity and femininity scales. Currently, such a pattern of scores is considered desirable, indicating sex-role androgyny (Bem, 1974). Finally, in the Heilbrun and Fromme (1965) study, the masculinity/femininity scores of only children did not differ significantly from those of children with siblings.

The fourth reference cited by Rosenberg and Sutton-Smith does, in fact, deal with the relative frequency of birth orders in a sample of lesbians and nonlesbians. However, this study did not find that only children were more likely than others to be found among the lesbian sample. Instead, Gundlach and Riess (1967) reported that a disproportionate number of only children, firstborns of a two-child family, and later-borns from large families were found among the lesbian sample. This finding is especially perplexing because only children have been found to be underrepresented among male homosexuals (Bieber, Dain, Dince, Drellich, Grand, Gundlach, Kreiner, Rifkin, Wilburg, & Bieber, 1962). A likely explanation for the Gundlach and Riess result lies in errors associated with the sample, rather than something intrinsic to birth order. This sampling error could be brought about by the smallness ($N = 217$) and self-select nature of the lesbian sample, and the questionable selection procedure undertaken in obtaining the nonlesbian sample.

Alternately, there is evidence that the presence of an opposite-sex sibling results in an increase of opposite-sex characteristics, especially if the opposite-sex sibling is older than the target child of the investigation. Using teacher ratings of tomboyism and sissyness, Brim (1958) found that children with an opposite-sex sibling were more tomboyish (if girls) or sissy (if boys) than children with same-sex siblings. This effect was more extreme if the opposite-sex sibling was older. Similarly, Rosenberg and Sutton-Smith (1964) found that children with opposite-sex siblings had more game preferences typical of the opposite sex than other children. Again, this effect was more extreme if the opposite-sex sibling was older. Finally, Rosenberg and Sutton-Smith (1968) reported that among undergraduate coeds, those with brothers had lower femininity scores. However, this result was unaltered by the relative age of the brother.

However, not all the evidence completely supports the opposite-sex sibling effect. Bigner (1972) found that the presence of an older brother elevated the preferences for male-typed items among both brothers and sisters. He also found that only children did not differ from children who had an older sister, but that only children made fewer male-typed choices than children who had an older brother. Overall, he reported the scores of only children were comparable to those of people with siblings.

Sutton-Smith and Rosenberg's (1970) statement about only children is another example of the impact of the popular assumption that siblings are necessary for healthy development. A cautious interpretation of the available literature does not support the conclusion that only children are more likely to be cross-sex-typed or homosexual than others. In fact, the available evidence suggests that cross-sex-typing or androgyny is more common among children with opposite sex siblings.

RECOMMENDATIONS

Overall, there has been little research devoted to only children. This is unfortunate because only children constitute a valuable comparison group for investigators who are interested in assessing the effects of having siblings. In order to avoid the potential contamination of research data with stereotype-induced effects, future research aimed at assessing the characteristics of only children should be guided by two rules. The first concerns devising data collection techniques that prevent the interviewer's (or other observer's) expectations about only children from altering the data. Whenever possible, people collecting data should be blind to the only–nononly child status of the subjects.

The second rule concerns the interpretation of the results. Many investigators attribute any difference between only children and others to the effects of siblings. While the presence or absence of siblings probably contributes to the development of distinguishing character- tics between only and other children, other factors, especially the associated parents, could also contribute.

Parents of only children have already demonstrated their deviancy by violating a strong social norm. According to Blake (1974) and Thompson (1974), having two children is the lower limit of socially acceptable family sizes. It seems likely that parents have just one child for several reasons and each of these reasons could have distinct effects on the only child. For example, one reason why parents have just one child is that the father is no longer present in the family. As reported earlier, the higher percentage of father absence among only children could at least partially account for the finding that only children score lower than expected on intelligence tests.

Another reason why parents have only one child is that they are subfecund. There is some suggestive evidence that only-child mothers are more likely to be subfecund than mothers of more children (Beckman, 1976; Falbo, 1976). It is possible that because of their awareness of their inability to have another child, subfecund or single parents of only children may be more protective of their child than parents of more children. Indeed, it is possible that one of the causes of the high clinic repeat rate of only children is the overprotective behavior of only-child parents.

Finally, some people may have just one child because they dislike the changes in their life-style that the presence of children requires. There is evidence that one-child homes are more adult-oriented than two or more child homes (Weisner, undated). Also, there is some evidence that one-child mothers rate the rewards of parenting as less important to them than mothers of more children (Beckman, 1976). Such parents would probably promote the precocious adoption of adultlike behavior in their sole child. In fact, only children have been described as behaving in more adultlike ways than their age would justify (Le Shan, 1960; Guilford & Worcester, 1930).

Conclusion

On the basis of a conservative assessment of available research, only children do not appear to live up to their reputation. As a group, there is no strong evidence that they are more selfish, lonely, or maladjusted than others. In fact, they may be prone to greater cooper- ativeness, autonomy, and leadership than those who grew up with siblings. Keep in mind, however, that our current knowledge about only children is limited. More research is needed to help clarify the questions raised by conflicting results or poorly executed research.

REFERENCES

Allen, V. L. *Children as teachers*. New York: Academic Press, 1976.

Beckman, L. J. Values of parenthood among women who desire an only child. In J. D. Goodchilds (Chair), *The Only Child: Problems and Prospects*. Symposium presented at the 84th Annual Convention of the American Psychological Association, Washington, D. C., 1976.

Belmont, L. Birth order, intellectual competence and psychiatric status. *Journal of Individual Psychology*, 1977a, *33*(1), 97–104.

Belmont, L. Personal communication, October 18, 1977b.

Belmont, L., & Marolla, F. A. Birth order, family size, and intelligence. *Science*, 1973, *182*, 1096–1101.

Belmont, L., Wittes, J., & Stein, Z. A. The only child syndrome: Myth or reality. Paper presented at the annual meeting of the Society for Life History Research in Psychopathology, Fort Worth, Texas, 1976.

Bem, S. L. The measurement of psychological androgyny. *Journal of Consulting and Clinical Psychology*, 1974, *42*(2), 155–162.

Berger, P. K., & Ivancevich, J. M. Birth order and managerial achievement. *Academy of Management Journal*, 1973, *16*(3), 515–519.

Berscheid, E., & Walster, E. Physical attractiveness. In L. Berkowitz (Ed.), *Advances in experimental social psychology* (Vol. 7). New York: Academic Press, 1974.

Bieber, I., Dain, H. I., Dince, P. R., Drellich, M. G., Grand, H. G., Gundlach, R. H., Kreiner, M. W., Rifkin, A. H., Wilberg, C. B., & Bieber, T. B. *Homosexuality: A psychoanalytic study*. New York: Basic Books, 1962.

Bigner, J. J. Siblings influence on sex-role preference. *Journal of Genetic Psychology*, 1972, *121*(2), 271–282.

Blake, J. Can we believe recent data on birth expectations in the United States? *Demography*, 1974, *11*, 25–44.

Blatz, W. E., & Bott, E. A. Studies in mental hygiene of children: I. Behavior of public school children—a description of method. *Journal of Genetic Psychology*, 1927, *34*, 552–582.

Breland, H. M. Birth order, family configuration, and verbal achievement. *Child Development*, 1974, *45*, 1011–1019.

Brim, O. G. Family structure and sex role learning by children: A further analysis of Helen Koch's data. *Sociometry*, 1958, *21*, 1–15.

Burke, M. O. A search for systematic personality differentiate of the only child in young adulthood. *Journal of Genetic Psychology*, 1969, *60*, 41–45.

Chapman, K. J., & Chapman, J. P. Genesis of popular but erroneous psycho-diagnostic observations. *Journal of Abnormal Psychology*, 1967, *72*(3), 193–204.

Claudy, J. G. Family size and life outcomes for young adults. In J. D. Goodchilds (Chair), *The Only Child: Problems and Prospects*. Symposium presented at the 84th Annual Convention of the American Psychological Association, Washington, D. C., 1976.

Connors, C. K. Birth order and need for affiliation. *Journal of Personality*, 1963, *31*(3), 409–416.

Corfield, V. K. The utilization of guidance clinic facilities in Alberta, 1961. *Alberta Psychologist*, 1968, 9(3), 15–45.

Dyer, D. T. Are only children different? *Journal of Educational Psychology*, 1945, 36, 297–302.

Falbo, T. Folklore and the only child: A reassessment. In J. D. Goodchilds (Chair), *The Only Child: Problems and Prospects*. Symposium presented at the 84th Annual Convention of the American Psychological Association, Washington, D. C., 1976.

Falbo, T. The only child: A review. *Journal of Individual Psychology*, 1977, 33(1), 47–61.

Falbo, T. Only children and interpersonal behavior: An experimental and survey study. *Journal of Applied Social Psychology*, 1978a, 8 (3), 244–253.

Falbo, T. Sibling tutoring and other explanations for intelligence discontinuities of only and last borns. *Population: Behavioral, Social and Environmental Issues*, 1978b, 1 (4), 349–363.

Farley, F. H., Smart, K. L., & Brittain, C. V. Birth order, rank, and branch of service in the military. *Journal of Individual Psychology*, 1974, 30(2), 227–232.

Grotevant, H. D., Scarr, S., & Weinberg, R. A. Intellectual development in family constellations with adopted and natural children: A test of the Zajonc and Markus model. *Child Development*, 1977, 48, 1699–1703.

Guilford, R. B., & Worcester, D. A. A comparative study of the only and nononly children. *Journal of Genetic Psychology*, 1930, 38, 411–426.

Gundlach, R. H., & Riess, B. F. Birth order and sex of siblings in a sample of lesbians and nonlesbians. *Psychological Reports*, 1967, 20, 61–62.

Hamilton, D. L. Illusory correlation as a basis for social stereotypes. In R. D. Ashmore (Chair), *Cognitive Biases in Stereotyping*. Symposium presented at the 85th Annual Convention of the American Psychological Association, San Francisco, 1977.

Hamilton, D. L., & Gifford, R. K. Illusory correlation in interpersonal perception: A cognitive basis of stereotypic judgments. *Journal of Experimental Social Psychology*, 1976, 12, 392–407.

Hastorf, A. H., Schneider, D. J., & Polefkka, J. *Person perception*, Reading, Massachusetts: Addison-Wesley Publishing Company, 1970.

Heilbrun, A. E., & Fromme, D. K. Parental identification of late adolescent and level of adjustment: The importance of parental model attributes, ordinal position, and sex of child. *Journal of Genetic Psychology*, 1965, 107, 49–59.

Hetherington, E. M. The effects of familial variables on sex typing on parent–child similarity, and on limitation in children. *Minnesota Symposia on Child Psychology*, 1967, 1, 82–107.

Hooker, H. F. The study of the only child at school. *Journal of Genetic Psychology*, 1931, 39, 122–126.

Hough, E. Some factors in the etiology of maternal over-protection. *Smith College Studies of Social Work*, 1932, 2, 188–208.

Howe, M. G., & Madgett, M. E. Mental health problems associated with the only child. *Canadian Psychiatric Association Journal*, 1975, 20(3), 189–194.

Kahneman, D., & Tversky, A. On the psychology of prediction. *Psychological Review*, 1973, 80(4), 237–251.

Kanouse, D. E., & Hanson, L. R. Negativity in evaluations. In E. E. Jones, D. E. Kanouse, H. H. Kelley, R. E. Nisbett, S. Valins, & B. Weiner (Eds.), *Attribution: Perceiving the causes of behavior*, Morristown, New Jersey: General Learning Press, 1971.

Ko, U., & Sun, L. Ordinal position and the behaviour of visiting the child guidance clinic. *Acta Psychologia Tiawanica*, 1965, 7, 1062–1965.

Kurth, E., & Schmidt, E. Multidimensional examinations of stuttering children. *Probleme und Ergebnisse der Psychologie*, 1964, 12, 49–58.

Le Shan, E. J. *The only child*. New York: Public Affairs Pamphlets, 1960.

Lynn, D. B. *Parental and sex role identification*. Berkeley: McCutchan, 1969.

Miller, N., & Maruyama, G. Ordinal position and peer popularity. *Journal of Personality and Social Psychology*, 1976, 33(2), 123–131.

Pfeiffer, J. W., & Jones, J. E. Nasa exercise: seeking consensus. *Handbook for structured experiences for human relations training*, Iowa City: University Associates Press, 1969, 69–79.

Rosenberg, B. G., & Sutton-Smith, B. Ordinal position and sex-role identification. *Genetic Psychology Monographs*, 1964, 70, 297–328.

Rosenberg, B. G., & Sutton-Smith, B. Family interaction effects on masculinity–femininity. *Journal of Personality*, 1968, 8, 117–120.

Rosenfeld, H. Relationships of ordinal position to affiliation and achievement motives: Directions and generality. *Journal of Personality*, 1966, 34(4), 467–479.

Rothbart, M. Judgmental heuristics in stereotype formation and maintenance. In R. D. Ashmore (Chair), *Cognitive Biases in Stereotyping*. Symposium presented at the 85th Annual Convention of the American Psychological Association, San Francisco, 1977.

Sells, S. B., & Roff, M. Peer acceptance–rejection and birth order. *American Psychologist*, 1963, 18, 355.

Smith, E. E., & Goodchilds, J. D. Some personality and behavioral factors related to birth order. *Journal of Applied Psychology*, 1963, 47(5), 300–303.

Snyder, M., Tanke, E. D., & Berscheid, E. Social perception and interpersonal behavior: On the self-fulfilling nature of social stereotypes. *Journal of Personality and Social Psychology*, 1977, 35(9), 656–666.

Snyder, M., & Swann, W. E. Behavioral confirmation in social interaction: From social belief to social reality. *Journal of Experimental Social Psychology*, 1978, 14, 148–162.

Solomon, E. S., Clare, J. E., & Westoff, C. F. Social and psychological factors affecting fertility. *The Milbank Memorial Fund Quarterly*, 1956, 34(2), 160–177.

Sutton-Smith, B., & Rosenberg, B. G. *The sibling*. New York: Holt, Rinehart, and Winston, Inc., 1970.

Thompson, V. D. Family size: Implicit policies and assumed psychological outcomes. *Journal of Social Issues*, 1974, 30(4), 93–124.

Tuckman, J., & Regan, R. Size of family and behavioral problems in children. *Journal of Genetic Psychology*, 1967, 111(2), 151–160.

U.S. Bureau of the Census, Census of Population: 1970, Subject Reports: Final Report PC (2)-3A. *Women by Number of Children Ever Born*.

Vogel, S. R., Broverman, I. K., Broverman, D. M., Clarkson, F. E., & Rosenkrantz, P. S. Maternal employment and perception of sex roles among college students. *Developmental Psychology*, 1970, 39(3), 384–391.

Weisner, T. Technical Report, NIMH, U.S. Public Health Service Grant #1R01MH24947-03.

World Health Organization. *Manual of the International Statistical Classification of Diseases, Injuries, and Causes of Death*, 6th Revision, Geneva, 1948.

Zajonc, R. B., & Markus, G. B. Birth order and intellectual development. *Psychological Review*, 1975, 82(1), 74–88.

8

Interaction between Young Siblings in the Context of Family Relationships

JUDY DUNN AND CAROL KENDRICK

Most babies grow up in families. They thus develop their powers of social understanding and communication within a web of relationships between mother, father, siblings, grandparents, and friends. Within this network, psychologists have turned their attention to the mother–child dyad, and recently to the father–child dyad, but we know very little about the other relationships that a child forms, or about the ways in which these various relationships interact. We are particularly ignorant about the relationship between young siblings, and about how this affects and is affected by the relationship between each child and the parents.

If we focus on early relationships between young siblings, there are two groups of questions concerning sibling interaction and the development of the young child that must be distinguished. In the first place we can ask whether, and to what extent, the interaction between siblings influences the course of development of the children. In what ways, for example, are only children different from children with siblings? How far are these differences a product of the "special" relationships with parents? Or of the fact that these children have not experienced a sibling

JUDY DUNN AND CAROL KENDRICK • Medical Research Council Unit on the Development and Integration of Behaviour, University Sub-Department of Animal Behaviour, Madingley, Cambridge, CB3 8AA, England. This work was supported by the Medical Research Council.

relationship? Are the differences between being an only child and being a firstborn generated by changes in the relationship with the parent? To what extent does the sibling relationship itself contribute? In the second place, we can examine the interaction between young siblings to see how far the interaction between them mirrors the interaction between parent and child, provides the "social functions" (Lewis & Feiring, 1979) the developing child needs, and overlaps the patterns of exchange we see between the child and other family members.

The first step towards answering either question involves describing the interaction between the siblings. An understanding of this process may well in itself teach us something of value about the development of social understanding in young children. Recent work on peer relationships among very young children has suggested a number of conclusions about their social competence, conclusions that imply that children respond to other children in a way that differs radically from their responses to adults. (Mueller & Lucas, 1975; Mueller & Vandell, 1979). This interesting work raises many intriguing questions. How far has the particular context in which age-mates have been studied affected the theoretical conception of the development of social relations between young children? Do infants of around a year old relate to other children largely through contact with objects, as this work has suggested? Such a view presupposes that young children have rather limited potential for social understanding, and hardly accords with what we would expect on the basis of the experience of parents with families outside laboratories or nurseries, or with what we know of the social skills of babies in relation to adults (Schaffer, 1978). In this chapter we discuss some of these issues, in the light of findings from a longitudinal study of siblings. The importance of imitative sequences, turntaking and co-action, the role of inanimate objects in social interaction between siblings, and individual differences in the affect involved in sibling interaction, teaching and empathy will be considered. Some of the ways in which the presence of a sibling affects the relationships between the firstborn and his mother will be discussed.

Outline of Study

Forty-three families were involved in the study. The ages of the first child when the second child was born ranged from 18 to 43 months. The sample was largely working class: the husband's occupation, classified according to the Registrar General, was IV for 7 families, III manual for 13 families, III WC for 15 families, and II for 8 families. An outline of the structure of the study is given in Table 1. Thirteen of the mothers delivered the second baby at home. Each observation lasted at least an hour; the observations were timed to include some time when the mother was busy with household jobs, and some time when she was more relaxed. The observers recorded precoded categories of behavior in lined notebooks, on a 10-second time–base. The method of recording was based on that of Clarke-Stewart (1973). Details of the observation categories can be obtained from the authors. All observations included a tape recording of the verbal interaction in the family, which was transcribed by the observer shortly after the observation. All observations were carried out by the authors, only one of whom was present at each observation. Since the study is still in progress, the analyses reported here that are concerned with data from the 14-month observations are based on an N of 20.

INDIVIDUAL DIFFERENCES IN FREQUENCY AND QUALITY OF INTERACTION

There was a considerable range of individual difference between sibling pairs, both in the quantity of social interaction, and in its affective quality. At the visits made when the younger sibling was eight

TABLE 1. OUTLINE OF STUDY

Mother pregnant with second child	Two prebirth observations: child with mother and father
	Interview
	Rating of temperamental characteristics[a]
Birth of second child 2 weeks postbirth 3 weeks postbirth	Observation Child with mother + sibling (includes feed)
	Observation (± father)
	Interview
Second child 8 months old	Two observations: siblings with mother (± father)
	Interviews
	Rating of temperamental characteristics[a]
Second child 14 months old	Two observations: siblings with mother (± father)
	Interviews

[a] This rating was developed by Dr C. Sturge of the Institute of Psychiatry; it is based upon that used in Thomas, Chess, and Birch's New York Longitudinal Study.

months old, the total time the siblings interacted ranged from 2 to 42% of the time they spent together, with a median of 13%. At the visits made when the younger sibling was 14 months, the time spent inter-actting ranged from 1 to 48% of the time together, with a median of 12%. The differences in the affective quality of the interaction in the sibling pairs were particularly striking, a point that can be illustrated by a crude categorization of positive or negative interactions. We catego-rized as positive interactions that included smiling, laughing, giving objects that were accepted, joint physical play, or affectionate tactile contact. We categorized as negative interactions any that included prohibitions, removal of the other child's toy, or physical acts that led to one child crying or physical agression. Not all the interactions were included in this classification. Mutual exchange of looks, without any other interactional behavior, for instance, would not be categorized as positive or negative. For the sample as a whole at the eight month observations, the proportion of positive interactions for the different pairs ranged from 8 to 95% of the interactions (median 56%); and the portion of negative interactions ranged from 0 to 80% (median 27%). At 14 months, the proportion of positive interactions for the different sibling pairs ranged from 10 to 80% of interactions (median 40%). The proportion of negative interactions ranged from 0 to 81%, with a median of 39%. Exchanges between the siblings were indeed often very strongly marked in their affective quality: either very warm and affectionate, with both siblings appearing to enjoy the contact very much, or at the other extreme, with almost every encounter involving dispute between the siblings. Such dispute very often involved inanimate objects. Neg-ative interactions were significantly more likely to involve inanimate objects than to be unrelated to these (Sign test, $z=4.37$, $p<.001$).

This range of affect raises many questions that further analysis, we hope, will help us to answer. Is the affective quality of the exchange associated with particular features of the family relationships before the second child was born? Is it a pattern of interaction predictable from the first child's response to the birth? Preliminary analysis indicates that there are indeed some consistencies in the relationships over time. For instance, there are associations between the response of the first child to the events surrounding the birth of the second and the sibling interactions at eight months and 14 months. There is a significantly higher proportion of positive interaction between the siblings in those families where the mother reports the first child as showing an interest in entertaining and in showing things to the new baby (Mann Whitney U-test: 8 months, $z=1.95$, $p<.05$; 14 months $z=2.29$, $p<.02$). There is also a significantly higher proportion of negative sibling interactions in those families where the mother reports the first child as showing an increase in negative behavior toward her (the mother) after the birth of the second (Mann Whitney U-test: 8 months, $z=2.26$, $p<.02$).

On Imitation and Replication of Actions

One of the notable features of the behavior of the siblings together was the frequency of sequences where one child apparently replicated the other's actions. Such sequences will be referred to as *replications* rather than *imitations* since imitation has a precise intentional connotation that may not be justified here. The importance of imitation in the development of communication has been elegantly demonstrated in a recent study by Pawlby (1977). She showed that imitation of the mother emerges gradually in the context of reciprocal social exchange between mother and child. She argued that imitative sequences between mother and child demonstrate that "a great deal of mutual understanding obviously comes about well before even the passive understanding of words." She sees the phenomenon of imitation "in terms of establishing a nonverbal communication code between an infant and an adult, and it is perhaps only through the use of such codes that the two are able to test the extent and nature of their mutual understanding." In answer to the question where does imitation begin, her study suggests that the process by which the baby comes to imitate his mother in an intentional way begins with the mother's readiness to imitate her infant. Mothers apparently select for imitation those acts to which they can attribute communicative significance, such as vocalizations. Pawlby shows that babies do pay special attention when their mothers imitate an act that they have just performed. The action is thus highlighted, and Pawlby suggests that the act is then produced on another occasion in order that the mother will imitate again. The developmental progression that the study revealed was that initially the number of infant–initiated, mother-imitated sequences was greater than the mother-initiated, infant–imitated sequences, but with age the number of the latter increased.

Our observations of infant-sibling interactions show a parallel progression, though at later ages. At 8 months most of the replication sequences are infant-initiated, sibling replicated I–S (Table 2). At the 14-month observations, however, the number of sibling-initiated, infant-replicated S–I interactions has increased. Table 2 shows that the sequences that increase most markedly are the replication of motor actions (rolling, crawling, running, and gestures, etc.) and manipulative acts involving objects (banging toys, poking or waving toys). The high

TABLE 2. REPLICATION OF ACTIONS

	Replication of motor actions		Replication of sounds		Replication of object manipulations	
	I–S	S–I	I–S	S–I	I–S	S–I
Infant 8 months (N = 20)	16 (9)[a]	5 (4)	25 (13)	8 (5)	15 (10)	10 (9)
Infant 14 months (N = 20)	15 (10)	35 (14)	7 (5)	8 (6)	13 (8)	39 (18)

[a]Number in brackets indicates N for that category.
I–S = infant initiated, sibling replicated.
S–I = sibling initiated, infant replicated.

frequency of these replicative acts shows first at 8 months the interest of the elder in the younger; the rapport between them in some pairs parallels that rapport that Pawlby describes in her study of mother and infant. Second, it underlines the power of the elder sibling as a model for the younger. It indicates that at both ages there may be considerable mutual understanding between the two underlying this particular type of communicative sequence, and that the developmental course of the communicative sequences follows a pattern similar to that described by Pawlby for mother and infant. It is not being suggested that the motivation of the elder sibling in imitating the younger at the 8-month stage is necessarily the same as that of a mother. It may well be that some of the replications of the acts of the baby by the elder child reflect an attempt to draw the mother's attention to the firstborn, rather than a desire to communicate with the younger. But it is suggested that such replications may be important to the younger child, and that such sequences form a distinctive feature of the way the relationship between the two develops.

There are marked differences between sibling pairs in the numbers of replication sequences, at both 8 months and 14 months. At 14 months, these differences are particularly evident when pairs of siblings that are the same sex are compared with pairs of siblings with one boy and one girl. If the siblings are the same sex, we find that there is a significantly higher frequency of replications at 14 months than there is between siblings of different sex (Mann Whitney U-test: $z=2.61$, $p<.02$). This difference holds, too, for those sequences where the younger child is replicating the acts of the older (Mann Whitney U-test: $z=2.27$, $p<.02$). At 8 months there is not a significant difference between the same sex and different sex pairs for replications of the older child's acts by the younger child, but there is for replications by the older of the acts of the younger (Mann Whitney U-test: $z=2.35$, $p<.02$). The interpretation of these differences is discussed below.

DIFFERENCES BETWEEN SAME-SEX AND DIFFERENT PAIRS

There are several other aspects of the social interaction between the siblings when the younger child is 14 months that in this small sample differentiate same sex from different sex pairs. Same sex pairs have a lower percentage of negative interactions than different sex pairs. (Mann Whitney U-test: $z=3.14$, $p<.001$). Same sex pairs have a higher percentage of positive interactions than different sex pairs (Mann Whitney U-test: $z=2.74$, $p<.01$).

These differences are open to a number of different interpretations. It could be that the elder sibling, recognizing the gender of his or her sibling (it is something that mothers continually talk about and refer to) is more drawn to play with and feel affection for the sibling if he or she is of the same gender, and that this early interest by the elder sibling promotes a continuing pattern of affectionate exchange. The greater number of replications at 14 months by the same-sex younger siblings would then be explained by the warm relationship promoted by the elder siblings' interest in the younger. Alternatively, or in addition, it could be that the younger sibling is at 14 months becoming conscious of her/his own gender, and is more interested in social encounters with the sibling if they share the same gender. Another interpretation could be that the higher frequency of positive interactions and the higher frequency of replication with same sex pairs arise because children of the same sex are likely to enjoy the same sorts of activities. For example, it could be that boys engage in more rough-and-tumble play than girls, and that two boys would be likely to enjoy playing such games together more than a boy and a girl, because of this common interest and not because there is any recognition of gender of self or of other by the younger child. However, analysis of the frequency of the incidence of joint physical play, and interactions involving gross motor activities shows, first, that there is no significant difference between boy–boy pairs and girl–girl pairs in such interactions; second, that same-sex pairs engage in significantly *more* of such interactions than different-sex pairs (Mann Whitney U-test: $z=2.61$, $p<.02$); third, that there is no significant difference between different-sex pairs with an elder boy, or with an elder girl, in such activities. In contrast to the findings on gross motor play, there was no significant difference between same-sex and different–sex pairs in the frequency of positive social interaction that involved manipulative play. The difference between same-sex and different–sex pairs in the frequency of replications, and of positive interactions, cannot then be interpreted in terms of a preference for boys to engage in particular activities of a gross motor kind, since these activities are as common among girl–girl pairs. However, it should be noted that these are the sequences that are particularly highly marked by excitement and positive affect. The second interpretation is certainly supported by studies such as that of Lewis and Brooks (in press), which demonstrates that some concept similar to self is present in the last quarter of the first year. And Money and Ehrhardt's (1972) work suggests very strongly that gender identity is acquired by 18 months. Given the small number of the children on which this preliminary analysis is based, we should be cautious about generalizing about these differences.[1]

TURN-TAKING AND CO-ACTION CONSIDERED

In the discussion of the development of social skills, the interactional model that had been very widely used is that of turn-taking, often termed "reciprocal interaction." The terminology of types of interaction is extremely confused, with the words "reciprocity" and "synchrony" being used in very different ways at different levels of analysis by different writers. Here "reciprocal" is used to refer to interaction with turn-taking. The term "complementary" is used to refer to interaction where each participant plays *different* roles (e.g., chaser–chased) and "interchangeable" where each partner plays identical roles.

In turn-taking interaction, each participant waits after his turn until the other has completed his turn, and each must be aware of the cues that indicate the end of a turn. This model is fundamentally a linguistic one, based on conversational exchange. Several studies have now described the gradual development in mother–infant interaction from a stage where the mother's contribution to the structure of the exchange is all-important—her sensitivity in timing her responses to pauses in the child's activity providing the structures of a reciprocal exchange—to a stage where each child becomes a real partner (Schaffer, 1978).

Because there has been so much emphasis on reciprocal behavior as the peak of communicative exchange, there has been a tendency to regard interaction that did not follow this pattern as "immature" disruption of an effective communicative sequence. Thus, sequences where both partners act together simultaneously have been regarded as

---

[1] These findings are strikingly similar to those reported in cross-cultural studies carried out in 13 communities in Africa, Asia, and the Americas by B. B. Whiting and colleagues (Whiting & Edwards, 1977), and in the Six Cultures study (Whiting & Whiting, 1975). Data on the interaction between siblings close in age showed that various types of sociable positive behavior occurred more frequently in same-sex interaction. In contrast, various types of negative aggressive behavior tended to occur more frequently in cross-sex interaction. These findings were based on the observation of children from a wide range of differing cultures; the range of ages represented was also wider than in the present study.

TABLE 3. STRUCTURE OF SEQUENCES WITH 14-MONTH-OLD INFANT
(N = 20 PAIRS)

		Interaction type	Number of interactions	
1.	(a)	B acts (not socially directed). A turns to game with different act. Mutual look + smile.	2	(2)[a]
		A acts (not socially directed). B turns to game with different act. Mutual look and smile.	1	(1)
2.	(a)	A acts, invites B to join. B joins. Both act together with laugh/smile. May/may not involve mutual look.	7	(4)
	(b)	B acts, invites A to join. A joins. Both act together with laugh/smile. May/may not involve mutual look.	2	(2)
3.	(a)	A acts-B joins. Both act together with laughs/smile.	14	(11)
	(b)	B acts-A joins. Both act together with laughs/smile.	10	(6)
4.	(a)	A initiates joint game (different roles: e.g., chasing–chased, hide-and-seek).	9	(5)
	(b)	B initiates joint game (different roles: e.g., chasing–chased, hide-and-seek).	10	(3)
5.		Parallel play becomes cooperative play (initiation uncertain).	7	(5)

[a]Number in brackets = N for that category.

"overlap" episodes. However, observation of the exchange between children of the same age (Camaioni, 1978) and the findings of the present study do suggest that it would be very misleading to regard the episodes where two children simultaneously produce the same behavior as unsuccessful episodes of reciprocal interactions. Table 3 shows how many of the more complicated social interactions between the 14-month-old infant with the elder sibling are of a form where one child joins the other in some activity and both continue in the activity together with much apparent enjoyment. Synchrony and mutual engagement between mother and infant have been beautifully described for us in the studies by Brazelton, Koslowski, and Main (1974) and Stern (1977), and Stern, Jaffe, Beebe, and Bennett (1975) have put forward a suggestion about the relationship between simultaneous "co-action," and alternating behavior that seems very relevant to our sibling observations. Stern and colleagues, studying the vocalizations between mothers and three–four-month-old infants, suggest that co-action and alternating interaction develop as separate modes of communication. Alternating vocalizations are seen as the mode from which conversational exchange develops, and "the co-action mode transmits emotional communications expressing the nature of the ongoing interpersonal relationships as well as contributing to the foundation of the relationship." This notion seems to fit well the observations of the sibling exchanges, where the sharing of the experiences often appears to fill both siblings with delight.

The co-action sequences appear to be of simpler structure than a reciprocal interaction would be. No knowledge of turn-taking rules is required, for instance. It is not surprising then that in some studies of interaction between age-mates such "specular" interaction, as Camaioni terms it, is observed *before* reciprocal interaction is observed. Camaioni (1978) notes in her study of conversation between two-year-olds that the performance of two identical actions simultaneously "constitutes a first, though elementary form of collaboration." In this study it was found that the greatest number of interactions consisted of sharing a common action or attention focus. But though it is simpler and developmentally earlier, co-action continues to be used as a mode of interaction by children (and by adults) who are adept turn–takers. Note that the elder sibling, who is certainly a sophisticated exploiter of the *alternating* mode, initiates many of the co-action sequences, and expresses enjoyment and often affection, in doing so.

Schaffer, Collis, and Parsons (1977) note, in discussing "overlap" episodes, that "simultaneous vocalising may under certain circumstances help further the interaction." And there is an interesting parallel here in the repetition of words that occurs in children's conversation with other children. Keenan (1975) suggests that the child uses the repetition of words in these child–child conversations not just to imitate, but as a means, admittedly very simple, of participating in the conversation. With sibling interaction, there is no doubt that replication and simultaneous action, as such, are highly enjoyable.

It is notable that among the positive interactions with or without objects outlined in Tables 4 and 5 for the eight-month observations, there are relatively few of the sequences where B joins A in an activity, while at 14 months there are many such sequences (Table 3). Does this reflect a developmental change whereby an increase in the younger sibling's ability to identify with and replicate the elder enables them to join in and synchronize more effectively? Before concluding that at 8 months the child's ability to recognize and replicate the elder's activity is limited by some aspect of his cognitive capacity, we should note that in fact many of the actions that A performs, and that B watches with apparent pleasure at 8 months, are actions that B is unable to perform because of his *motor* development. Several of the 8-month-old children were not yet able to crawl, and the acts that they watched included leaping, rolling, and running acts quite impossible for B to replicate. But there are some interactions (Table 4, 11a, Table 5, 4b) where B does

Table 4. Positive Interactions with 8-Month-Old Infant Not Involving Objects (A = Elder Sibling; B = Infant). (N = 40 Pairs)

Interaction type		Number of interactions
1.	(a) A acts. Mutual look, B smile/laugh.	9
	(b) B acts. Mutual look, A smile/laugh.	5
2.	A acts and deliberately repeats act. Mutual look, B smile/laugh.	14
3.	Mutual look and laugh.	7
4.	A caretakes or helps. Mutual look, B smile/laugh.	2
5.	A initiates game (e.g., peep-bo, pat-a-cake).	2
6.	A joins in mother-B game (peep-bo, pat-a-cake).	4[a]
7.	A imitates B. Mutual look/smile.	17
8.	A affectionate tactile contact B. mutual look; smile/laugh.	2[a]
9.	(a) A initiates joint physical play; both laugh/smile.	18 + 14[a]
	(b) B pulls/touches A. Leads to joint physical play.	7
10.	(a) A greets B. Mutual look; B smile/laugh.	1
	(b) B voc. + look A. Mutual look; A smile/laugh.	3
11.	(a) A acts. B looks, laughs joins (imitates).	4
	(b) B acts. A looks, laughs joins (imitates).	

[a]Mother involved in interaction.

join A in his/her actions. The 8-month-olds in some of these instances were mobile and very active. This suggests that for some 8-month-olds at least, the limitation on the number of actions that the child joins is not a limitation in the ability to replicate and join. Indeed Pawlby's material suggests that comparatively complicated imitative sequences are quite common in mother–infant interaction by 8 months.

In their analysis of peer interaction with toddlers in a play-group, Mueller and Lucas (1975) analyzed the changes in the structural organization of the interactions they observed, and drew attention to the important distinction between role-diffuse interchanges, and true role-reversal. It was not until the third stage of their model of the development of peer interaction that the children were involved in interchanges where each child did different but intercoordinated things, for instance, playing the role of "chaser" and the role of "the one being chased."

Now, categorizing the sequences of interaction between the siblings in this fashion does present some problems. By the 14-month visits most sibling pairs were engaging in several interactions of the type where each child acted in different but complementary ways, the

TABLE 5. POSITIVE INTERACTION WITH 8-MONTH-OLD INFANT INVOLVING
OBJECT
(A = ELDER SIBLING; B = INFANT.) (N = 40 PAIRS.)

Type of interaction	Number of interactions
1. (a) A gives B object. Mutual look, B smile.	$38 + 4^a$
(b) B gives A object. Mutual look, A smile.	3
2. (a) A puts object on B. B look + smile.	8
(b) B puts object on A. A look + smile.	1
3. A entertains B with object. Mutual look. B smile. A continues.	2
4. A initiates to-and-fro game (cars, bricks, etc.).	$6 + 1^a$
5. A joins Mother-B game with objects.	1^a
6. (a) B acts on object. A imitates. Both act together, laughing.	5
(b) A acts on object. B watches; B initates. Both act together, laughing.	4
7. A acts on object. B watches. Mutual look + smile. A continues.	3
8. B joins Mother-A game with objects.	1^a

[a] Mother involved in interaction.

"chaser" and "being chased" distinction. But it was not clear that such sequences provided evidence of true role-reversal. For instance, in one observation the 14-month-old girl acted as "chaser" in one sequence, and as "being chased" in another, but she did not reverse the roles within any one sequence, and her elder sister initiated the majority of the chasing sequences, taking the different roles first herself. The younger sibling clearly knew how to play the complementary role when the game was initiated, but we cannot conclude that she could have switched roles effectively in the course of a game. Mueller and Rich (1976) suggest that "if the child who receives immediately offers back, and the child who previously offers now receives, it is possible to infer that each child comprehends both roles, and that the children seek to elicit the complementary role when they act."

But with the sibling pairs it is not always so clear that the younger child is seeking the complementary role, since the elder sibling may be providing the necessary scaffolding for role complementarity. Take the following observation of two girl siblings, Chrissy (B) aged 14 months and Tessa (A) 3 years old:

> B is being held by her mother; she is holding a piece of paper which 3 minutes ago had been the focus of a chasing game between the siblings. A starts running round and round her mother. B watches and laughs at A, leans over her mother's shoulder and offers the paper to A as she runs round

behind her mother. A, laughing, looks (mutual) as B, takes the paper and continues to run round her mother. As she passes in front of her mother she offers the paper back to B, who takes it, then as A passes round to the back of her mother on the next circuit, B again leans over her mother's shoulder and offers the paper to A. A again takes it, laughing, and continues to run round her mother. The whole pattern of passing the paper to and fro, first over the mother's shoulder and then in front of her, is repeated 3 times, with both children laughing and vocalizing.

The exchange illustrates the elaborate sequence of turn-taking that a 14-month-old can take part in with an older sibling, but since it was the elder child who first reversed the give-and-take sequence it would not be justified to infer that the younger would have initiated a similar role-reversal with an age-mate.

There are by 14 months a number of elaborate sequences between the siblings, like the paper-passing game, sequences of a complexity not seen at 8 months. But it must be emphasized that among the 8 month-old observations there were interchanges that suggested that the younger sibling could take part in social exchanges with other young children that reflected a degree of social competence quite different from that shown in the play-group observations of age-mates. Take the following observation of Tim, who is 8½ months old, and his sister Bella.

B (Tim) is playing with bricks in a wooden truck, banging them repeatedly with his hand. A (Bella) watches, joins him at the truck; mutual look, and she starts banging bricks, too, in concert. Both continue to bang bricks with mutual look and vocalization.
Two minutes later in observation.
B goes back to truck with bricks. Looks at A, simultaneously vocalizes and bangs bricks. She looks (mutual), comes over to join him as before and starts banging the bricks with him.

How should we interpret B's acts in the second sequence? Would it be justifiable to assume he is attempting to start a repeat of the previous game? We have been cautious and simply coded the interaction as "A joins B in acting on bricks." But the whole question of *when* we impute intentionality in these exchanges is a very delicate one. If the same sequence had been carried out by an 18-month-old, it would probably have seemed justifiable to code it as "B attempts to start repeat of game."

Empathy

During our observations of the families we noted a number of incidents that suggested that one of the siblings (almost always the elder) was concerned about, or understood well the other's state or situation, and acted toward the other in a manner that reflected this empathy. It would, of course, be very easy to read too much into such incidents: in categorizing them as showing empathy or concern for the other's state we have been extremely conservative. For instance, several of the sequences where the elder child gave the younger a toy could have indicated some interest in his or her welfare. Such incidents were, however, not included in the group as we have classified as showing empathy, unless the elder child gave the toy (unsolicited) after the younger had hurt himself, or for some other reason was distressed.

In 16 out of the 20 families observed when the younger child was 14 months, there were incidents we classified as showing empathetic concern for the younger child. These included helping the younger with a toy when he or she was frustrated by it, offering toys or food when he or she was crying, bringing the younger child toys, unsolicited, when he or she was on the potty, going to ask the younger child if he or she wanted a drink, then fetching one, showing concern that the younger child should be included in games, etc., and some incidents that reflected quite subtle "reading" of the younger child's expression. For instance, Becky, a 14-month-old girl, was fascinated by a bag that a visitor had brought to the house; she stood very close to it, but did not dare to touch it. The visitor said to her, "It's all right, you can play with it." Becky looked very doubtful, and still did not touch. Sarah, her elder sister aged 35 months, said to Becky, "You *can* play with it, look," and gave it to her.

It is, of course, not surprising that the elder children in the sample who were aged between 32 and 57 months by the time that the younger sibling was 14 months should show such concern and understanding. It is worth noting, however, that several of these incidents, at the visit when the sibling was 8-months old, involved children younger than 30 months, and that there have been very few laboratory studies of empathy or prosocial behavior reporting such behavior in children under 3 years. Hoffman (1975) noted 2 incidents, similar to the incidents observed in the present study, involving children under 2 years; these were observed when the children were at home. He commented that "role-taking in familiar natural setting may precede laboratory role-taking by several years." He suggests that children may have the capacity to take the perspective of others at an earlier age than is usually assumed, and that this competence may be demonstrated in performance only in particuarly highly motivating natural circumstances.

There were, too, a few incidents from the observations at 14 months, and from a few later observations that suggested that the younger child becomes capable of some degree of understanding of the other's wishes quite early in the second year. One incident with a 14-month-old boy, Gary, reflected the *opposite* of empathy.

> B (Gary) repeatedly reaches for, and manipulates the magnetic letters which
> A (Tracey, 37 months) is playing with. A repeatedly says NO gently. B goes
> on trying to reach the letters. Finally, A picks up the tray on which the letters
> are, and carries it to a high table which B cannot reach. B is furious, starts to
> cry. Then B turns, and goes straight to the sofa where A's comfort objects, a
> rag doll and a dummy, are lying. He takes the doll and holds tight, looking
> at A. A, for the first time very upset, starts crying and runs to take the doll.

Seeing this incident, it was very difficult not to conclude that B had a
pragmatic understanding of what would upset A very much. Another
incident, this time reflecting a concern for the older child, involved 16-
month-old Len. Len at this time played a particular game with his
mother and father, which unfailingly made them laugh. He was a stocky
boy with a big stomach, and his game was to come to them, pulling up
his T shirt and showing his fine stomach.

> A (Martin), aged 40 months, falls off climbing frame, cries vigorously. B (Len)
> watches solemnly. B then approaches A pulling up his T shirt and showing
> A his tummy, vocalizing and looking at A.

Such incidents do suggest that during the first half of the second year
some children do develop considerable concern over the distress of other
children and some pragmatic understanding of how to cheer up others.
There are also indications that this sort of concern for the younger child
on the part of the elder may have important consequences for the way
in which the younger child relates to the elder. Only two of the twenty
14-month-olds that have been observed so far do go to be comforted to
the elder sibling; the elder sibs in these families are two children who
rank very high on initiating positive exchanges with their siblings.

THE ROLE OF INANIMATE OBJECTS IN SIBLING INTERACTIONS

It has been argued that inanimate objects play a special role in the
development of social interaction between peers. Mueller and Vandell
(1979) suggest that objects play the roles of both "carrot" and "stick" in
social encounters: they both force an infant to notice a peer (when, for
example, he takes a wanted toy), and in other circumstances, they
"encourage and invite contacts." Mueller and Brenner (1977) found that
88% of the contacts between infants aged 12–24 months involved "nonsocial objects." Mueller proposes that toys, and objects in general,
"provide a kind of fulcrum for the emergence of transactions between
peers." Observation of same-age peers in a play room suggested that
the first stage of interaction between peers was a stage of object-centered
contacts in which the child appeared to be unaware of other children
manipulating the object. As a second stage, the child became aware of
the control of the toy exercised by the other child, and so began to relate
more directly with the child.

There are some studies, however, whose findings do not support this developmental hypothesis. Lewis, Young, Brooks, and Michalson (1975) observing unacquainted toddlers in a play room found that objects played little part in social encounters. Lichtenburger observed social encounters between his twins long before objects were involved in their interactions (quoted in Mueller & Vandell, 1979). The findings of his study suggest that real familiarity between the infant and the other child might be important in determining the difference in results, and that careful observation in a home setting might be necessary in order to identify the cause of such differential patterns of interaction.

Our own observations of siblings do certainly suggest that objects are less important in social encounters than has been reported by most studies of age-mate toddlers in a play-group situation. First, there are many positive exchanges between the 8-month-old infant and his or her sibling in our observations that do not involve inanimate objects at all. In Table 4 an outline of the different categories of encounter without objects at eight months are given. Note that encounters were only classified as category 2 (A acts and deliberately repeats act for B) if there was good evidence (usually verbal) that A was deliberately drawing B's attention to his exaggerated or vigorous manner and actions. For example:

Observation of Case 2 (eight months)
A (Tim aged 33 months) jumps and falls. B (Robert aged 8 months) watches, roars with laughter. Mutual look, A jumps and falls again, saying, "Look, Rob, look at me," continues to jump and fall round room, laughing too, repeated mutual looks and laughter.

In Table 5 an outline of positive social encounters involving objects at 8 months is given.

At the observations made when the second child is 14 months we find, again, that there are many positive social encounters that do not involve objects. At this stage we are particularly interested in the more complicated social encounters that we have termed "Sequences" (Table 3). We distinguished encounters where A and B take different roles (categories 4a and 4b) from sequences where the one child joins the other in an activity, and both act together, with mutual looking, smiles, and/or laughter. We also distinguished sequences where one child acts and then invites verbally, or appears to invite vocally or by gesture, the other to join. Do objects play an important part in these comparatively complicated interactions? The answer is not necessarily. For 20 sibling pairs we observed 25 such sequences with objects, and 37 without objects.

Confirmation of the idea that objects are not necessary for social interaction between age-mates is provided in a recent study by Eckerman

(1978). She observed 44 pairs of infants aged 10–12 or 22–24 months in two play conditions, one with toys, one without toys, and she found that a number of peer-related social activities occurred more frequently without objects. Without toys, the infants vocalized, smiled, and gestured more to each other, contacted one another more, and duplicated each other's actions more often.

TEACHING AND PATTERNS OF PLAY

In discussion of the birth-order effects on intellectual development Zajonc has drawn attention to the mutual influence of siblings. The value of the role of teacher for the first child, and the effects of a second-born on the quality of the intellectual environment for the first are important features of his confluence model (Zajonc & Markus, 1975).

In the course of our observations we have noted several examples of teaching, and of caregiving by the elder. But there are two even more striking features of the family interaction that were related to this model. First, the effects on the quantity and quality of parental attention the first child receives after the birth of the second, and second, the tendency of the first to play at a less "mature" level when he is interacting with his sibling than when he plays with his parents. In an earlier study we showed that the effect of adult involvement on children's play was to increase the child's pattern of attention, and that the joint attention of adult and child tended to be in the context of relatively complicated and "advanced" activities (Dunn & Wooding, 1977). The profile of play for an only child receiving a lot of attention was a pattern of long spans of play at a relatively "mature" level. We have reported elsewhere the sharp decrease in the quantity of such parental attention after the birth of the second child (Dunn, in press; Dunn & Kendrick, in prep). And when young siblings play together, the firstborn tends to play relatively simple games; he approaches a level of play more appropriate for the younger child. One exception to this involves the pretend play in which the elder involves the younger.

INTERACTION BETWEEN RELATIONSHIPS

Hinde (in press) has outlined a number of ways in which one individual can affect the relationship between two others. We want here to illustrate just a few of these, showing how the presence of the second-born affects the relationship between the mother and the first-born, both directly and indirectly.

1. The presence of the second-born can affect the amount of time the mother has available for interacting with the first-born. We found a sharp decrease in the amount of time spent in joint attention and play by mother and child (Dunn & Kendrick, in press).

2. The presence of the second-born is associated with a significant decrease in the frequency of the mother's initiations of bouts of joint play and attention, and conversational episodes (with the exception of prohibitive comments). This change in maternal behavior may be a result of her tiredness (the majority of mothers suffered a sharp decrease in hours of sleep after the birth, and reported extreme degrees of tiredness (Dunn & Kendrick, in press); it may be the result of her lack of time available, (1. above), or it may be a response to changes in the first-born's behavior.

3. There are changes in the behavior of the first-born after the birth of the second, so that he interacts differently with the mother. We found that there were increases in demanding behavior, and negative behavior to the mother, and changes in bodily function, with increases in sleeping problems, toileting problems, and feeding difficulties (Dunn & Kendrick, in press).

4. There are also more positive changes. Most of the first-born children took a greater responsibility for initiating joint play and conversational episodes. Many of them showed signs of being more "grown-up." Some of them started feeding themselves, others went to the toilet on their own, others dressed themselves. Some of these changes suggested that becoming the first-born, rather than being the only child, had a marked effect on the child's self-image, and this was reflected in their conversation with their mothers. The change in family structure was accompanied by a constellation of changes in the environment for the first child, many of which could have contributed to these changes in bodily function and behavior.

5. At the later visits we found that there are several families where direct effects on the interaction between mother and first child could be linked to the interaction between mother and second child. One pattern that occurs in several families is that the probability that the first child will make a verbal demand to the mother is significantly increased by an interaction sequence between mother and second child, e.g., Case 38:

> Verbal demands by elder child were observed to be significantly more common than expected in intervals following an interaction between mother and baby ($\chi^2 = 4.9$, $p < .05$).

In some families, this effect is so marked that, if one is interested in the interaction between mother and first child, it would be absurd to try to

analyze this interaction without taking account of the interaction between mother and second child.

In other families interaction sequences between mother and younger
child increase the probability of the mother prohibiting the elder child.
This pattern arises because when the mother interacts with the baby,
the elder child frequently changes his activities in a way that leads to
prohibition, e.g., Case 29:

> Maternal prohibitions were more common in the interval following an
> interaction between mother and baby than would be expected ($\chi^2 = 7.32$,
> $p<.01$).

A third common pattern is that after interactions between the siblings
the frequency of prohibition by the mother is increased above the
expected value: Case 23, at eight-months visit $\chi^2 = 18.5$, $p<.001$).

It is also notable that in some families the mother's conversation
with the elder child makes continual reference to the younger, so that
even when the younger is not present the elder is continually reminded
of him. In one family (Case 24), 25% of the mother's utterances to the
elder child were direct references to the second–born.

DISCUSSION

There are marked disparities between our observations made on
young siblings at home, and the findings of studies of age-mates in
laboratories or play-groups. The importance of inanimate objects in
mediating the exchange, the lack of distal interactions among the
younger children, and the comparatively simple structure of the exchanges in the play-group are features that are much less evident in the
sibling observations. If we think about the possible reasons for these
disparities, it leads us to consider the rather different developmental
questions to which the two types of study might provide answers. First,
the disparities between the studies. In their discussion of the development of social relations between age-mates, Mueller and Lucas (1975)
outline three stages in the organization of interactions. It was only by
the second stage that the toddlers performed an action on a toy in part
for its effect on the other child. The toddler in stage 1 "lacked an
orientation towards influencing the behavior of peers themselves, an
interest in re-creating interpersonal contingency—for example, in causing another child to repeat his actions on an object rather than merely
reproducing that action himself." All of our 14-month-olds, and some of
our 8-month-olds, however, do show such an orientation toward their
siblings. (For example, Table 4 categories 9b, 10b, and possibly obser-

vations such as that on page 155). The play-group observations also suggested that interchanges even at stage 2 involved the toddlers keeping in close physical proximity. Only by stage 3 could the children sustain interaction over a distance. Yet, in many of our observations the 8-month-olds interacted with their siblings over a distance: for instance, several of the instances of categories 1, 2, 3, 7, 10, and 11 in Table 4. What explanation could there be for such disparity between studies?

It could be that the 8-month-old would only initiate the more complex sequences with an adult or an older child, and that the differences between the findings of the two studies reflect the differences between looking at age-mates and looking at an infant with an older child. It is quite possible that 8-month-old twins would not initiate such games with each other, though Lichtenberger's observations, quoted in Mueller and Vandell (1979), suggest that they do.

Alternatively, the disparity could reflect the much greater familiarity between the siblings or the contextual differences between studies carried out in the home situation or in day-care. Mueller and Lucas do stress that the generality of the pattern they describe, where physical objects play a major role, remains untested. They suggest that children in different settings or at different ages may not contact each other through objects. If there are observations of siblings in a laboratory context, which indicate that objects play a major role in friendly contacts, then this would suggest that it is the context in which the children are observed that influences the importance of objects in mediating the social exchange. That contextual differences do make a dramatic difference to the patterns of interaction between age-mates has been shown in a study by Becker (1977), who observed pairs of 9-month-olds brought together twice, once in the home of each infant. She found that infants directed significantly more behavior toward the other peer, mother, and observer when the play session was in their own homes, and that they paid significantly more attention to the toys when they were away from their own homes. The tendency for the infant to pay more attention to his play-session mate when in his own home was shown at all levels of behavioral complexity.

Now, if the questions in which we are interested center on the issue of which sorts of experience and which patterns of interaction with the young child are likely to be developmentally significant, we choose to study those situations or those interactions that we assume to have developmental importance. The recent film and video studies of mother with infant have begun to show us just how important the early exchange between mother and baby is in the development of communication. The work by Trevarthen, (1977), Bruner (1977), Newson (1974), Brazelton et al. (1974), and Stern (1977) has demonstrated clearly that in the development of shared understanding and intentional behavior the context of interaction can be of great significance. The observations on siblings at home do suggest that the interaction between siblings at home may well also have some influence, not only directly, through the emotional impact of the interactions with their marked affectional coloring, through the modeling and teaching of the elder, but indirectly, through the change in patterns of parent–child interactions that follow the arrival of a sibling. These observations bring us back to the two questions about developmental significance that were distinguished in the introduction. Although such findings cannot enable us at this stage even to begin to answer the first question (which asked what are the developmental consequences of the interaction between siblings), they can go some way toward answering the second. We can see in which ways the social exchange between siblings parallels and overlaps the patterns of communication observed in parent and child, and in which ways they reveal a distinctive mode of interaction. But can we answer such developmental questions, concerned with understanding how human infants become *humans*, if we examine the infant with age-mates in situations outside the family circle in which the child grows up?

Here we are confronted with an issue that parallels the dispute over the relative importance of peers and mothers in the development of infant rhesus monkeys, and in this dispute Hinde (1971) has outlined the problem in a particularly helpful way. This issue centers on the problems presented by classifying interaction patterns according to the age/sex class of the infant's social companions. Hinde points out that while classification is an essential stage of description and analysis, it involves the observer imposing divisions on the behavior studied, and marking discontinuities that may have no given base in the phenomena. Such divisions may well be no better than artifacts, a matter of conven-ience to the observer that may in fact obscure the most important questions. He notes, for instance, that categorizing the interaction between an infant rhesus and the different members of the social group within which it is raised in terms of their age/sex class/peers, adult females, adult males, etc.—has been very useful, but has led to dispute over the issue of the relative importance of each class of social companion in the infant's development. The dispute he suggests is in part a consequence of the artificial nature of the categories themselves, since the infant interacts with each type of companion in many different ways, and these overlap between the categories. The important ques-tions about development concern the nature and extent of the different types of interaction necessary for the infant's social development. We can also ask which companions usually provide these, under which circumstances, and how far one class of companion can substitute for another. The significance of these questions may easily be obscured if we classify interaction according to the age/sex class of the companion.

The observations of infants with family members, and with age-mates present very similar problems. Our observations suggest that there is great potential in sibling interaction for the younger child to learn about role-taking skills, to get a sense of role–complementarity and role-reversal. They also indicate qualities of social understanding on the part of the elder child that are much less likely to be revealed in interaction between child and adult: gentle concern and caring for the younger child, teaching and helping, cooperation, and a quality of physical affection, and enjoyment of mutual play that is very moving to observe. Watching a young child with different family members can then be very revealing, in that different facets of his social understanding will become evident in the varied exchange with siblings, peers, and adults. But we should be cautious about classifying such different patterns of social interaction as different *systems* according to the age/sex class of the companion. It is plain that each family member will interact with the child in several ways, and that there will be much in common between the patterns of interaction with different companions. The overlap between the patterns of interaction of an infant with his mother, and those with father and siblings is, for example, considerable. (Some of the elder sisters in our sample "mothered" their infant siblings continually.) Moreover, the range of interaction patterns shown by the sibling pairs is, as we have noted, extremely large: for some pairs it is characteristically warm and playful, for others it is neutral, and for others it is frequently hostile. To answer some developmental questions it would clearly not be helpful to lump all these interactions in one category.

But the question about the relative importance of the social companion performing the "social function" still remains important. What sort of difference does it make to the course of a child's development if it is his *mother* who is his chief playmate, or his sibling? Hinde's paper comments that it is also possible that it is important for the child to have a companion with whom he (say) rough-and tumble plays, who is *different* from the companion from whom he suckles. That is, distribution of functions may also be important. That this is a very real question can be illustrated by Figure 1, which represents the initiations of positive social interactions within two families when the younger sibling was 14 months old. In Family I, on the left of the figure, each of the siblings initiates many social interactions of a complex sort with her sister. (Complex interactions include sequences as in Table 3, and bouts of joint physical play.) Simple interactions include all others of not more than three "turns."

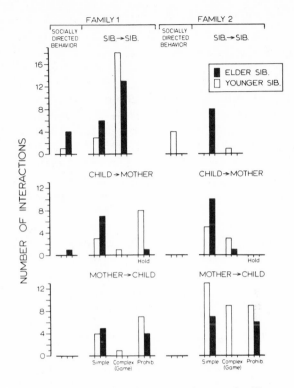

Fig. 1. Initiation of positive interaction: two families.

In contrast neither child initiates much play with the mother, and the mother initiates very little with B and none with A. There is a very different pattern of interaction in Family II. Here the elder child A initiates no complex sequences with the younger child B, and the younger only one with the elder. The mother, on the other hand, initiates many games and sequences with the younger child, though little with the elder. The elder child initiates several interactions with the mother, but these do not develop into complex sequences or games.

The point we want to emphasize is the *difference* in the experience of the two 14-month-old children. In Family I the little girl's experience of complex interaction sequences is almost entirely with her sister, 20 months older than she. In Family II, the little boy's play is almost entirely with his mother, and inevitably these games are rather different. What are the developmental consequences of these different experiences?

Figure 1 illustrates another general feature of the differences between interaction with a child and with a parent. This concerns the number of unsuccessful attempts at initiating interaction occurring when one child emits a "socially directed behavior" (S.D.B.), and the person to whom it is directed does not respond. The left-hand column of the data for each family illustrates the number of these S.D.B.'s. For these two families none of the mother's initiations were not responded to, and only one initiation directed *to* the mother was not responded to. However, several of the children's initiations were "unsuccessful." We should note that in Family II, the elder child A has no S.D.B.'s, or "unsuccessful" initiations: this does not reflect the success of interactions between A and B in this family, but rather it reflects the fact that the elder sister initiated very few interactions with her brother, and appeared to be rather uninterested in him. He, on the other hand, attempted to initiate interaction with her on several occasions when she did not respond.

The difference between child–child and child–adult interaction in the numbers of "unsuccessful" interactions does appear to be a general feature of the family interactions analyzed so far. It is interesting that the same difference has been noted for conversations between children, and between child and adult. Camaioni (1978) notes that engaging in conversation, which involves collaboration between both interlocutors, is not an easy task for two young children. The child has to learn to use a series of routines that will secure the companion's involvement and participation. Often these approaches fail, and in Camaioni's data there are several examples of sequences in which attempts to create mutual involvement fail.

If we are to understand the way in which such experiences influence the individual course of development of a child, it is surely important to examine them in the context of the child's own social world. The task of describing how interaction between the siblings affects and is affected by the relations between the parents and each sibling individually is one that we are only just beginning, but already it is clear that to acquire a clear understanding of the relations between the two individuals in any of the dyads within the family we must also be concerned with the other family members. A similar argument stressing the importance of describing and understanding the different social "functions" important in development as well as the different social "objects" involved, has recently been put forward by Lewis and Feiring (this volume).

It is trivial to emphasize that the laboratory context of study cannot provide us with a full description of the context within which humans develop. But it is far from trivial to stress that laboratory studies, interpreted with anything but caution, may easily lead us to distort the developmental significance of particular types of interactive episodes. A similar point is made by Suomi (this volume) on the basis of his precise analysis of the behavior of young rhesus monkeys raised in different environments, and by White (1977) in an analysis of the developmental course of play activities in rhesus monkeys. Until we possess fuller and more extended analyses of the variety of interactive episodes occurring within the family context in which most human babies are in fact reared, it will necessarily remain extremely difficult to distinguish issues of developmental significance from simple considerations of frequency of occurrence in different situations.

Acknowledgments

We would like to thank the families in the study for their generous help, and Robert Hinde for his helpful comments on the manuscript.

References

Becker, J. M. T. A learning analysis of the development of peer-orientated behavior in nine-month-old infants. *Developmental Psychology*, 1977, *13* No. 5, 481–491.

Bruner, J. S. Early social interaction and language acquisition. In H. R. Schaffer (Ed.), *Studies in mother–infant interaction*. London: Academic Press, 1977, pp. 271–289.

Brazelton, T. B., Koslowski, B., & Main, M. The origins of reciprocity: the early mother–infant interaction. In M. Lewis & L. Rosenblum (Eds.), *The effect of the infant on its caregiver*. New York: Wiley, 1974.

Camaioni, L. Child–adult and child–child conversations: An interactional approach. In E. Ochs Keenan (Ed.), *Studies in developmental pragmatics*, New York: Academic Press, 1978.

Clarke-Stewart, A. Interactions between mothers and their young children: Characteristics and consequences. *Monographs of the Society for Research in Child Development*, 1973, no. 153.

Dunn, J. The arrival of a sibling: Approaching the study of a developmental context. *Atti del IV Congresso Internationazionale della I.S.S.B.D.* (Vol. 1). Milan: Franco Angeli, in press.

Dunn, J. & Kendrick, C. The responses of first-born children to the arrival of a sibling, in prep.

Dunn, J. & Wooding, C. Play in the home and its implications for learning. In B. Tizard & D. Harvey (Eds.), *The biology of play*. London: Heinemann Medical Books, 1977, pp. 45–58.

Eckerman, C. O. The human infant in social interaction. In. R. B. Cairns (Ed.), *Social interaction: methods, analyses & illustrations*, 1978, in press.

Hinde, R. A. Some problems in the study of the development of social behavior. In E. Tobach, L. R. Aronson, & E. Shaw (Eds.), *The biopsychology of development*. New York: Academic Press, 1971.

Hinde, R. A. How X may affect the relationship between A and B. In *Atti del IV Congresso Internazionale della ISSBD*. (Vol. 1). Milan: Franco Angeli, in press.

Hoffman, M. L. Developmental synthesis of affect and cognition and its implications for altruistic motivation. *Developmental Psychology*, 1975, *11*, No. 5, 607–622.

Keenan, E. O. Making it last: Repetition in children's discourse. *Papers of the Berkeley Linguistic Society*, Vol. 1, 1975.

Lewis, M., & Brooks, J. *Social cognition and the acquisition of self.* New York: Plenum Press, 1979.

Lewis M., & Feiring, C. The child's social network: Social object, social functions, and their relationship. In M. Lewis & L. Rosenblum (Eds.), *The child and its family.* New York: Plenum Press, 1979.

Lewis, M., Young, G., Brooks, J., & Michalson, L. The beginning of friendship. In M. Lewis & L. Rosenblum (Eds.), *Friendship and peer relations.* New York: Wiley, 1975, pp. 27–66.

Money, J., & Ehrhardt, A. A. *Man and woman, boy and girl.* Baltimore, Maryland: The John Hopkins University Press, 1972.

Mueller, E., & and Brenner, J. The origins of social skill and interaction among playgroup toddlers. *Child Development*, 1977, 48.

Mueller, E., & Lucas, T. A developmental analysis of peer interaction among toddlers. In M. Lewis & L. Rosenblum (Eds.), *Friendship and peer relations.* New York: Wiley, 1975, pp. 223–257.

Mueller, E., & Rich, A. Clustering and socially-directed behaviors in a playgroup of 1-year-old boys. *Journal of Child Psychology and Psychiatry*, 1976, *17*, 315–322.

Mueller, E., & Vandell, D. Infant–infant interaction. In J. Osofsky (Ed.), *Handbook of infant development.* New York: Wiley Interscience, 1979, pp. 591–622.

Newson, J. Towards a theory of human understanding. *Bulletin of the British Psychological Society*, 1974, *27*, 251–257.

Pawlby, S. Imitative interaction. In H.R. Schaffer (Ed.), *Studies in mother–infant interaction.* London: Academic Press, 1977, pp. 203–224.

Schaffer, H. R. Acquiring the concept of the dialogue. In M. H. Boorstein and W. Kessen (Eds.), *Psychological development from infancy.* New York: Lawrence Erlbaum, 1978.

Schaffer, H. R., Collis, G. M., & Parsons, G. Vocal interchange and visual regard in pre-verbal children. In H.R. Schaffer (Ed.), *Studies in mother–infant interaction,* London: Academic Press, 1977, pp. 291–324.

Stern, D. *The first relationship: Infant and mother.* Cambridge: Harvard University Press, 1977.

Stern, D., Jaffe, J., Beebe, B., & Bennett, S. L. Vocalising in unison and in alternation: Two modes of communication within the mother–infant dyad. *Annals of the New York Academy of Sciences*, 1975, *263*, 89–100.

Trevarthen, C. Descriptive analyses of infant communicative behaviour. In H.R. Schaffer, (Ed.), *Studies in mother–infant interaction.* London: Academic Press, 1977, pp. 227–270.

White, L. On the nature and development of social play in the rhesus monkey. Unpublished Ph.D. thesis. University of Cambridge, 1977.

Whiting, B. B., & Edwards, C. P. (Eds.). The effect of age, sex, and modernity on the behaviour of mothers and children. Report to the Ford Foundation, January, 1977.

Whiting, B. B. & Whiting, J. *Children of six cultures: A psychocultural analysis.* Cambridge: Harvard University Press, 1975.

Zajonc, R. B., & Markus, G. B. Birth order and intellectual development. *Psychological Review*, 1975, *82*, No. 1, 74–88.

9

(Toddlers + Toys) = (An Autonomous Social System)

Edward Mueller

> In the majority of cases, infants in the second half year of life will come into contact. They will touch each other, smile, squeal, and utter sounds, and perhaps they will begin to play with each other's clothes or feet, or make movements in front of each other. They may forget each other after a while. Persistent contact, however, will be formed only on another basis, that is, the presence of a material in which both children are equally interested. (Bühler, 1931, p. 399)

Pretend you are in New York City. It is 1925. You stand in the gloom of a narrow, dirty street. Except for the snow falling, everything is brown: the buildings are brown; the horse manure-littered street is brown; the house sparrows are brown fluff, huddled in the sooty eaves. Horses' hooves and carriage wheels clatter against cobblestones. Immigrant children—one barefoot—rush out one door, screech at the slushy snow, and disappear in the neighboring door. Shapeless women with bundled babies tred through the slush and enter an undistinguished building. The temporary sign beside its door reads "MILK DEPOT." Here the mothers receive medical aid and milk for their babies.

Suddenly a black-chauffeured Model-T thunders down the street, stopping at the milk depot. The chauffeur almost falls in the slush as he rounds the car. He opens the passenger doors. A bevy of young women, all wearing the latest New York fashions, emerge from the car. They

Edward Mueller • Psychology Department, Boston University, Boston, Massachusetts 02215. This chapter is based on a lecture in honor of Charlotte Bühler, given at the Fourth annual Child Development Conference, U.C.L.A., Los Angeles, November 5, 1977. Playgroup Project was supported by a grant from the National Institute of Mental Health.

carry new notepads. Last to emerge is a dignified young woman in European dress. The others vie to escort her to the building. One burdened immigrant mother, mouth agape, stops in her slushy tracks. Never has she seen such fine ladies on Lasalle Street!

The European woman, her assistants holding the heavy oak door, hurries into the depot; the assistants follow in chattering excitement. The door slams closed, and the immigrant mother, uncomprehending, again makes tracks in the snow across the treacherous cobblestones.

The European woman was Dr. Charlotte Bühler, only thirty-two but already a leading child psychologist of Vienna. Inside the milk depot, she began the world's first systematic study of the social aspects of early child development. Given the mother–infant orientation of so much recent research, you may be surprised to learn that this earliest study was of infant *peer* relations. Why did she study peer relations and why in New York City rather than in Vienna?

In her day, the dominant theory of intellectual development was maturationalism. The child's intelligence was given by heredity; the psychologist's role was to carefully describe its pattern of unfolding and individual differences in endowment. Gesell (1925) had just applied the maturational research program for the first time to infant mental development. Bühler's interest was in adolescent personality types, not intelligence. Yet, when she studied these personalities using diary records, she found that the "complications" (Buhler, 1930, p. 16) introduced into personality by experience made analysis difficult. Thus, like the foremost students of mental development in her day, she turned to infancy as the best place to observe the natural personality types, uncomplicated by later experience. And why introduce the mother's complicated personality into the assessment? Instead she placed pairs of babies together in a crib and observed their social relations. In relying on the contemporaneous theories of mental development, Bühler began a tradition in social development research that continues today.

Why New York City? In 1924, using the Laura Spelman Rockefeller Memorial funds, Lawrence K. Frank began setting up the famous child-study institutes (Senn, 1975). His first grant was to Teachers College, Columbia University, then under the intellectual leadership of Edward L. Thorndike. It appears that Thorndike's first action with the new funds was the invitation to Charlotte Bühler: "Come to New York, talk with me, conduct a model study for our students. We can supply all necessary equipment, assistants, and facilities." Bühler took the only reasonable course: she accepted.

With the study completed, she returned to Vienna. The results were published in German in 1927, more than 50 years ago. Thus, in 1979, I salute Professor Charlotte Bühler (1893–1974), the founder of peer study, and the originator of a largely forgotten history of research in early social development (Vandell and Mueller, in preparation).

Among the most famous peer studies of the period before World War II is Maudry and Nekula (1939). They were among other American women who traveled to Vienna and continued the peer research under Bühler. Bühler had concluded that three main infant personality types existed; they were the socially blind, socially dependent, and socially independent child. She hoped that Maudry and Nekula would independently confirm these types. Yet, they did not meet her wishes. What appeared to Bühler as personality types appeared to Maudry and Nekula as developmental stages. They believed that much more careful normative analysis was necessary before individual personality types could be understood. They took a first large step in providing such an analysis.

There matters rested for thirty years. Research in social development was dominated by the ideas of Sigmund and Anna Freud. Charlotte Bühler notes that the Freuds "regarded my husband (Karl Bühler) and me as opponents whom they refused to meet. Anna Freud refused to be together with me on a panel to discuss child development" (1973/4, p. 204).

When I began to study toddler–peer relations in 1971, the zeitgeist in mental development theory was very different. Gesell was gone and in his place stood Piaget, the cognitivist. Trained in Piaget, I saw the toddler as a curious investigator of the unknown. Initially "peers" were in the class of noncontrollable, and in this sense "unknown" objects. The toddlers' job was to "master" peer relations. In other words, they had to discover which available skills were effective in controlling peer behavior, and they had, perhaps, to invent new skills. Such concerns may seem removed from core topics of social development such as friendship and attachment. Yet, attachments and friendships must have some sort of developmental antecedents. Before toddlers can come to like their age-mates, they need ways of becoming familiar and sustaining their interactions with them. This chapter points to social participation and skill as crucial factors in this process. Thus, they also serve as basic steps on the pathway to peer friendships and attachments.

Before these results can be understood, however, I must explain how toddler social skill and peer social structure were identified. While developing these concepts, my goal was always to utilize the instant replay features of video tape for recovering the remarkable complexity and velocity of toddler–peer social interactions.

The first problem was to identify toddler social skill itself. For me neither IQ tests, nor even Piagetian tests of cognitive level made much sense for assessing social skill. Both seemed overfocused on skills for control of the *physical* environment rather than the social environment.

Given their vastly different interactional affordances, skills for people and skills for things are at least potentially very different types of achievement. For example, in observing toddler play, DeStefano (1973) stressed that people afford "action at a distance" while most interaction with physical objects is direct. Tests also had an overly manipulative quality for the study of infant-peer relations; so little was known that observation of the quality of early peer skills was required first.

The general theory of scheme development (Piaget, 1952) seemed most relevant to analysis of the infant's social skills. In fact, the assessment of social skill in this chapter is a simple extension of one dimension in Piaget's approach. The dimensions in Piaget's analysis are easily reviewed by use of a familiar example.

Recall for a moment Laurent, aged three months, whose hands were bandaged and tied by string to his bassinet, preventing his sucking (an example of a child-rearing practice so dramatic as to distract from the point!). Piaget decided to experiment with this apparatus: he attached the strings to celluloid rattle-balls hanging from the hood.

For about a week, Laurent shook the balls only by chance. But later, the infant intentionally reproduced the movement of the balls. Piaget cites four types of evidence:

1. Refinement: There was refinement in the infant's movements themselves. Where before both arms were shook, now only the arm actually attached to the ball was moved. Furthermore, it was moved in a particular direction (backward), which optimized the effect.
2. Anticipation: Eye blinks occurred just as the arm moved, as though anticipatory to the movement of the ball.
3. Resilience under Interruption: The action could be spontaneously resumed after brief pauses during which irrelevant acts were performed.
4. Coordination of Actions: Laurent came to look at the ball at the same time as he swung his arm, showing an appreciation of where to seek the result.

Fischer (1978) measured and interrelated many of these dimensions in studying skill acquisition by rats and pigeons. By manipulative interventions he could, for example, interrupt the animal midway through its task performance. In this way he could systematically examine the effects of *interruption on skill resilience* at different stages in the learning process. No comparably multivariate approach was attempted in the present relatively naturalistic study of children.

Instead, relying on its central place in Piaget's sensory-motor stages, its reliable occurrence, and its ease of observation, I studied only the *coordination of actions* in assessing peer social skill. I labeled as simple *socially directed behaviors* (SDB) those actions where a toddler coordinated looking at a peer with one other discrete action (e.g., smiling, banging a toy, vocalizing). *Coordinated SDBs* simply took the idea one step further, noting that a child can both vocalize and smile, all while looking at a peer. This method of studying a child's average social behavioral complexity is not unlike the concept of *mean length of utterance* (MLU) so frequently mentioned today in child language research. Of course, words must be strung together in linear fashion rather than simultaneously. I do not know whether toddler–peer behavioral complexity correlates with later mean MLU, though as shall become clear, I have reason to predict that it will not.

I have already suggested dangers in following too closely on the coattails of the current intellectual development theory. Thus, given this direct tie to Piaget's research, let me next consider how the present approach differs from Piaget's. For all his emphasis on the role of social interaction in development, Piaget seldom devoted much time to the direct analysis of social interaction itself. Instead he focused chiefly on cognitive systems, internal systems of action and understanding. In fact, his structuralist position demanded no separate analysis of social interaction or society, because mind and society were both reflections of the same logic:

> The important question is not how to assess the respective merits of the individual and the group (which is a problem just like that of deciding which comes first, the chicken or the egg), but to see the logic in solitary reflection as in cooperation . . . . Whatever Tarde may say, there are not two kinds of logic, one for the group and the other for the individual; there is only one way of coordinating actions A and B according to relationships of inclusion or order, whether such actions be those of different individuals A and B or of the same individual (who did not invent them single-handed, because he is a part of society as a whole). Thus, cognitive regulations or operations are the same in a single brain or in a system of cooperations. (1971, pp. 368–9)

Given our current ignorance of the logic of children's social interaction, such a reciprocal assimilation of mind and groups seems premature. A central tenet of our toddler research is that a separate analysis of social skills and social structure is both possible and necessary. Not only does toddler social structure exist in a manner unrelated to their initial social skills, but social skills themselves derive from participation in peer social structure. In other words, social structure is a source of social skill, not merely its product.

Perhaps an example will help clarify these central but abstract ideas. Ever since Bühler first placed unfamiliar babies together, they have been failing their one-session peer skill "tests." Initially they cannot relate to one another like older children; there are no peek-a-boo games, no run-chase, nor is there even much peer-directed protest when a toy is stolen. Thus, tests of *skill* could lead to the conclusion that no enduring social structure is possible in the earliest years. More sociological approaches, however, reveal that when toddlers first meet, a primitive social structure appears immediately. In the child development literature, it is called *parallel play with toys.*

This first peer social structure does not depend on peer-related skills; instead it relies on the toddler's attachment to toys and skill with toys. From the start, toddlers find themselves coming together because they share skills for things like opening the jack-in-the-box or sliding down the slide. For too long this parallel play was simply discounted as an inadequacy of role-taking or other social-cognitive skill. Yet, our data suggest that across several months of peer experience, parallel play is a cradle for the evolution of a peer-skilled toddler (Mueller & Brenner, 1977). A social structure reflective of incompetence turns out to foster the spontaneous (nontutored) growth of peer competence. In the opening quotation, Bühler reaches the same conclusion. Yet, only through a careful separation of individual skill and social organization could the present study support her hypothesis.

Space here does not allow a full analysis of the developmental interactions between toddler skill and peer social structure (Vandell & Mueller, in preparation). Here I have only cited an example to suggest the value of keeping skilled action and social structure clearly separate. While a joint analysis of both skill and interaction is necessarily complex, we compensate by studying toddler–peer relations, surely among the simplest natural social systems in normal child development.[1]

Once committed to the direct analysis of peer interaction, one finds a variety of models available for its analysis. Should interactions be seen as synonomous engagement or reciprocal alternations? Sustained, reciprocal attention is a necessary part of interaction; yet, most toddler interaction also includes simple alternation of actions in an act–watch rhythm. Are the social ties between behaviors in interaction more usefully defined as "contingencies" or as "elicitations"? Contingency implies only spatial and temporal contiguity, while elicitation implies a causal tie: the second behavior would not have been likely to have occurred in the absence of the first.

Mueller and Vandell (1979) note that there are no universal answers to these questions; that in fact infant development may progress from interaction as sustained reciprocal engagement to interaction as engaged alternation sequences. Thus, the definitions *must vary* depending on whom one is studying. For toddler relations I now define interaction as "an elicitation (or series of elicitations) between the behaviors of two

---

[1] *Infant* peer relations (i.e., children under 12 months) would even be simpler, and I regret not starting with them. Fortunately, Vandell is presently applying a similar analysis to infant peer relations.

children." The underlying alternation model of interaction seems "forced" on the toddler data only in run-chase interactions. Here, the chaser must constantly adjust rate of movement and direction to maintain the chase. The lead child must signal his participation by vocalizations and by looks over the shoulder. Only the repetition of a path around the room serves to break this interaction into cyclical units. Clearly, the form of social interaction follows from the communication requirements of different types of play. The meaning of the interchange run-chase versus verbal exchange, dictates interaction structure; structure follows from meaning.

Socially directed behavior and interaction are two primary concepts in this research; a third is contact. Peer social interaction and even parallel play remain fairly infrequent events in toddler playgroups. Yet, I wanted to identify all such events and subject them to a microscopic examination. I came to call such events *contacts*. A specific contact could be totally noninteractive play with a common toy; alternatively it could be a sequence of pure social interchange with no toys present. In fact, many contacts contained a mixture of parallel toy play and social interaction. Thus, we found it useful to distinguish as "object-centered" those contacts where over half the time was spent in noninteractive toy play. While similar to Stern's (1924) concept of parallel play (Parten contributed the label), object-centered contacts may include some interactions.

Operational definitions of these three main concepts appear in Mueller and Vandell (1979). Together, they formed the basis of a longitudinal, observational study of toddler playgroups.

METHODS

Design of Playgroup Project

A pilot playgroup studied in 1971 (Mueller & Rich, 1976) had already convinced us that social skills grew among toddlers in a playgroup setting. We also suspected that the playgroup itself was nurturing these skills. Boston University's Playgroup Project, conducted 1973–1976, provided an experimental test of our suspicions. We varied extent of playgroup experience (and thus peer acquaintance) while holding chronological age constant. We asked: "Given two groups of same-age acquainted toddlers, which vary considerably in the length of acquaintance, will the more experienced group be more social with each other?" Consider the meaning of four possible results: (1) The groups are similar in showing no social interaction. Such a result would confirm the cultural stereotype that toddler–peer relations do not exist. (2) The groups are similar in showing much social interaction. This result would mean that while toddler interactions are possible, they stem from the parent–toddler relations or from maturation but not from peer practice. (3) The groups are dissimilar with more interaction generated by the *less* peer-experienced toddlers. Such a result suggests that toddler–peer relations are dysfunctional. Peer practice serves only to extinguish peer relations. (4) The groups are dissimilar with more interaction generated by the more experienced toddlers. This result suggests that peer practice enhances peer social interaction. If the less experienced toddlers show no interaction, or qualitatively simpler interaction, it suggests that the playgroup forms a separate, yet important, channel of social development.

The operational design testing these possibilities is shown in Figure 1. Basically, two boy-toddler playgroups met each weekday morning across seven months. At the first session Playgroup 1 (PG1) toddlers were aged 12 months. Playgroup 2 (PG2) toddlers began at age 16½ months. The ages permitted two comparisons between PG1 and 2 when the children were of similar age but varied by 4½ months in actual peer familiarity. In the actual comparisons, shown in Figure 1, the less experienced boys (PG2) were actually older, working against the hypothesis that participation with peers was a crucial element in the genesis of toddler–peer relations.

PLAYGROUP 1 (PG1)
122 MORNING SESSIONS
ACROSS 7 MONTHS

12 MONTHS
(± 15 DAYS)

CROSS-
GROUP
COMPAR-
ISONS AT
SIMILAR
AGES

16½ MONTHS
(± 26 DAYS)

PLAYGROUP 2 (PG2)
128 MORNING SESSIONS
ACROSS 7 MONTHS

12   13   14   15   16   17   18   19   20   21   22   23

AGE (MONTHS)

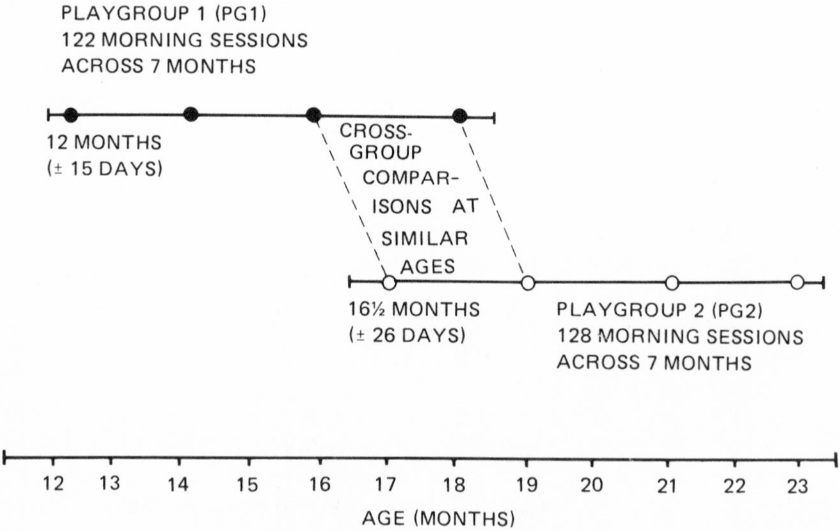

FIG. 1. Design of playgroup project (see text).

Subjects

The selection of boys was fortuitous. All children in the pilot playgroup had been boys even though children of both sexes were welcomed. We sought to confirm the ideas generated there with additional boys. Both playgroups included three firstborn and three later-born unacquainted boys. None had prior peer experience defined as playing once or more per week with children under three years of age.

Setting, Television Facility, and Playgroup Organization

The description of the playroom and television apparatus is summarized by Mueller and Brenner (1977). We found that a two-camera system with split-screen capacity aided us in showing both faces of an interacting pair.

Two teachers were with the children at all times. Because we sought to demonstrate the spontaneous emergence of peer relations, the teachers avoided teaching the children interactional games like ring-around-the-rosie or hide-and-seek. They also allowed the children to resolve disputes on their own; however, if a child persisted in hitting many children, the teachers intervened. While dominated by free play periods, the morning routine also included "snack time" and "activity periods" when special materials like finger paints or dress-up clothes were introduced.

Systematically Sampled Behavioral Contexts of Playgroup Project

While limited to a small carefully selected sample of children, Playgroup Project studied their behavior across a variety of contexts. Within the playgroup, we studied behavior both in dyadic and full group situations. Additionally we studied the quality of both toddler–mother and toddler–father interaction at several points across the play year. This report is the first to consider these cross-situational findings of the project; however, a much more detailed summary is needed and is in preparation (Vandell & Mueller, in preparation). The three principal situations in the study were the peer–peer dyad situation, the peer-peer group situation, and the parent–toddler situation.

Peer–Peer Dyad Situation

Each morning the playroom was divided in half by a folding wall. Two children accompanied a teacher for 15 minutes of play apart from the rest of the group. The teachers read, knitted, or simply watched as the two children played. Usually two dyads were videotaped on a given morning. When all 15 possible dyads had been recorded, a procedure requiring two to three weeks, the play equipment and toys present were changed, and the next dyad "pass" was begun. In the present analysis, four even–spaced passes were selected from each group. The superior technical quality of the dyad videotapes made them the data of choice for most analyses.

Peer–Peer Group Situation

Each week free play sessions of the entire group were videotaped. Because the activities of six toddlers could not be followed at once, we followed each child's play for five minutes, thus generating a 30-minute videotape when all were present. Over 50 such tapes were recorded in each playgroup. To date the group situation has been analyzed only in PG2 (Vandell, 1977). The sample represents 30 minutes of behavior (6 days, 5 minutes/day) for each child at each of three periods in the play year. In these situations, each child may interact with up to seven other persons, five peers and two teachers.

Parent–Toddler Situation

In PG1 parent–toddler relations were studied only in a pilot fashion. In PG2 mother–toddler and father–toddler dyadic play sessions were recorded at the beginning, middle, and end of the playgroup. These 30-minute sessions were conducted in a large comfortable room in the building where the toddlers attended playgroup. Each session opened with 10 minutes of free play followed by 20 minutes of semistructured play. In the latter, the parents were asked to devote some time to playing with their sons with each of four different toys. The toys were crayons and paper, picture book, a miniature cash register with pennies, and a "surprise box" (a commercial toy that resembles a row of jack-in-the-boxes opened in various ways). These objects afford a variety of interactions (e.g., verbal-symbolic versus motoric-inactive) while still allowing considerable freedom in parent–child interaction. They increase the comparability of individual parent–toddler dyads, while allowing statistically significant family influences to emerge even given the small number of subjects. All parent–infant interaction data in this report derives from videotapes of this semistructured situation. (see also Vandell, in press).

RESULTS

No comprehensive picture of the playgroup results is possible here. Instead, today, I will draw selectively from the five completed studies (four of them are unpublished dissertations) in the service of a small number of points. These are:

1. Peer social interaction and social skill displayed significant growth in the playgroups; on the other hand, activity with things remained the predominant mode of play.
2. The conceptualization of socially directed behavior as an index of toddler social skill (given above) was supported.
3. Toddler group size and toy properties both influenced peer social interaction.
4. Toddler–peer relations in playgroup was an autonomous system in early social development. While influenced by toddler–parent relationships, they developed from experience in playgroup, relied on object mediation, focused on different content, and influenced toddler–parent social interactions.

While omitting interesting father–mother comparisons, as well as an analysis of toddler–peer sympathy (Marvin, 1977), these four points allow a fairly comprehensive summary of the completed research.

1. Peer social interaction and skill displayed significant growth in the playgroups; on the other hand, activity with things remained the predominant mode of play.

If the toddler's visually directed gaze mirrors his thought, then visual attention may provide a simple index of the toddler's preoccupation. The relative pattern of visual gazing at different target objects in 16 months-old dyads[2] is shown in Figure 2. Reflecting the overall pattern shown in the figure, all six children in PG1 watched toys more than people. All but one averaged more time watching an active peer than a normally inactive teacher. A comparison of the duration and frequency data of Figure 2 reveals that looks at people were of relatively brief duration compared with looks at things. The toddler appears *to check* what the peer and teacher are doing, but to *watch* physical objects.

The toy-centered quality of toddler orientation is further confirmed by examining the relatively small proportion of dyad time spent in contact with a peer (Figure 3). The percentage of total dyad time spent in contact reached a maximum of 23% and 21% in the respective playgroups. The rest of the time the toddlers were either playing with toys or simply watching other people without actively participating in their activities.

When we look "inside" contacts, the toy-focused nature of boy toddlers' play is confirmed. For contacts, as Stern (1924) has suggested, were chiefly times of object–focused parallel play with a common toy. Figure 4 shows that a maximum of 30% of contact time (= 7% of total dyad time) was spent in actual social interaction between peers.

---

[2] The dyad situation was analyzed because it offered the most accurate data on gaze direction.

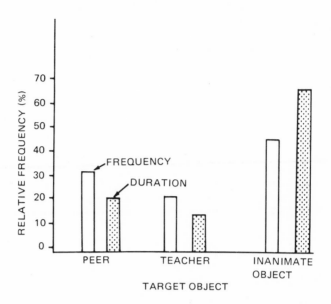

FIG. 2. Mean relative frequency and duration of looking at various target objects in dyad situation (age = 16 months).

While much of this analysis will focus on these social interactions, it is crucial to remember them in the larger context. They were new and unstable events emerging in play sessions dominated by the toddler's passion for *things*.

Yet, emerge they did. In both playgroups the frequency of interactions showed significant overtime linear growth (Figure 5). The nonsig-

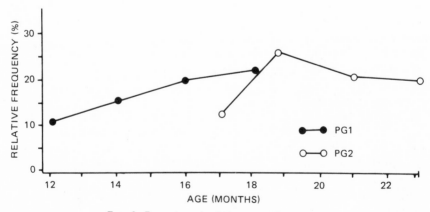

FIG. 3. Percentage dyad time spent in contact.

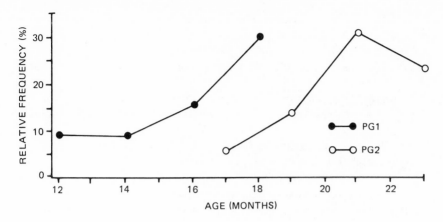

FIG. 4. Percentage contact time spent in social interaction.

nificant decline in interaction frequency at the end of PG2 is attributed to the specific toys present; a review of the videotapes suggested that these particular toys were less supportive of interaction.

The frequency of socially directed behavior shows similar growth trends to that of interaction (Mueller & Brenner 1977). Only "isolated

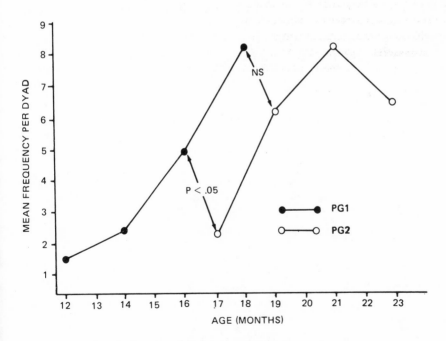

FIG. 5. Overtime change in social interaction frequency.

SDBs," (i.e., those receiving no response and thus seen as "unsuccessful initiations") showed no overtime frequency changes. Finally, studying only PG2, Vandell (1977, Table 66) reports that the mean length of interactions (as measured in number of component SDBs) also increases in significant linear fashion.

In summary, studying the dyad situation, we found that social behavior and interaction grew in both playgroups, yet always remained infrequent compared with object play.

2. The conceptualization of socially directed behavior as an index of toddler social skill was supported.

A central feature of skill (as opposed, for example, to memory) is instrumental effectiveness. "Even in the case of such relatively imprecise concepts as 'social skills,' the essence of the skill lies in the ability to achieve a goal" (Elliott & Connolly, 1974, p. 135). A skilled action should do the job better than an unskilled action. Thus, if coordination of social behaviors represents skill, coordinated SDBs should elicit more peer responses than simple SDBs. Bleier (1976) found that they did so; this result is shown here in Table 1. Furthermore, skilled actions should elicit the desired type of response. If the desired response is taken to mean "interaction maintaining," again the evidence is confirmatory. It is only after five months of peer experience, however, that SDB coordination becomes significantly related to the quality of response (Table 2).

Coordinated SDBs also were found to display both cross-situational and intersubject overtime stability. Both results are compatible with the "basic skill" interpretation given here. Vandell (1977) found that the child's proportional frequency of coordinated SDBs was invariant across a variety of social partners and situations. Rates ranged from about 20–30% at 16 months to about 30–40% at 22 months (Table 3). This table also illustrates the greater average coordination in parental behavior to toddlers. While the mothers simplify their messages across time (linear trend, $p = <.05$), the mother never reaches (and the father never comes close to reaching) the simplicity of their son's messages to them. We

TABLE 1. PROBABILITY OF PEER RESPONSE BY SDB COORDINATION[a]

Peer response	SDB coordination[b]	
	Simple	Coordinated
No elicited response (or can't tell)	.74	.62
Elicited response	.26	.38

[a]Data source: Bleier (1976), Table 37, p.134.
[b]Intercorrelation of variables shown: $d = .14$: $p<.0001$.

Table 2. Probability of Various Elicited Responses by SDB Coordination and Period[a]

Elicited response	SDB coordination	
	Simple	Coordinated
	Mean age: 14.6 months	
Non-SDBs	.66	.63
SDBs	.34	.37
Total	1.00	1.00
	Mean age: 17.8 months[b]	
Non-SDBs	.56	.33
SDBs	.44	.67
Total	1.00	1.00

[a]Source: Bleier (1976), Table 38, p. 135.
[b]Somer's $d = .24$; $p < .05$.

also found significant rank stability over time in individual differences in toddler peer-directed coordinated SDBs. Children who used such messages frequently in playgroup at 22 months were the same children who had used them frequently at 16 months (see Tables, 33, 47, and 72 in Vandell, 1977).

These three types of evidence—instrumental effectiveness, cross-situational invariance, and cross-subject overtime stability—together point toward the coordination of action as a useful approach to toddler social skill.

3. Toddler group size and toy properties both influenced peer social interaction.

Size of group influences amount and quality of interaction in both children and adults (Bales & Borgatta, 1965). Its effects on toddler–peer relations were pronounced. Comparing the dyad and group situations in PG2, we found striking differences in interaction growth rates. Near the start of PG2, both situations produced similar, low rates of interaction. Comparisons after three and six months of playgroup revealed a more rapid growth of interaction in the dyad situation. This pattern of significant linear growth in dyads and nonsignificant increases in the group setting characterized nine of the twelve social behavioral and interaction measures examined (Vandell & Mueller, in preparation). Figure 6 illustrates the relative growth rates for one of these nine measures, coordinated SDBs.

Bühler's students were the first to observe that all one-year-old interaction was dyadic in character. We had confirmed this finding in an earlier study (Mueller & Rich, 1976). Now we see that the expression of dyadic interaction is fostered in a dyadic context. Why should this be?

TABLE 3. MEAN PERCENTAGE COORDINATED SDBs BY ACTOR, PARTNER, SITUATION, AND PERIOD[a]

Period (months)	Toddler behavior			Parent behavior to toddler	
	To peer (dyad group)	To mother (dyad group)	To father (dyad)	By mother (Dyad group)	By father (Dyad)
16	30 24	26 28	29	62 56	58
18	— 30	— 33	—	— 63	—
19	44 —	31 —	28	53 —	58
20	— 26	— 35	—	— 58	—
22	34 31	38 37	34	47 66	55
Significance of linear trend	ns ns	$p < .1$ ns	ns	$p < .05$ ns	ns

[a]Source: Vandell (1977), Table 19, p.224.

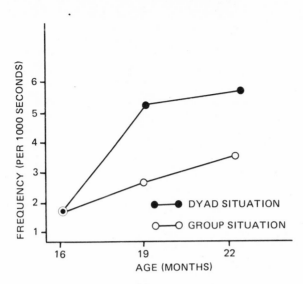

Fig. 6. The effect of group size on the frequency of coordinated socially directed behavior.

Perhaps toddlers in groups interrupt, and thus disrupt, each other's interactions. Vandell and Mueller (1977) examined this hypothesis. In over five hundred minutes of social interaction, there were fewer than five instances of interruption by a nonparticipant. Thus, some other property of the group situation—perhaps each child's monitoring of every novel event in the room—must be responsible for the smaller occurrence of interaction in the group setting.

This finding helps explain why some recent toddler–peer studies find interaction growth while others report little or none. The studies reporting growth tend to look at interaction in dyadic settings (see Mueller & Vandell, 1979). While the toddlers are learning to interact in the group setting, they can express their skills much more frequently when alone with one other child. This result points toward breaking up the toddlers' playroom into discrete play areas where a few children can play together in isolation from the larger group.

De Stefano (1976) experimentally varied the presence of play materials in PG2 dyads. In a cross-sectional study of 19-month-old toddlers, he compared four conditions. They were (1) all objects present, (2) small portable objects present, (3) large, nonportable objects present, and (4) no objects present. Table 4 gives the mean frequency of contact, social interaction, and selected interaction properties under these four conditions. Without reviewing the exact pattern of significance here, De Stefano found that small, portable objects when present alone or with

TABLE 4. MEAN FREQUENCY OF CONTACT AND SOCIAL INTERACTION VARIABLES BY TOY CONDITION[a]

	All objects present	Small objects present	Large objects present	No objects present
Contact	18.3	18.3	31.7[c]	23.3
Social interaction	20.0	21.0	41.0[c]	38.0[c]
Positive affect in interaction[b]	.08	.04	.28[c]	.26[c]
Negative affect in interaction[b]	.07	.19[c]	.05	.16[c]
Physical contact[b]	.27	.27	.24	.44[c]
Nonaccommodatory interaction[b]	.15	.28[c]	.09	.34[c]

[a]Data Source: De Stefano (1976), Table 1, p. 66.
[b]Expressed as relative frequency.
[c]Significantly ($p < .05$) larger than means by Newman-Keuls multiple comparisons.

large objects depressed interaction rates. Both the "large objects present" and "no objects present" conditions generated more social interaction. This interaction, however, was more likely to be physical, nonaccommodatory, or contain crying and other negative affect in the "no objects" conditions. Thus, De Stefano's results point toward large nonportable objects, more familiar under the name "play equipment," as especially facilitative of both toddler contact and prosocial interaction. The message to the playgroup director seems clear enough: to facilitate peer relations, don't let the room get cluttered with small toys. Experiment with periods when only the slide, jungle gym, rocking boat, and the like are present. According to De Stefano the natural outdoor "playground" should be a facilitating setting for early peer relations. Unfortunately, today's playground equipment is scaled too large for use by toddlers.

Besides group size and toy size, Playgroup Project examined other environmental factors (Vandell & Mueller, in preparation); undoubtedly child physical health, ordinal status, and especially teacher behavior all have their impact on peer social relations. Teachers (or parents) who constantly seek to direct or control peer relations probably make it difficult for toddlers to evolve peer relations (Kennedy & Mueller, 1972). Schools of education at times seem to neglect training their students for a major observational role in the preschool setting routine.

The previous factors were seen as accounting for the day-to-day variations in social interaction in playgroup. Yet, given the present setting, what can we say about the central processes in the growth of peer relations? Are peer relations generalized from parent–toddler relations? What role does participation in peer relations play in the emergence of skilled peer-directed action? Our answers will be given as we consider the autonomy of toddler peer society.

4. Toddler–peer relations in playgroup were an autonomous system in early child development. While influenced by toddler–parent relationships, they developed from experience in playgroup, depended on object mediation, focused on different content, and influenced toddler–parent social interactions.

In Playgroup Project, the influence of parent–toddler relations on peer–peer relations was studied. Using PG2 families and cross-lag correlational methods, Vandell (1977) asked which features of parent–toddler interaction at one time influenced peer–peer interaction at a later time. Influences were found but they had nothing to do with the central structural features of interaction; rather, they concerned individual differences in behavioral style. Thus, a child who offered objects frequently to his peers had both mothers and fathers who had frequently offered things to him (Cross lag: $p<.01$ for both parents). Conversely, toddlers who took relatively many objects from their peers, had mothers who had taken things relatively often from their sons.

Yet, beyond a handful of relations similar to these (Vandell, 1977) and relating only to individual differences in style, if we ask how toddlers come to form relations with their peers, all our evidence suggests their autonomous growth in the play setting.

The most direct evidence stems from the project research design. The playgroups were designed to allow several comparisons of toddlers similar in age but differing in length of playgroup experience—six months versus two months (see Figure 1). If we consider the global measure the "average frequency of interactions," the more experienced toddlers were initially ahead but the less experienced toddlers eliminated any significant difference after two months (Figure 5). Yet, a more detailed examination of the results showed this result to oversimplify the actual operation of peer experience. When the social interactions were broken into brief versus sustained ones, all effects of experience were attributable to the sustained interactions. Peer-experienced toddlers produced significantly more sustained interactions in both the first and second comparisons; they never produced more simple interactions. Similarly, in both comparisons, experienced toddlers produced significantly more coordinated SDBs than less experienced age-mates (Mueller & Brenner, 1977). In other words, better-acquainted toddlers were often participating in longer interactions with their peers, and these interactions were composed of more complex social messages.

Both these fundamental changes occurred after peer experience; toddlers not receiving such experience were relatively retarded in their toddler–peer relations.

How does such interaction and skill evolve "inside" playgroups? Like Bühler fifty years earlier, we found that play materials were the contextual basis of toddler social interaction. Elsewhere (Mueller & Vandell, 1979) we have called play materials the "mother love" of toddler–peer relations. Unlike the ever-accommodative mother, infants and toddlers don't see peer adjustment as their central developmental task. Nevertheless, they are drawn into contact by their reciprocal interest in physical things. They initiate each other's toy play and gradually learn to control each other and not only the toy. At age 12 months, in PG1 dyads, 92% of all peer social interactions appeared during object-centered contacts. All interaction was nested in contacts where objects played some mediating role. Up through the second birthday, not more than 17% of all social interactions ever occurred in contacts *not* involving physical objects (Mueller & Brenner,1977). Thus, we have come to see play materials as a natural catalyst of toddler social relations. Parallel play is not merely some expression of child egocentricity; instead in earliest childhood, it is a natural birthplace of peer relations. Yet, it doesn't resemble the direct engagement attained by a mother and infant (Brazelton, Koslowski, & Main, 1974). The purposive source of contact in parent–infant relations (the parent) contrasts with the fortuitous source of contact in toddler–peer relations. This contrast indicates that the autonomy of peer social relations extends to the source of peer relations in a different "pathway" or "channel" of social development (Vandell & Mueller, in preparation).

Mother–toddler and peer play also differs in the growth of general modes of social communication. Table 5 shows that toddlers used increasing numbers of vocal behavior to mothers only, and increasing numbers of motoric social behavior to peers only. Stated differently, the toddlers were growing in different ways in the two relationships. This separation in the domains of toddler growth also points toward the autonomy of toddler–peer relations. Incidentally, the failure of father–toddler dyads to show any significant growth in Table 5 is typical of our results across a wide variety of measures. In the second year of life father–toddler social relations appeared to be growing less dramatically than either mother–toddler relations or peer relations. We consider these results in more detail in Vandell and Mueller (in preparation).

A final reason for considering peer relations as autonomous is that they have important influences on mother–toddler relations. Toddlers who developed long interactions with their peers early in playgroup later came to engage in long interactions with their own mothers. This result was reflected in four significant crosslag correlations all reflecting

Table 5. Summary of Overtime Linear Trend Analysis for Vocal and
Motoric Behavior in Three Dyadic Relationships[a]

Dyadic relation	Behavior of	Frequency of vocal behavior	Frequency of motor behavior
Mother–toddler	Mother	ns	ns
	Toddler	F lin. $(1,5) = 89.2$, $p<.001$	ns ns
Father–toddler	Father	ns	
	Toddler	ns	ns
Toddler–toddler	Toddler	ns	F lin. $(1,5) = 20.8$, $p<.01$

[a]Data Source: Vandell (1977), Tables 34 and 74.

interaction duration (Table 81 in Vandell, 1977). Such a result stands a commonly held assumption about mother–toddler interaction directly on its head. Sustained toddler–peer play was found to be a source of, rather than product of, mother–toddler sustained play. We saw earlier that individual differences in toy-taking and other specific social actions stemmed from mother–toddler relations. Yet, individual facility in sustaining interaction with peers, a skill we demonstrated as emerging in playgroup itself, led to longer sustained mother–child interactions. Perhaps the toddlers learn from their peers how to hold up their end of "a game." Alternately, their mothers, watching their sons' peer play through our one-way vision mirrors, may have learned how to better accommodate their own behavior to their sons. Internal support for this hypothesis was found in the mother's simplification of her own messages to her toddler over the duration of playgroup (Table 3).

To summarize, in its *origins* in the object-centered contact (parallel play); in its *contentive focus* on motoric interactions; in its *consequences* for mother–toddler relations; and in a *direct test* of the role of peer experience in peer social skill, toddler–peer relations were found to be an autonomous system in early child development.

Discussion

What does it mean to consider toddler–peer relations as "autonomous"? It means that, while growing in parallel across the same period of time, one social system was not the direct and immediate source of the other. It does *not* mean that earlier social experience in infancy played no role in the toddlers' "readiness" for a playgroup experience. An infant's original curiosity about its world (Hebb, 1949) is nutured by adults during the first year of life; if it is not, the baby may show the "learned helplessness" in novel situations described by Lewis (1976). In the earliest months, peer contact cannot substitute for accommodating adults (Mueller & Vandell, 1979).

Early attachments to both persons and physical things reflect the infant's sense of control over these objects. Too often attachment is seen only as a system for remaining close to the mother, a biological system with an evolutionary basis only in predation reduction. Yet, the child uses the familiar in exploring the novel. Security in controlling part of its world is what allows "sorties" (Anderson, 1972) into the unknown. As part of Playgroup Project, we studied the children's reactions to maternal departure each morning. This evidence (Vandell & Mueller, in preparation) plus the growth of peer relations themselves both suggest the secure, curious quality of our toddlers, ready to master a new environment.

It is a pity that Sigmund Freud and Charlotte Bühler were opponents. Had the two founders of social-personality development been friends—as was possible, at least geographically—we would not have to speculate today on the relations between attachment and competence. Their integrated model would have generated the needed research years ago.

Models of Early Social Development

While this chapter does not focus on theory, it is worth noting that the model underlying the reported work differs from both the constructivist and interactional models. These familiar models, together with the present model, each oversimplified, are shown in Figure 7. The constructivist model focuses mainly on the cognitive restructuring of the individual across development. Interactions with the environment are important, but the major developments are based in psychic reorganization. Interactions influence the rate more than the course of this development.

The interactional model is more behavioral than cognitive. The concern is how two individuals developing together influence each other's behavior. Causation is efficient and is characterized in direct processes such as elicitation and imitation. Each behavior is related to the others in a network of probabilistic, Markovian connections.

The cross-systems model, employed here, derives something from both the constructivist and interactional traditions, yet it differs from both. From the constructivist model comes the belief that a wide variety of specific actions share the same organization, here called socially-directed behavior. From the interactional model comes the view that social interaction is efficient causation, and that peer responsiveness is a cumulative, probabilistic function of both participants' behavior (see Mueller, Bleier, & Krakow, 1977).

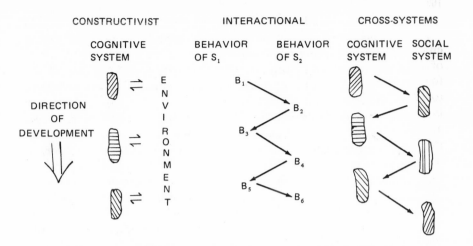

FIG. 7. Three models of the early development of social relations (see text).

The cross-systems model differs from the others in several ways. Besides cognitive structure, this model identifies social structure. Object-centered contacts, simple imitative interactions, and role-reversed interactions are three main structural types of social relation in toddler–peer contacts (Mueller & Lucas, 1975). These structural forms are a source of cognitive growth, not only its product. Rather than stemming chiefly from endogenous change, cognitive growth stems from participation in structured interactions. The interactions change the child, and after several children have changed in similar ways, new forms of social structure are created; these in turn foster further cognitive change. Both brain and social system are organized and each reorganizes the other over again across development. For example, object-centered contacts (a social structure) are a consequence of object skills (a cognitive structure). Yet, coordinated SDBs (a cognitive structure) are products of the social interactions of playgroup (a social structure). Only the cross-systems model reflects this interplay between mind and society, while also describing the changing structural features of each (Vandell & Mueller, in preparation).

Functional Significance of Spontaneous Peer Relations in Child Development

Most human relations serve multiple functions. Caregivers don't only give care and peers don't only play. Yet, play *is* the predominant activity in spontaneous peer relations throughout childhood. Thus, the normative, functional significance of peer relations and of play are closely tied together.

What is play? Is play some mere catharsis, some release of excess energy? Is play some imbalance in cognitive equilibrium, some excess of assimilation? The present results support a more positive, function for play, one described by Bruner, Jolly, and Sylva (1976): "What appears to be at stake in play is the opportunity for assembling and reassembling behavior sequences for skilled action" (p. 15). While such language accurately reflects the type of social skill growth reported here, it also may be an overly technical way of saying that play is imaginative. Play is imagination at work in the service of mastery (Vandell & Mueller, in press). Play is going beyond the known and seeking to master the novel. The toddler imagines how a peer might respond, and ignoring its visible dissimilarity to familiar social objects, the toddler delivers a first peer message. "We make believe that we may believe" is the way James Mark Baldwin summarized the importance of imagination in child development. When we remember the role of peers in the make-believe of all ages, we begin to see the functional significance of peer relations. Howes and Mueller (in press) treat this topic more fully.

Just as social play crosses the domains of cognitive and social psychology, so it enters the domain of psychotherapy. Therapists sometimes state that only in play is the child or adult free to be creative (Winnicott, 1971). Anthony (quoted in Grunebaum & Solomon, 1977) goes so far as to say that " . . . play for me at least is therapy and therapy is play." He means that play is the vehicle of personal growth and that therapy is a way of teaching people to play.

Here is a philosopher of mental development (Baldwin), respected therapists (Winnicott & Anthony), and empirical studies of toddler–peer relations all pointing towards the functional significance of play in human development. Perhaps a bridge of "play" can at last be erected between clinical and experimental psychology. Such a bridge has been needed ever since those Viennese founders, Charlotte Bühler and Sigmund Freud, went their very separate ways.

ACKNOWLEDGMENTS

I am ever grateful to the families who participated in Playgroup Project. I also wish to thank Fred Massarik and Isolde Loewinger for helpful information about Bühler's life.

REFERENCES

Anderson, J. W. Attachment behaviour out of doors. In N. Blurton Jones (Ed.), *Ethological studies of child behaviour*. London: Cambridge University Press, 1972.

Bales, R., & Borgatta, E. Size of group as a factor in the interaction profile. In P. Hare, E. Borgatta, & R. Bales (Eds.), *Small groups: Studies in social interaction.* New York: Alfred Knopf, 1965.

Bleier, M. R. *Social behavior among one-year-olds in a playgroup.* Unpublished doctoral dissertation, Boston University, 1976.

Brazelton, T. B., Koslowski, B., & Main, M. The origins of reciprocity: The early mother–infant interaction. In M. Lewis & L. A. Rosenblum (Eds.), *The effect of the infant on its caregiver.* New York: Wiley, 1974.

Bruner, J. S., Jolly A., & Sylva, K. (Eds.). *Play.* New York: Basic Books, 1976.

Bühler, C. Die ersten sozialen Verhaltungsweisen des Kindes. In C. Bühler, H. Hetzer, & B. Tudor-Hart (Eds.) *Soziologische und psychologische Studien über das erste Lebensjahr.* Jena: Gustav Fischer, 1927.

Bühler, C. *The first year of life.* New York: John Day, 1930.

Bühler, C. The social behavior of children. In C. Murchison (Ed. *A handbook of child psychology.* Worcester, Mass.: Clark University Press, 1931.

Bühler, C. Humanistic psychology as a personal experience. *Interpersonal development.* 1973/ 4, 4, 197–214.

De Stefano, C. T. *Environmental determinants of peer social behavior and interaction in a toddler playgroup.* Unpublished doctoral dissertation, Boston University, 1976.

De Stefano, C. T., & Mueller, E. Sources of toddlers' social interaction with their peers. Unpublished manuscript, 1973.

Elliott, J., & Connolly, K. Hierarchical structure in skill development. In K. Connolly & J. Bruner (Eds.), *The growth of competence.* New York: Academic Press, 1974.

Fischer, K. W. Learning and problem-solving as the development of organized behavior. Journal of Structural Learning, 1978.

Gesell, A. L. *The mental growth of the pre-school child: A psychological outline of normal development from birth to the sixth year, including a system of developmental diagnosis.* New York: Macmillan, 1925.

Grunebaum, H., and Solomon, L. F. A peer theory of group psychotherapy. Paper presented at the meetings of the Northeastern Society for Group Psychotherapy, Boston, December, 1977.

Hartup, W. W. Toward a social psychology of childhood. Presidential Address to Division 7, American Psychological Association, Washington, D.C., September, 1976.

Hebb, D. O. *The organization of behavior.* New York: Wiley, 1949.

Howes, C., & Mueller, E. Friendship: Its sigificance for development. In W. Spiel (Ed.), *Psychology in the 20th century.* Zurich: Kindler, in press.

Kennedy, J. M., & Mueller, N. Only doves dwell in the sandbox. *Early Years,* 1972, 3(3), 52–56.

Lewis, M. The orgins of self-competence. Paper presented at the NIMH Conference on Mood Development, Washington D.C., November, 1976

Marvin, C. *Sympathy and affection in the peer interaction of one-year-old boys.* Unpublished doctoral dissertation, Ohio State University, 1977.

Maudry, M., & Nekula, N. Social relations between children of the same age during the first two years of life. *Journal of Genetic Psychlogy,* 1939, 54, 193–215.

Mueller, E., Bleier, M., Krakow, J., Hegedus, K., & Cournoyer, P. The development of peer verbal interaction among two-year-old boys. *Child Development.* 1977, 48, 284–287.

Mueller, E., & Brenner, J. The origins of social skills and interaction among playgroup toddlers. *Child Development,* 1977, 48, 854–861.

Mueller, E., & Lucas, T. A developmental analysis of peer interaction among toddlers. In M. Lewis & L. A. Rosenblum (Eds.), *Friendship and peer relations.* New York: Wiley Interscience, 1975

Mueller E., & Rich, A. Clustering and socially-directed behaviors in a playgroup of 1-year-olds. *Journal of Child Psychology and Psychiatry*, 1976, *17*, 315–322.

Mueller, E., & Vandell, D. Infant–infant interaction: A review. In J. D. Osofsky, (Ed.), *Handbook of infant development*, New York: Wiley-Interscience, 1979, pp. 591–622.

Parten, M.B. Social participation among preschool children. *Journal of Abnormal and Social Psychology*, 1932, *27*, 243–269.

Piaget, J. *The origins of intelligence in children*. New York: International Universities Press, 1952.

Piaget, J. *Biology and knowledge*. Chicago: University of Chicago Press, 1971.

Senn, M. J. E. Insights on the child development movement in the United States. *Monographs of the Society for Research in Child Development*, 1975, *70*, No 3–4.

Stern, W. *Psychology of early childhod up to the sixth year of age*. New York: Henry Holt, 1924.

Vandell, D. L. *Boy toddlers' social interaction with mothers, fathers, and peers*. Unpublished doctoral dissertation, Boston University, 1977.

Vandell, D. L. A micro-analysis of toddlers' social interaction with mothers and fathers. *Journal of Genetic Psychology*, in press.

Vandell, D. L., & Mueller, E. The effects of group size on toddlers' social interaction with peers. Manuscript submitted for publication, 1977.

Vandell, D. L. & Mueller, E. Peer play and peer friendships during the first two years. In H. Foot, T. Chapman, and J. Smith (Eds.), *Friendship and Childhood Relationships*. Sussex: John Wiley Ltd., in press.

Vandell, D. L., & Mueller, E. *The role of peer relations in infant development*. In preparation.

Winnicott, D. W. *Playing and reality*. New York: Basic Books, 1971.

10

The Effect of Adults on Peer Interactions

Leonard A. Rosenblum and Edward H. Plimpton

"We're all drifting and things are going rotten. At home there was always a grownup. Please, sir; please, miss; and then you got an answer. How I wish!"
"I wish my auntie was here."
"I wish my father . . . . Oh, what's the use?"
"Keep the fire going."
The dance was over and the hunters were going back to the shelters.
"Grownups know things," said Piggy. "They ain't afraid of the dark. They'd meet and have tea and discuss. Then things 'ud be all right-"
"They wouldn't set fire to the island. Or lose-"
"They'd build a ship-"
The three boys stood in the darkness, striving unsuccessfully to convey the majesty of adult life.
"They wouldn't quarrel-"
"Or break my specs-"
"Or talk about a beast-"
"If only they could get a message to us," cried Ralph desperately. "If only they could send us something grownup a sign or something."

William Golding, Lord of the Flies[1]

---

[1] William Golding. *Lord of the Flies*. New York: Capricorn Books, 1959. Reprinted with the permission of the publisher, Putnam's • Coward, McGann & Geoghegan, Inc. • Marek, New York, New York. Reprinted outside the United States with the permission of Faber and Faber, Ltd., London, England.

Leonard A. Rosenblum and Edward H. Plimpton • Downstate Medical Center, Department of Psychiatry, Brooklyn, New York 11203. This research was supported by NIMH grant #22640.

William Golding in his classic novel examines the behavioral and emotional disruption observed in a group of English schoolboys who find themselves confronted with the need to live together and survive in the absence of the adult society to which they are accustomed. The situation he created and the reactions he envisioned dramatically illuminate many of the basic issues with which this chapter will deal. While the novel has many levels of interpretation, it does suggest that in the absence of adults and the structured interaction that generally characterizes their behavior, the behavior of young children may become more disorderly, less focused, and—perhaps as a by-product of these factors and their consequent emotional impact— ultimately highly aggressive. Except during the ravages of war (Freud & Dunn, 1951) in both primitive and technologically advanced societies, it is quite unusual for children to function and attempt to survive without adults. In most instances in which children are observed interacting with one another, they are deeply immersed in the characteristic social patterns of their society or have only been briefly and temporarily separated from it. Thus, despite the fact that most early peer relations occur within an adult social network, as Lamb (1977) has pointed out, there has been little systematic research on the effect of the presence or absence of adults on peer interaction. Since in the majority of nonhuman primates development also occurs within the context of a social group, it would be valuable to consider these issues from a comparative perspective.

It is important at this point to reflect briefly upon our perspectives concerning the utility of animal models in forming our conceptualizations regarding the role of adult social structure at the human level. Given our present state of knowledge, a comparative perspective cannot serve as the basis for isomorphic comparisons between nonhuman and human primates. It is unwarranted even under the best of circumstances to leap too quickly from branch to branch across the phylogenetic tree. Nonhuman primate species differ widely from each other in terms of their characteristeristic individual behavior patterns, the pace of infant development, and the nature of their adult social structure. Even within species, recent field and laboratory studies indicate that marked differences in social behavior and structure emerge as a function of group size, composition, and the particular ecological demands confronting the group. Indeed, the capacity for such varied social adaptation may be considered one of the distinguishing characteristics of the primate order. Therefore, it is only through the development of a variety of animal models, based on different species observed in a variety of settings, that broad behavioral principles of considerable generality can be generated. At present, it is impossible to attempt to draw conclusions regarding human social behavior and its development based on even the best of nonhuman primate data. This is not to say, however, that such material is of no heuristic value for the study of human phenomena in this area. Indeed, it is our view that the lessons at the nonhuman primate level can effectively serve as the basis for reordering the priority of hypotheses considered appropriate for testing at the human level.

As a starting point in this effort, unlike many of the papers in this volume that deal with specific relationships between infants and non-mother social objects, the current chapter will focus instead on the manner in which a specific class of individuals, mature adults, may by their presence and behavior influence the form of social interaction within peer groups of infant and juvenile nonhuman primates. In order that these data be most readily applicable to hypothesis generation at the human level, we will focus primarily on studies undertaken under relatively controlled laboratory conditions.

ADULT STRUCTURE AND PEER INTERACTIONS

On the most global level, the structured patterns of the adult interaction can influence the form and direction of peer social behavior. In our laboratory we have made a series of comparisons between social behaviors of pigtail (*Macaca nemestrina*) and bonnet (*M. radiata*) macaques. Under laboratory conditions, while living in large pens, pigtails maintain relatively pronounced individual distances between themselves. Unrelated adults rarely make contact with one another unless engaged in some active form of behavior such as grooming, agression, or sex. In contrast, unrelated bonnet adults brought together in the laboratory show marked tendencies to sit in close contact with one another for long periods of time (Rosenblum, Kaufman, & Stynes, 1964). Furthermore, pigtails are regularly observed as more aggressive toward one another, more competitive for various incentives, and in general, function within a social structure that is more hierarchically organized than is true for bonnets. Mother–infant interaction and infant development is also dramatically different between the two species. In contrast to bonnet mothers, pigtails restrict and protect their young infants more, and in the first months of life, actively prevent others in the group from touching, exploring, or playing with their infants.

As a consequence of these differences in social organization and maternal behavior, the way in which the young bonnets and pigtails begin peer interactions differ markedly. A bonnet infant grows up in close proximity to a wide variety of adults and other infants. As a result, two bonnet infants, while each is still sucking at its mother's breast, can begin active peer interaction. In contrast, pigtail infants must leave their mother before they will be in close enough proximity to begin interacting with another peer. As a consequence of these differences in the behavior of their mothers, a far greater proportion of bonnet infant play is socially directed toward peers than is true of pigtails. Even though the overall level of play may be similar in the two species across development, the proportions of social and nonsocial play within the play category differ. Thus, compared to the pigtails, the bonnet infant plays earlier with peers, plays with them more often as it matures, and appears to remain more consistently involved with unrelated social partners throughout life.

THE ROLE OF KINSHIP IN PEER RELATIONS

The role of familial factors in organizing adult, and consequently infant and juvenile social behavior, has been the object of considerable interest in recent years. As long-term studies of nonhuman primate social groups have developed over the last 10 to 20 years, various observers have grown sensitive to the role of kinship relationships, not just at the infant–mother or young sibling level, but among mature adults as well (Kurland, 1977). Thus, in most circumstances, in addition to age and gender classifications, most adult social groups of primates must be considered as structured along another dimension, i.e., matrilineal kinship groups. Indeed, it is worth noting that contemporary theories have given great emphasis to the role of kin selection in various forms of behavior as an important aspect of the evolution of the primate order (Wilson, 1975).

A study in our laboratory indicates the potential impact of strong kinship bonds on various aspects of peer relations in infant and juvenile macaques. For this study, we allowed one group of each species to breed undisturbed for a period of almost nine years (Rosenblum & Nadler, 1971). At the end of this time each group, which had initially contained only an adult male and four or five adult females, had grown to more than two dozen members each. Each female had produced 2–5 offspring that continued living with her in the group; in addition, several second-generation infants had been born into these familial groups. Several new findings relating to the issues of adult structure and infant social development emerged in these two species groups. The pigtail group showed evidence of strong kinship-related patterns, whereas bonnets showed minimal evidence of this factor. Pigtail offspring, even after puberty, oriented an overwhelming proportion of their social behavior toward other members of their own kinship line. Bonnet infants, however, after about the first year or so of life, essentially interacted with members of their own kinship group at about the same rate they did with the nonkin group. If a kinship group represented 20% of the total number of animals available, in pigtails as much as 50–80% of all social behavior for that kinship group would be confined to interaction among its members. Bonnets, under the same circumstances, directed perhaps 20–25% of their behavior toward other members of their kinship group. Even social play, generally interpreted as a peer or age-mate behavior, showed a similar distinction. Pigtail offspring involved both younger and older siblings in their social play often in apparent preference to nonrelated age mates; bonnet infants showed no such proclivity. Furthermore, in marked contrast to our previous findings on the dramatic species differences between pigtails and bonnets in their tendency toward passive physical contact with one another, there was a breakdown in this distinction with the emergence of the kinship groups in pigtails. In previous studies, using strangers that were brought together as adults from the wild, pigtails rarely sat together, whereas in the presence of developed kinship groups, pigtail juveniles and adults manifested almost exactly the same levels of passive contact behavior that were characteristically observed between nonkin members of bonnet groups.

Thus, the difference between bonnets and pigtails is not in terms of a general propensity to engage in contact behavior, but in the selection of partners to express it with. Our current results indicate that pigtails restrict close physical contact to members of their own kinship group while bonnets are relatively promiscuous in this regard. These species differences in the patterns of adult spacing and contact behavior influence both the form and direction of early peer interaction.

MATERNAL STATUS AND INFANT SOCIAL BEHAVIOR

Looking within the structure of a given species group reveals another way in which the adult structure may influence the pattern of social behavior in the young. Data suggest that within a social group the status of the mother is an important influence on the type of interactions in which her offspring can engage. Field research on the rhesus monkey has suggested that the offspring of dominant females will in turn become dominant themselves. Koford (1963) noted that the male offspring of dominant, as opposed to low-ranking, rhesus females were more likely to stay within the center of the troop and would often be dominant over older animals. In contrast, the male offspring of low-ranking females were found to become low-ranking group members, and ultimately, to move to the periphery of the troop. Generally, female offspring of all mothers remained within the central core of the troop, but as they matured, their own hierarchy paralleled that of the mothers. In this vein, Sade (1967) found that offspring of high-ranking rhesus females generally defeated lower-ranking ones in aggressive encounters. It is interesting to note, that in recording aggression between yearlings, these data consisted only of those fights in which the mother was at a distance or not "paying attention." The implication behind this finding is that these yearlings had already acquired a "dominant" personality and had established an independent status of their own among their peers. However, at present, we know little about the point at which an infant acquires a status of its own, independent of his mother's presence, and the extent to which such acquired status is maintained in various situations.

Some work done previously in our laboratory (Stynes, Rosenblum, & Kaufman, 1968) demonstrates quite explicitly how maternal dominance will influence interaction between peers. For this study, two mixed species groups, each containing two bonnet and two pigtail mother–infant dyads were established. Dominance between the two species was manipulated by introducing either a bonnet or pigtail male into the group, or having no male present. In the absence of a male, the pigtails, a larger and more aggressive species, dominated over the bonnets. The presence of a pigtail male basically sharpened the dominance of the pigtail females. However, when a bonnet male was introduced to the group there was an immediate reversal in dominance. The expression of dominance assumed several forms for these mother–infant dyads. First, it should be noted that there were virtually no interactions between the two species except for infrequent aggressive exchanges. Rather, the expression of the status of the mothers, and consequently that of their infants, was more indirectly demonstrated. The upper shelves of the pens, which were the preferred area of the pen, were utilized predominantly by the dominant species. When no male or a pigtail male was present, the pigtail mothers and their infants exclusively occupied the upper shelves while the bonnet dyads remained confined primarily to the floor of the pens. With the introduction of the bonnet male, this situation was immediately reversed. With the conspecific male, the bonnet dyads displaced the pigtails from the upper shelves, and it was the pigtail in this condition that occupied the less desirable floor area. In conjunction with the mothers' choice of preferred areas, infants would spend more time off mother, and engage in more play and object exploration in the condition in which their mothers were dominant.

As Figure 1 illustrates, peer interaction was dramatically affected by the relative status of the mothers; this in turn depended upon the

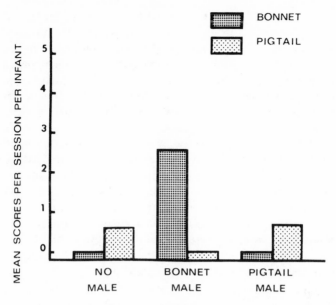

FIG. 1. The mean scores for social play among bonnet and pigtail infants as a function of the presence or absence of bonnet and pigtail adult males.

presence or absence of an adult male of their own species and its consequent impact on the interactional structure of this mixed-species group.

This influence of maternal dominance on peer play and its effects on aggressive encounters (Koford, 1963, Sade, 1967) can also be extended into sexual behavior. It is not unusual to see, in a structured social group, a small preadolescent male offspring of a dominant female mount a much larger mature adult female. However, when a two-year-old male is introduced to an adult female in an acute testing situation, where his mother is not present, he will not attempt to mount the female (Rosenblum & Nadler, 1971). In these acute tests, the adult female is larger than the young male and she rapidly emerges as dominant over him. This in turn inhibits his sexual behavior. In the same study, the males were also presented with receptive young females of appreciably smaller size than the adult-female stimulus animals. The young males immediately mounted, and copulated frequently with the young female, over whom they could readily establish their own dominance. Adult males in this test situation, being larger than both females, quickly mounted each of them on all tests. These observations indicate a transference of status from dominant females to male offspring. Under a dominant mother's protection, a male gains a degree of her status over a chosen female and is able to mount that female with impunity. In the absence of the support gained from the mother functioning within the structure of her adult group, the young male must attempt to dominate on his own a task that can be accomplished with a smaller female, but not a fully adult one. Thus, the social network within which the young male finds himself can clearly modify the effects of one aspect of dominance, physical size, and the extent to which it will regulate various forms of behavior.

We have seen a few of the ways in which adults may indirectly influence peer interaction through their relationships with each other. On the most global level, the characteristic social organization of the species influences the way in which peers come together. Bonnets will interact with a wide variety of age-mates regardless of genetic relationship. In contrast, pigtails will spend a greater proportion of their time interacting with peers who are related. In addition, the mother's position in the social network will influence the expression and direction of such behaviors as play, aggression, and mounting.

Adult Interaction Patterns and Infant Socialization

While the previous discussion has indicated how adult–adult relationships can impinge directly on peer interactions, very little is known about the effects of the actual presence or absence of an intact social structure. One suggestion in this regard is found in studies of the squirrel monkey *(Saimiri scuireus)* (Coe & Rosenblum, 1974; Rosenblum & Coe, 1977). In the squirrel monkey, there is a marked tendency among adults toward sexual segregation. Males and females tend to separate into distinct same-sex groups, in which the spatial distance between opposite sex individuals is always greater than between same sex partners. However, the normal pattern of sex segregation is not maintained in either a heterosexual group of subadults (33–39 months) or juveniles (21–23) when mature adults are not present. When adults are placed into groups of young animals of this type, however, there are clear age differences in response to their presence. The subadults, in particular the females, made frequent attempts to approach the adults. The adult females were more tolerant of the approaches by the subadult females than those by the subadult males. Similarly, the adult males, although initially avoiding all the youngsters, showed more tolerance to the approaches of subadult males than females. As a consequence, by the second week in the presence of the sexually segregated adult structure, the subadult group split along the male–female line; by increasingly attaching themselves to the same sex adult subgroup, the subadults were soon showing as sexually segregated a pattern as the

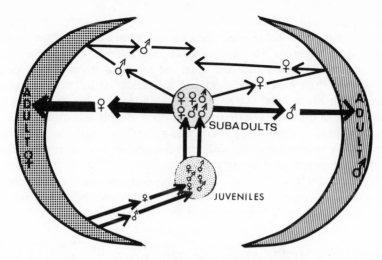

FIG. 2. The ontogeny of sexual segregation with specific reference to the differential responsiveness of adult males and females to the approach of same or opposite sex subadults. Larger arrows reflect greater tendencies to approach. Note the lack of approach by either male or female juveniles and the repulsion of opposite sex subadults by the adult males and females.

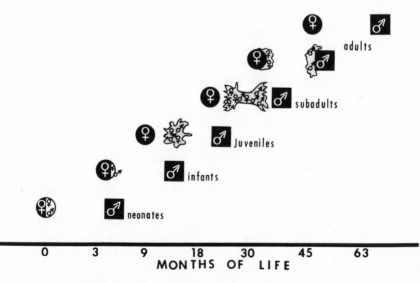

FIG. 3. The ontogeny of sexual segregation in squirrel monkeys. Note the gradual splitting of the juvenile subgroup, as developing males and females move closer to the same sex adults, and reproduce the segregated adult pattern around the time of puberty (40–50 months).

adult males and females. In contrast to the subadults, the younger
juvenile group did not change their pattern of social organization when
adults were present. The adults were not tolerant to approaches by
juveniles who in turn did not continue to make them. The juveniles
maintained their heterosexual grouping pattern at relatively large distances from the adults. As reflected in Figure 2, there are age-related
differences in the efforts of developing squirrel monkeys to move toward
groups of their own and opposite sex adults. In addition, adult males
and females respond differentially to the approaches of younger animals.
With increasing age of the infant, as depicted in Figure 3, the initially
segregated structure of the adult group reproduces itself, and by the age
of puberty, males and females function within the selective pattern of
interaction characteristic of adults in this species.

The Effects of Mothers and Nonmothers on Peer Interaction

In a variety of ways, we have seen that adult–peer interaction will
influence peer relationships. However, very little is actually known
about how specific behavior patterns between peers may be influenced
by the presence or absence of adults. In the following study, an attempt
is made to analyze peer interaction in the presence or absence of a
variety of adults.

Subjects were 12 one-year-old bonnet macaque infants, 6 males and
6 females, which had lived with their mothers and another mother–infant
dyad during the first year of life. For a given mother–infant dyad, their
living companions during the first year were alternated every two weeks,
so that the infant lived successively with a same sex, and then an
opposite sex peer and its mother. This "alternating double–dyad"
situation was one of moderate social complexity somewhere between
isolation or "single-dyad" rearing and social group rearing.

In the current study, subjects were placed in one of three treatment
conditions; a peer-only group, a peer–mother group, or a peer–other
females group. All groups contained two male and two female peers
who were unfamiliar with each other at the beginning of the study.
However, the condition under which they came together differed dramatically in terms of the total social situation. In the peer-only group
(Figure 4), there were no adults; in the peer–mother group, each infant
had its own mother (and therefore three additional unfamiliar adult
females, see Figure 5); and, in the peer–other group, four adult females
were present with whom all peers were unfamiliar (see Figure 6). Prior
familiarity between adults was not systematically controlled. The objec-

FIG. 4. The peer-only group with males sitting on the right and females on the left.

tive in creating these groups was to manipulate the presence or absence of adult females and their relationship to the infants such that "adults" would not necessarily be synonymous with "mother."

Subjects were housed in pens that measured approximately 6 ft. wide, 7 ft. high, and 12 ft. deep. Two shelves were located at the back of the pen, the first one 3 ft. above the floor and the second 3 ft. above the first. Two one-way vision mirrors were located in the front of the pen for observations. Food and water were available continuously.

After the subjects had been living in their respective groups for five weeks, the mothers of the peer-only and adult–peer group were returned to their offspring for a two-week period. This reunion was an attempt to control for separation effects before beginning a replication of the test conditions. For the replication, 10 of the original subjects were reassigned to new treatment groups and two new subjects of the same age and experience were added in order to maintain the unfamiliarity of peers at the time of group formation.

Observations began after the first week that the subject had been placed in their treatment groups. Behaviors were recorded using a 30-second time sample, in which each peer was the focus of observation for 14 minutes a day, four days a week. The recorded behaviors and their definitions are given in Table 1.

FIG. 5. The peer–mother group with each infant adjacent to its mother.

FIG. 6. The peer–other female group, with peers on the lower shelf and adults on the upper level.

TABLE 1. BEHAVIORAL TAXONOMY[a]

Social play	Both rough and tumble wrestling as well as chase and follow sequences
Exercise play	Vigorous jumping, climbing, or running without social referents
Social exploration	Close visual, oral, or olfactory inspection and/or tentative manipulation of the body of another animal
Mounts	Both partial and complete foot-clasp mounts
Aggression	Intense visual states, facial threats, and physical attacks
Bounce display	A violent, repetitive shaking of the environment such as the shelves of the pen that produces a loud noise
Distress	Vocalization, lipsmack, fear grimace, or raised-tail
Grooming	Careful picking through and/or slow brushing aside of the fur of another animal with one or both hands
Object exploration	Close visual, oral, or olfactory inspection of an inanimate object, or vigorous chewing of an inanimate object

[a]Derived from Kaufman and Rosenblum. 1966.

In addition to the time-sample behavior, the location of each subject in the pen was recorded on spatial maps nine times during each observational day. These maps were used to compute a measure of environmental usage and the relative constraint of the mobility of the infants in the pens. Behavioral data from the two parts of the experiment were combined to do a two-way Anova with sex and groups as independent variables.

The three groups appeared dramatically different from each other from the moment they were put together. In the formation of any nonhuman primate group, there is an initial period of aggression that may last several minutes or hours or even several days depending on the species. In the laboratory, new bonnet groups generally stabilize after a day of living together. During the initial period of aggression, the yearlings in the peer–mother group tended to remain quite close to their mothers. If, however, a particular mother was the object of the rest of the group's aggression, its offspring would readily separate from her. There was practically no interaction or contact between peers during this intense period. In the peer–other group, the youngsters were frequently drawn together during periods of intense fighting between adults. While the adults were fighting among themselves, the young animals would often huddle together in a corner. In contrast to the adult groups, there was no immediate aggression in the peer-only group. Upon entering the pen, the youngsters would sit on a shelf, look around briefly, and then begin moving around the pen, often passing other peers in the process. Only after several minutes had passed would a period of aggression ensue between the members of the young peer group.

On a variety of behaviors, the peer–mother group seemed to occupy an intermediate position between the total absence of adults, as in the peer-only group, and the presence of unfamiliar adults as in the peer–other female group. On the most global level, the presence of adults seemed to restrict the activity of the infant peer group. Infants were not able to move around to different parts of the pen to the same degree in the presence of adults as in their absence. Utilizing the location maps, the frequency with which each infant was observed in each of 10 portions of the pen was tabulated. The variance of scores for pen location for each subject was calculated as a measure of the infant's mobility in the pen. The smaller the variance for a given subject's location scores, the greater the constraint on its mobility. As reflected in Figure 7, constraint of mobility was greater in the peer–other condition than in the peer–mother condition. Mobility of the peer-only group was least constrained.

One behavior that requires the utilization of large amounts of space is exercise play (Figure 8). Reflecting the constraint of mobility measure, the mean exercise-play score was higher in the peer-only group (24.09), a little less in the peer–mother group (18.75), and dramatically less in the peer–other adult female group (9.38).

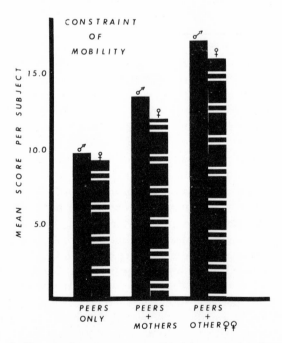

FIG. 7. The overall mean score per subject for constraint of mobility.

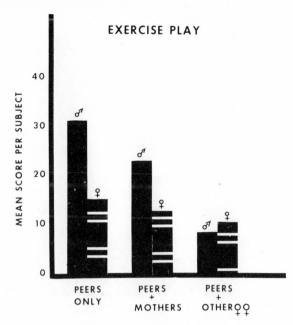

FIG. 8. The overall mean score per subject for exercise play.

In addition to this significant group effect, males engage in significantly more exercise play than females. This sex effect held across the three treatment groups. Distress measures indicated that these lower levels of mobility and exercise play in the adult conditions were the result of the adults actively frightening the peers (Figure 9).

There was significantly more distress in the peer–other adult-female group (6.15) than in either the peer–mother (11.13), or peer-only conditions (5.92). In all three of these measures, constraint of mobility, exercise play, and distress, the peer–mother group occupied an intermediate position in the level of peer activity. The peer-only and peer–mother group engaged in about twice as much play as the peer–other adult-female group; there were no overall significant differences in social play (Figure 10).

In the second replication, one of the females in the peer-only group became ill and subsequently died after the completion of the study. Although the data from the sick infant were excluded from the analyses, her presence seemed to depress play activity within the group as a whole.

A number of both nonsocial and social behaviors such as object exploration, social exploration, and grooming showed no significant differences across the treatments. Each of these behaviors involves rather

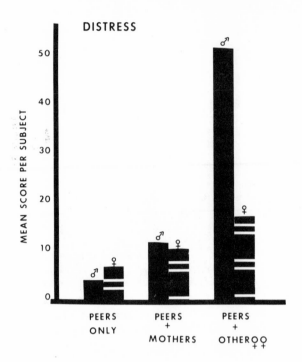

FIG. 9. The overall mean score per subject for distress.

quiescent behavior on the part of one or two animals, and can readily occur without provoking much attention from others in the group. Perhaps for this reason they escaped the inhibitory action of the adults that affected more vigorous forms of activity.

Consistent with the theme of Golding's *Lord of the Flies,* in the absence of adults, there was a significant increase in aggressive–assertive behaviors such as aggression, mounting, and bounce displays. These assertive and aggressive behaviors were more than twice as frequent in the peer-only group as compared to either of the peer–adult groups.

As reflected in Figure 11, males were responsible for virtually all mounts and bounce displays in each of the treatment groups, but both males and females showed their highest levels of aggression in the peer-only condition.

These results, with the possible exception of play, are similar to those reported by Suomi (in this volume) in his comparison of peer interaction in the nuclear-family and pen conditions. In the nuclear-family apparatus, adults had visual but very limited physical access to peers, while in the pen conditions, adults had continual physical access to them. In the absence of adults (the nuclear-family apparatus), aggression, sex, and play were significantly greater than in their presence (the pen condition). Furthermore, in the presence of adults, there was significantly more huddling between peers than in their absence. It is significant that in two different species of monkey, observed at comparable ages but in rather different settings, the absence of adults produced similar behavioral changes.

In general terms, perhaps the major effect of adults on peer interaction is to act as a suppressor of certain types of vigorous activity. Locomotion, as expressed in exercise play and the constraint of mobility measure, were dramatically reduced in the presence of adults. Vigorous social interaction such as that involved in aggression, sex, and in some cases play, were also reduced when adults were part of the social network.

The manner in which vigorous activity is suppressed by adults will vary as their characteristics are considered in more detail. When a young monkey is in the presence of its mother, as in the peer–mother group, a decrease in mobility tends to be correlated with increased time spent

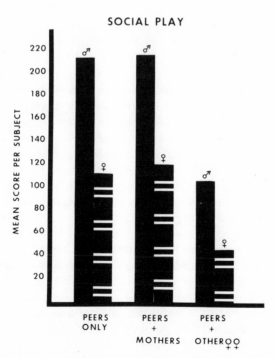

FIG. 10. The overall mean score per subject for social play.

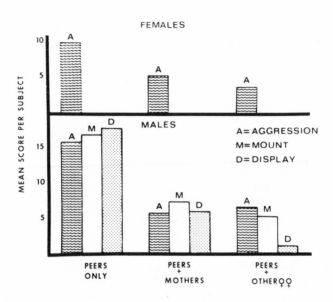

FIG. 11. The overall mean score per subject for aggression, mounts, and display. Females did not engage in any mounts or displays.

in contact with mother. In a previous study in our laboratory, the influence of mother and peer on adaptation to a novel environment supported the same correlation. One-year-old bonnet infants were exposed to novel environments in the presence of a familiar peer or with their mother, and then retested alone in these situations. The acute postexposure tests revealed no differences between prior adaptation with the mother and with the peer. However, in the adaptation period itself, it was found that infants engaged in more locomotion in the presence of a peer, and higher amounts of contact while with the mother. It is noteworthy that behaviors such as object exploration, social exploration, and grooming, for which no significant differences between conditions were found, could still be performed while the infants remained in contact with the mother.

The adult females in the peer–other adult female group were not uniform in their behavioral characteristics. Consequently, they suppressed peer activity in different ways. All the adults used in the first replication had recently been separated from their own infants as part of another experiment. One of these recently separated females occasionally allowed two of the peers, a male and a female, to make ventral contact with her. In contrast, two of the adult females used in the second replication of the peer–adult group, had not been in contact with any infants in over a year. The peers, in this group, were not allowed to come near the adults. As reflected in Figure 6, in the peer–adult group, adults stayed primarily on the top shelf, while the peers remained on the bottom one. When the youngsters would attempt to move to the top shelf they would often, but not always, be threatened and displaced by the adults.

The type of adults such as mother versus nonmother around which peers interact will suppress vigorous activity in different ways. It is important to consider the functional significance of these types of behavioral suppressors by adults. If adults, in a more natural environment, also tend to inhibit vigorous activity, such inhibition may well be valuable in preventing juveniles from straying too far from the troop, in reducing disruptions in group communication, and in decreasing visibility of infants to outsiders. This would limit the danger of predation, maintain group cohesion, and prevent infants from becoming lost. An extreme example of this inhibition of vigorous activity could be observed in the peer–other adult female group. The high degree of distress in these young monkeys suggests that in the absence of the modulating effects of the mother, the adults were overly severe in their suppression of peer activity. On the other hand, the high degree of aggression in the peer-only group might be indicative of a difficulty in regulating interactions between themselves without the help of adults. Indeed, Wallen, Bielert, & Slimp (1977) have suggested that one effect maternal intervention in peer interaction may have is to decrease the infant's fear of the approach of another infant. As a result of this intervention, aggressive interactions between peers are kept to a minimum. The intermediate position which the mother–peer group occupied with regard to the occurrence of so many behaviors suggests that the presence of mothers and other adults simultaneously modulates and facilitates peer interaction.

OVERVIEW OF ADULT EFFECTS ON PEER INTERACTION

As a matter of convenience, rather than as a valid dichotomy, the presence of adults can be viewed as having a variety of indirect and direct effects on peer interaction. These have been summarized in Table 2. Direct effects are conceived of here as those discrete behavioral acts that adults direct at particular peers or groups of infants. Alterations in peer interaction, which can be seen as a by-product of adult–adult interactions or merely the presence of adults, are considered as indirect effects.

Adults can directly alter the affective state of the infant adversely by overt threat or attack, or can alleviate distress, usually in the case of the

Table 2. Effects of an Adult Social Structure on Peer Interaction

Direct (influence through actions towards individual infants)	Indirect (influence because of their presence or adult–adult interaction)
1. Alter general affective states	1. The choice of social partner (such as nonsibling peers)
2. Serve as alternative social objects	2. Conferral of social status (maternal dominance)
3. Restrict or expand the effective boundaries of the environment	3. Inhibit or facilitate differentiation of the social group
4. Inhibit or facilitate specific behaviors	

mother, by offering it "contact comfort." Mason (1965) compared the preferences of young chimpanzees to a costumed person who either played with them or held them. Arousal reduction through interaction with the "contact" figure would typically precede engagement with the "play" figure. In the peer–other adult female group, high amounts of distress accompanied a depression in a variety of behaviors. When mothers were present, contact with them reduced negative reactions and higher levels of positive peer interaction ensued. Thus, through direct behavioral intervention, adults can alter the infant's general affective state and consequently his willingness to interact with others.

Adults may also serve as alternative social objects in a variety of ways. Although absent in the current study, bonnet males in the field as well as the laboratory have been reported to engage in play with juveniles (Simonds, 1965). Similarly, adults participate in exploration and grooming activity with juveniles. In this vein, as Konner (1975) has pointed out, strict age-mate peer groups in primates are more an artifact of culture or laboratory manipulation than a naturally occurring phenomenon. Thus, under field conditions there is rarely the neat division that we have presented between a peer and an adult social structure. In fact, the majority of early social interactions in primates occur within the context of mixed-aged groups, with various forms of interaction occurring between subjects of differing ages.

The effective boundaries of the environment within which infants and juveniles can move are also directly affected by the presence or absence of adults. The older juveniles and adults in nature have learned the traditional pathways and feeding areas used by a troop, and it is these older animals that restrain, retrieve, and lead the younger subjects in moving through the environment. In our study, the presence of adults constrained the mobility of peers in the usage of the restricted laboratory environment. On the one hand, infants will stay near adults, in particular the mother, because they restrain them and also offer them protection. On the other hand, adults, in the limited space of the laboratory pen, will actively prevent infants from invading their personal space. It is common, for example, to see an adult threaten an infant that has just jumped on its head or tail, or has merely bounded close by in the midst of a vigorous play bout.

Finally, in terms of direct affects, adults may inhibit or facilitate specific behaviors of the infants. In the presence of adults, highly vigorous activities such as aggression, bounce display, mounting, and play were dramatically restricted; however, less active behaviors such as grooming and object exploration were not similarly affected. Since many of the highly vigorous activities are engaged in more by males, one could hypothesize that males would be more affected by the presence or absence of adults. This inhibition of male behavior may be even more pronounced in the presence of adult males in the group (a potentially important factor not as yet investigated). Such male-specific constraint may serve as the prelude to the relatively high levels of subadult male rejection from the troop that occurs in many macaque groups at the time the juvenile approaches puberty. Finally, it should be noted that peers can also influence specific behavior patterns of adults. The acquisition of new habits such as potato washing in Japanese macaques spread most rapidly among juveniles, and then only after a period of time did some adults adapt these behaviors (Itani, 1958).

The social context in which the adults are embedded will also influence peer interaction in a more indirect manner. Adults may influence peer interactions either through their presence alone or as a by-product of adult–adult interaction. The characteristic form of adult social relations can affect the range of infant behavior and bias the infant's choice of social partners. Thus, in species in which the adult structure well demarcates into genetic lineages, such as the pigtail macaque (Rosenblum, 1971), the peers with which an infant will interact will be strongly influenced by kinship factors, and a majority of interactions will involve sibling groups. On the other hand, in species within which lineage appears less important in adult interaction, such as the bonnet macaque, developing infants interact freely with both siblings and nonsibling peers. Similarly, within the various types of primate social groups, in which hierarchical factors are prominent, the status of an infant's mother in the adult structure will influence the possible range of behaviors in which her offspring can engage. The

success of an infant in winning competitive encounters, the choice of
sexual partners, and the infant's eventual position in the troop will all
be influenced by the mother's dominance status (Koford, 1963). Other
aspects of the adult structure may also influence peer interactions
indirectly. In squirrel monkeys, as discussed above, subadult peer
groups in which males and females intermingle freely in the absence of
adults rapidly showed a species-typical pattern of sexual segregation
when an adult structure was present.

In conclusion, social development in primates does not normally
occur within a social vacuum. In nature, peer relationships are enmeshed
in the total social network, which includes juveniles, subadults, and
adults, as well as peer groups. This total social structure directly and
indirectly influences the behavior of individual infants as well as the
nature of peer interaction as a whole. Further research on social development must weigh carefully the potentially distorting impact of an
environment from which adults are excluded and the role of particular
adult social structures in shaping the fabric of peer social relations.

ACKNOWLEDGMENT

We would like to thank Jayne S. Rand for her assistance in collecting
data and reading the manuscript.

REFERENCES

Coe, C. L., & Rosenblum, L.A. Sexual segregation and its ontogeny in squirrel monkey
    social structure. *Journal of Human Evolution*, 1974, 3, 551–561.
Freud, A., & Dunn, S. An experiment in group upbringing. In R. Eisler (Eds.), *The
    psychoanalytic study of the child* (Vol. 6). New York: International Universities Press,
    1951, 127–162.
Golding, W. *Lord of the Flies.* New York: Capricorn Books, 1959.
Itani, J. On the acquisition and propagation of a new food habit in the natural group of
    the Japanese monkey at Takasaki-Yama (English Summary). *Primates*, Vol. 1, No. 2,
    1958, 84–86.
Kaufman, I. C., & Rosenblum, L.A. A behavioral taxonomy for *Macaca nemestrina* and
    Macaca radiata based on longitudinal observations of family groups in the laboratory.
    Primates, Vol. 7, No. 2, 1966, 205–258.
Koford, C. B. Ranks of mothers and sons in bands of rhesus monkeys. *Science*, 1963, 141,
    356–357.
Konner, M. Relations among infants and juveniles in comparative perspective. In M. Lewis
    & L. A. Rosenblum (Eds.), *Friendship and peer relationships*. New York: John Wiley
    & Sons, 1975, 99–129.
Kurland, J. A. Kin selection in the Japanese monkey. In F. S. Szalay (Ed.), *Contributions to
    primatology* (Vol. 12). Basel: Karger, 1977.

Lamb, M. E. A re-examination of the infant social world. *Human Development*, 1977, *20*, 65–85.

Mason, W. Determinants of social behavior in young chimpanzees. In A. Schrier, H. Harlow, & F. Stollnitz (Eds.), *Behavior of nonhuman primates* (Vol. 2). New York: Academic Press, 1965, 335–365.

Rosenblum, L. A. Kinship interactions in pigtail and bonnet macaques. In J. Biegert (Ed.), *Proceedings of 3rd International Congress of Primatology, Zurich 1970*, (Vol. 3). Basel: Karger, 1971, 79–84.

Rosenblum, L. A., & Coe, C. L. The influence of social structure on squirrel monkey socialization. In S. Chevalier-Skolnikoff & F. E. Poirier (Eds.), *Primate bio-social development*. New York and London: Garland Publishing, Inc., 1977, 479–499.

Rosenblum, L. A., Kaufman, I.C., & Stynes, A. J. Individual distance in two species of macaque. *Journal of Animal Behavior*, 1964, *12*, 338–342.

Rosenblum, L. A., & Nadler, R.D. The ontogeny of sexual behavior in male bonnet macaques. In *Influences of hormones on the nervous sytem. Proceeding of the International Society of Psychoneuroendocrinology, Brooklyn, 1970*. Basel: Karger, 1971, 388–400.

Sade, D. S. Determinants of dominance in a group of free-ranging rhesus monkeys. In S. A. Altman (Ed.), *Social communication among primates*. Chicago: University of Chicago Press, 1967, 99–114.

Simonds, P. E. The bonnet macaque in South India. In I. Devore (Ed.), *Primate behavior*. New York: Holt, Rinehart and Winston, 1965, 175–196.

Stynes, A. J., Rosenblum, L. A., & Kaufman, I. C. The dominant male and behavior within heterospecific monkey groups. *Folia Primatologica*, 1968, *9*, 123–134.

Suomi, S. J. Differential development of various social relationships by rhesus monkey infants. In M. Lewis and L. Rosenblum (Eds.), *The child and its family*. New York: Plenum Press, 1979.

Wallen, K., Bielert, C., & Slimp, J. Foot clasp mounting in the prepubertal rhesus monkey: Social and hormonal influences. In S. Chevalier-Skolnikoff & F. E. Poirier (Eds.), *Primate bio-social development*. New York and London: Garland Publishing, Inc., 1977, 439–462.

Wilson, E. *Sociobiology*. Cambridge, Mass.: Belknap Press of Harvard University Press, 1975.

11

Differential Development of Various Social Relationships by Rhesus Monkey Infants

Stephen J. Suomi

Introduction

The social network of the infant is one of ever-expanding complexity in a number of respects. Far from being a tabula rasa, the typical neonate enters its postnatal world equipped with substantial perceptual capabilities and behavioral predispositions, and it rapidly becomes the focus of widespread social activity by those within its immediate environment. Few contemporary developmental researchers would argue with the view that in the succeeding weeks, months, and years, the infant's perceptual systems become considerably more sophisticated, its behavioral repertoire expands enormously, and its cognitive capabilities increase qualitatively as well as quantitatively. Those arguments that do exist tend to deal instead with the degree to which such advancement is a function of the "normal" maturation of the infant's brain and CNS, as opposed to a function of the infant's interaction with its social and nonsocial environment. Perhaps as a result of this continuing controversy, models of social development involving either one or, to a growing extent, both of these sets of factors have become increasingly sophisticated in recent years (e.g., Sameroff, 1975).

STEPHEN J. SUOMI • Psychology Department, University of Wisconsin, Madison, Wisconsin 53706. The research described in this chapter was supported in part by USPHS Grant number MH–11894 from the National Institute of Mental Health and by the Grant Foundation.

Consideration of the infant's social world has likewise tended toward greater complexity. In previous years both theoretical and empirical studies of infant social behavior focused almost exclusively on interactions with the mother or mother "substitute." This emphasis seemed justified by the fact that in most mammals, mothers are the primary (and often exclusive) caretakers of neonates. Hence, an infant's initial social encounters appeared most likely to involve its mother, rather than any other individual in its social environment. Indeed, some investigators regarded the infant's relationship with its mother as the prototype for most, if not all, future social relationships that would be developed, further justifying intensive studies of mother–infant interactions. Such studies, representing fields as diverse as ethology, psychoanalysis, and behaviorally oriented experimental psychology, yielded detailed and often elegant accounts of emerging relationships between mothers and infants.

During the past decade, however, investigators have become increasingly aware of the fact that the social world of the developing infant includes other individuals besides its mother and that its relationships with at least some of these individuals may be substantially different from that with its mother. Among the first in recent years to emphasize this point were Harlow and his co-workers, working with rhesus monkeys. These researchers documented the infant monkey's growing relationship with its peers as an important factor in its social development. Contemporary investigations of the social activities of human infants have focused on interactions with peers, fathers, siblings, and even strangers. The contents of this volume give ample testimony to the fact that the social network of the maturing infant can be complex indeed.

Acknowledging that infants ordinarily encounter and interact with other individuals besides their mothers from early in life is one thing; specifying the nature of such relationships and determining the extent to which they might contribute to the infant's emerging social capabilities is quite another. One might begin by detailing the specific behavior patterns that constitute the interactions between the infant and the various individuals that are in its social network, as well as measuring the relative amount of time the infant spends in interactions with each individual or class of individuals, e.g., mothers or peers. Of course, it is possible to describe each set of interactions in considerably greater detail, such as specifying the patterns or sequences of the component behaviors characterizing each set of interactions. Alternatively, one might consider different sorts of questions regarding such interactions: Does the infant tend to initiate more interactions than its partner? Are more than one individual involved in any given interaction? Or, are changes that develop over repeated interactions due more to changes in the infant's behavior than to those of its partner?

At any rate, by characterizing the various interactions that the infant has with those around it, one can develop an empirical basis for describing the various social relationships, i.e., the products of those sets of interactions (Hinde, 1976a), that the infant develops with each of the individuals that constitute its social network. One can then begin to determine to what extent the various social relationships that the infant develops differ from one another, and if so, what effect each relationship may have on the infant's emerging social repertoire. Indeed, Lewis and Feiring (this volume) have argued that in order to understand the processes that are important in the socialization of the infant, one should begin by establishing a taxonomy of not only the identity of the various individuals that make up the infant's social network but also the various social roles that each individual provides for the infant. This, of course, becomes an empirical, matter.

To date, such a taxonomy has not been completely constructed for human infants. While individual relationships, e.g., those between mothers and infants or those between fathers and infants, have been examined in detail in numerous studies, such studies have not simultaneously considered *all* of the relationships encountered by any infant in its social network. Moreover, those relationships that are examined are usually viewed only in a few contexts, e.g., in the home or in a contrived laboratory setting. Of course, this state of affairs is quite understandable, given that infants are hardly "captive" subjects (except, perhaps, those in institutions), making a complete accounting of all forms of interaction with all individuals across all situations in which such interactions take place virtually impossible from a purely practical standpoint.

However, compiling such a taxonomy for a member of a nonhuman primate species living within a laboratory setting is considerably more feasible. Because such subjects can be raised in "captive" environments in which all social interactions can be monitored, at least in theory, as often and as completely as an experimenter desires, a relatively complete "ethogram" can be constructed for a developing infant. At the very least, principles that might be applied to consideration of the human infant's social network can be developed and tested through careful, detailed study of such captive nonhuman primate infants (Harlow, Gluck, & Suomi, 1972; Hinde, 1976b).

Unfortunately, to date most nonhuman primate studies of this sort have chosen to focus exclusively on a single type of social relationship developed by the infant, e.g., with its mother (Hinde & White, 1974; Dienske & Metz, 1977), with its father (Redican, 1978; Suomi, 1977), or with peers (Chamove, Harlow, & Rosenblum, 1973, Ruppenthal, Harlow, Eisele, Harlow, & Suomi, 1974), rather than simultaneously considering all the relationships entered into by the maturing infant. In this respect they have been similar to the above-described studies of human infant social relationships. As a result, it has been impossible to make direct comparisons between relationships involving the infant regarding such factors as the particular behavior patterns utilized, relative time committed to each relationship, or relative form and rate of change in the dynamics of the relationship. Moreover, such limited approaches have largely precluded meaningful consideration of how changes in one relationship might affect the infant's participation in other social relationships. One undesirable side-effect has been that many authors, either implicitly or explicitly (e.g., Harlow, 1969) have pitted one type of relationship against another in terms of which is "more important" for the infant, rather than considering the ways in which they might complement or interact with one another in contributing to the infant's overall social competency.

In view of these facts, for the past several years I have been conducting detailed longitudinal studies of rhesus monkey infants growing up in a variety of complex social groups. Each infant is observed several times each week, and during each observation period all of the infant's interactions with each member of its social group are sequentially recorded. In the pages that follow, I will present some of these data in order to address the following issues regarding the social relationships that young rhesus monkeys develop during their first two years of life:

1. To what extent do different behavior patterns characterize the infant's different social relationships?
2. Does the distribution of these behavior patterns change as the infant grows older, and if so, are such changes similar or parallel across its various social relationships?
3. To what degree do characteristics of each form of social relationship vary across different social environments, i.e., are some relationships more influenced by certain factors in the environment than are others?

SUBJECTS, SOCIAL ENVIRONMENT, AND DATA COLLECTION PROCEDURES

Most of the data to be presented were collected on rhesus monkeys living in nuclear family units, artificial laboratory apparatuses each containing four adult male–female pairs and their various offspring. A nuclear family unit is illustrated in Figure 1, and a more detailed description can be found in Harlow (1971). As shown in the figure, each

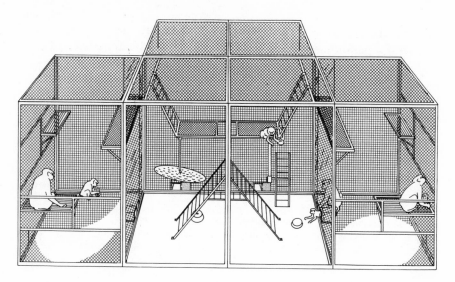

——— = 1 Foot

FIG. 1. Nuclear-family apparatus. Adult male–female pairs are confined to outer living cages, but infants have access to central play area and to all living cages via the connecting tunnels.

adult pair was confined to one of four 1.3 × 1.3 × 2m living cages that surrounded a 2.6 × 2.6 × 2m play area. The only access to the play area from the living cages was through tunnels large enough for infants but too small for adults to squeeze through. Thus, unlike their parents, the infants living in nuclear family units had access to all portions of the apparatus and therefore they could interact with any other monkey in the unit at any time they pleased. Further, these infants could escape or avoid interactions with any adults by simply staying out of those animals' living units.

Behavioral data gathered on 12 infants, 6 males and 6 females reared from birth in these nuclear family units, comprised the primary data base for the discussion that follows. These data were collected during 5-minute observations of each infant 4 days each week for the first 24 months of its life. During each observational session the frequency and sequence of all behaviors that were initiated by the subject, as well as those directed toward the subject by others in its social group, were recorded by two trained observers employing an exhaustive category observational scoring system. In all social interactions involving the focal subject, the identities of the participants were recorded and all of their behavioral responses coded. Details of this observational scoring system, including operational definitions of the behavioral categories and classification of response patterns, are presented in Table 1.

TABLE 1.   Operational Definitions of Categories of Initiates and Response
Patterns

Categories of Initiates

Contact: Any ventrally oriented contact or behavior that serves to maintain contact between any two animals. Motor patterns include nipple contacts, clinging, clasping, embracing, and cradling.

Protection: Movement toward the infant by the mother or the father (or vice versa) caused by some interference on the part of other animals or an extraneous source. Motor patterns include retrieval, running toward another while showing signs of fear, restraint.

Groom-exploration: Manipulatory inspection of the fur of another animal other than while in maternal contact.

Huddle-sit: Moving to and remaining within 6 inches of another animal. Motor patterns include dorsal or lateral surface contact, proximity with orientation toward another animal.

Play: Animated movements, gestures, facial expressions, and contacts of varying intensity and duration directed toward another subject. Motor patterns include low-intensity, mouth-open "threat" face, cuffing, "boxing," wrestling, chasing, running from, carom movements in response to, clasp-pulling, or nipping another animal.

Sex: Male or female sex patterns, movements, and postures directed at another animal. Motor patterns include hindquarter positioning, pelvic thrusting, hindquarter posturing, foot clasping.

Hostility: Intense and protracted threatening, displays, or brief contactual assertions. Motor patterns include retracted threat face, "hard" cuffing, single bite or slap, cage shaking, barking.

Defense: Hostile or aggressive behaviors directed at the protagonist of an interaction involving a third subject.

Categories of Response

Reciprocate: Response in kind and context to the behavior initiated by another animal (as acceptance in the case of a maternal context).

Ignore–accept: No response or attention directed at a subject initiating an interaction.

Reject–withdraw: Any behavioral pattern or action that seeks to terminate or restrict the initiations of another subject; motor patterns include movement away from (other than in play context), maternal punishing.

Fear–submit: Assumption of a "frozen" posture of fear grimacing in response to the initiations of another subject.

GENERAL FINDINGS

Preliminary analyses of these data indicated that major differences in frequency of occurrence among categories of behaviors and in target distribution were displayed by both male and female infants. Furthermore, these levels and targets changed substantially during the first two years of the subjects' lives. Figure 2 presents behavioral profiles of initiations by male and female infants during their first four months of life (upper left panel), contrasted with comparable profiles during months 21–24 (upper right panel).

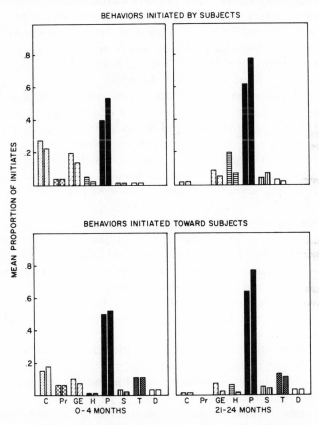

FIG. 2. Proportional distribution of categories of initiates by infants toward group members when 1–4 months old (upper left panel) and when 21–24 months old (upper right panel); proportional distribution of categories of behaviors directed by group members toward infants when 1–4 months old (lower left panel) and when 21–24 months old (lower right panel). Left bar of each pair represents female subjects; right bar represents male subjects. C = contact, Pr = protect, GE = groom-explore, H = huddle-sit, P = play, S = sex, T = threat-aggression, and D = defend.

During their first four months, play was the predominant behavior for both male and female infants, followed by contact and groom-explore; the remaining categories accounted for less than 10% of the subjects' social initiations. Sizable sex differences were evident for play and groom-explore behaviors, while lesser sex differences were found for contact and huddle-sit categories. By months 21–24, the proportion of both male and female initiates encompassed by play increased substantially. Groom-explore levels displayed corresponding declines, while contact and protect initiates all but ceased entirely. Significant increases over four-month levels were found in huddle-sit, sex, and threat-aggression categories. Most of the sex differences apparent earlier in life were exaggerated by 21–24 months in these subjects. Such developmental changes in behavior profiles are consistent with most previous reports of macaque social development in laboratory settings, e.g., Hansen, (1966), Hinde and Spencer-Booth (1967), and in feral environments, e.g., Kaufmann (1966), Lindburg (1973).

Summary proportions of behavioral categories directed *by* group members *toward* infants during months 1–4 and during months 21–24 are presented in the lower left and lower right panels of Figure 2, respectively. As was the case for initiates by infants, the predominant behavior directed toward infants during their first four months of life was social play, but levels of contact and groom-explore were lower and levels of threat-aggression were substantially higher. Moreover, there were no major differences in levels of any behavior directed toward male versus female infants. By the time the infants were 21–24 months of age, the relative amount of play directed toward them had increased substantially, with higher levels directed toward males than females. In contrast, females were the target of more grooming and huddling activities. Contact and protection behaviors were no longer being directed toward these subjects, while proportions for the remaining categories were basically unchanged from the levels recorded when the infants were 1–4 months old.

Thus, during the first two years of life, these infants exhibited substantial changes in the proportional distribution of their behavioral initiates, as well as in the proportional distribution of behaviors directed toward them by other monkeys in the group. In general, sex differences in the behavioral repertoires of the infants were of greater magnitude than were sex differences in proportions of behaviors directed toward them throughout the two-year observation period.

Figure 3 presents the distribution of initiates by infants according to the identity of the targets (mother, father, etc.) at 1–4 months of age (upper left panel) and at 21–24 months of age (upper right panel). It also presents the relative frequencies of behaviors directed toward the infants

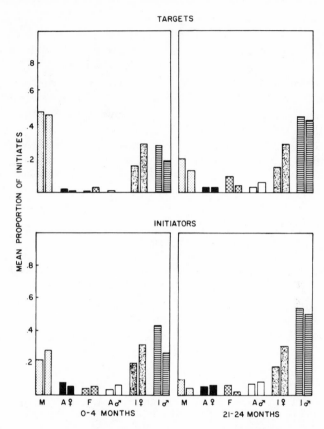

Fig. 3. Proportions of total initiates directed toward each class of group member by infants when 1–4 months old (upper left panel) and when 21–24 months old (upper right panel); proportions of total initiates by each class of group member toward infants when 1–4 months old (lower left panel) and when 21–24 months old (lower right panel). M = mothers, A ♀ = other adult females, F = fathers, A ♂ = other adult males, I ♀ = female peers, and I ♂ = male peers. Sex of subject code same as in Figure 2.

by various members of the social group during the same two time periods (lower panels). It is clear from the figure that the infants were relatively selective toward whom they directed their behaviors, and it is equally clear that some members of their group directed more activities toward them than did others. Furthermore, both sets of distributions changed considerably during the period of study.

Specifically, during their first four months of life infants of both sexes directed over half of their total initiates toward their mothers and virtually all of the rest of their initiates toward peers. Very few behaviors were directed toward fathers or other adults of either sex. By the time the infants were 21–24 months old, their initiates toward their mothers had dropped by more than 50% for females and 65% for males. Most of the "slack" was taken up by increased amounts of activity directed toward all other classes of social objects, except female peers. Similar but even more dramatic changes over this two-year period were evident in the relative proportions of activities directed toward infants by various members of the social units. For example, by the time they were 21–24 months old, male subjects were the targets of fewer initiates from their mothers than from all other classes of individuals except fathers.

The data presented in Figures 2 and 3 clearly show that as they grew older these rhesus monkey infants changed both their behavioral repertoires and the degree to which they interacted with various individuals in their social unit. Moreover, there were largely parallel changes both in the types of social activities and in the sources of social activities directed toward the infants as they matured. Formal statistical analyses of the data corroborate these points. ANOVAs were performed for each category of behavior initiated by the subjects, as well as for each category of behavior directed toward the subjects. In each ANOVA, sex of subject was an independent variable, and 4-month time periods and class of target (initiator)—mother, father, other adult females, other adult males, female peers, and male peers— were repeated measures. Significant (p < .05) time block and target (initiator) main effects were disclosed for 15 of the 16 analyses. Significant time block × target (initiator) interactions were found in 14 of the 16 analyses. By way of comparison, significant sex of subject main effects were obtained in only five analyses, while significant interactions involving this variable occurred in eight analyses.

Such findings lend considerable credence to the observation that both the relative incidence of behaviors and the distribution of these behaviors toward various targets (and by various initiators toward the subjects) were undergoing major changes as the infants grew older. For these reasons, it was decided to examine in greater detail the behavioral profiles of activities directed by subjects toward each class of social object in the group, as well as profiles of behaviors initiated toward the subjects by these various classes of social partners.

PROFILES OF SOCIAL RELATIONSHIPS: DESCRIPTIONS AND DEVELOPMENTAL CHANGES

Figure 4 presents the proportional distributions for categories of behaviors initiated by male and female subjects during their first four months toward their mothers, fathers, other adult females, other adult males, female peers, and male peers, respectively. It can be clearly seen

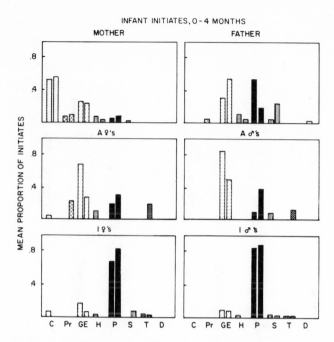

INFANT INITIATES, 0 - 4 MONTHS

Fig. 4. Proportional distribution of categories of initiates toward each class of group member by infants when 1–4 months of age. Category and sex of subject code same as in Figure 2; target code same as in Figure 3.

from the figure that profiles differed considerably across target type. For example, interactions with mothers were characterized by high proportions of contact initiates and lower proportions of play initiates than displayed toward any other animals in the group. In contrast, infants initiated relatively few behaviors *except* play toward peers of both sexes. In addition, there were major differences between male and female infants with respect to initiates toward fathers, other adult females, and other adult males, but there were relatively small sex differences with respect to initiates toward female peers and no significant sex differences in initiates toward mothers and male peers. It is obvious that by as early as four months of age, both male and female infants were displaying quite different patterns of initiates, depending on whom they were interacting with.

Proportional distributions of behaviors directed toward infants during the same time period by each class of group members are presented in Figure 5. As was the case for initiates by infants, the various classes of monkeys differed considerably from each other in how they directed their activities toward infants. For example, the great

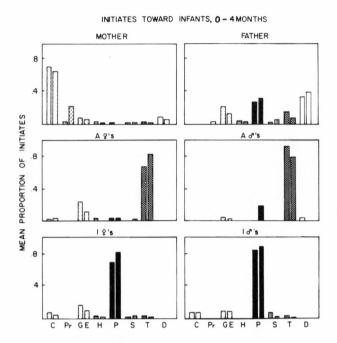

FIG. 5. Proportional distributions of categories of initiates toward 1–4 month-old infants by each class of group member. Category and sex of subject code same as in Figure 2; initiator code same as in Figure 3.

majority of initiates by mothers were of a contact nature, most initiates by peers consisted of social play, while the most common behaviors directed toward infants by other adults of both sexes were threat and aggression. In contrast, fathers appeared to defend, play with, and groom their offspring with approximately equal frequency.

The findings presented in these two figures strongly suggest that very early in life these infant rhesus monkeys were well on their way toward establishing quite different social relationships with various members of their social group. This is reflected not only in terms of the relative amount of time they spent with various individuals, but also with respect to the specific behaviors they tended to direct toward various group members, and vice versa. During succeeding months these relationships did not remain static. However, as will be evident from the analysis that follows, they did not all change to the same extent, or even in similar directions.

Figure 6 presents the proportional distributions of behaviors initiated toward each class of group member by the subjects when 21–24 months of age. Major changes from patterns exhibited during their first four months were evident for initiates directed toward mothers, other adult females, other adult males, and (for male subjects) fathers. In contrast, the proportional distributions of behaviors directed toward male and female peers were virtually unchanged from previous levels. Changes for specific categories within specific relationships will not be detailed here. However, it is interesting to note a certain convergence in the manner in which the infants, particularly male infants, apportioned their activities toward other adult females and female peers, and toward other adult males and male peers, as they grew older.

Figure 7 presents the proportional distribution of behaviors directed toward infants by each class of group member when the infants were 21–24 months old. A comparison with these sets of proportions with those displayed in Figure 5 indicates differential changes, depending on the relationship examined. For example, mothers and fathers changed their patterns of initiates toward offspring of both sexes to an enormous extent, as did adult males toward nonoffspring male infants. In contrast, adult females, male peers, and female peers apportioned their activities toward 21–24 month old infants in much the same fashion as they did

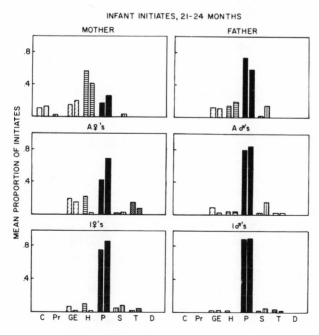

FIG. 6. Proportional distributions of categories of initiates toward each class of group member by infants when 21–24 months old. Category and sex of subject code same as in Figure 2; target code same as in Figure 3.

INITIATES TOWARD INFANTS, 21-24 MONTHS

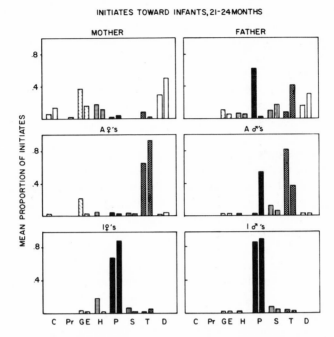

FIG. 7. Proportional distributions of categories of initiates toward 21–24-months infants by each class of group member. Category and sex of subject code same as in Figure 2; initiator code same as in Figure 3.

when the infants were only 1–4 months of age. Again, I will not dwell on changes in particular behavior patterns within specific relationships, except to point out that close examination of many of these changes leads to rather interesting speculations regarding the development of different social relationships.

The data presented thus far indicate that not only are very young monkeys capable of forming qualitatively different, behaviorally complex social relationships with different members of their social group, but also that the relationships that are established can change differentially as the animals grow older. The degree and direction of change depend on the particular relationship in question. Furthermore, the various changes in the form of relationships that do occur are not solely dependent on changes in the patterns of initiates by the infants, or in changes in activities directed toward them by their partner in each relationship, but rather reflect changes on the part of both participants. In this respect, it is clearly an oversimplification to talk about "effects produced by a changing social environment" or "maturational changes displayed by an infant in a constant social environment," even though the same particular individuals make up the social environment. Instead, more complex transactional models, e.g., Sameroff (1975), appear to be more appropriate for describing the present situation.

Stability of Different Social Relationships

Given the fact that different changes in various social relationships did occur for the present subjects during their first two years, one can ask whether these changes occurred at the same rate or took place within similar chronological periods across the various relationships. One way to address this issue is to examine the chronological points at which each behavior initiated by an infant (or toward an infant) within a given relationship became stable with respect to its relative frequency of occurrence in the individual's repertoire. "Stabilization points" for various behaviors could then be compared across relationships.

This procedure was carried out on the present data set. Proportions of total initiates by subjects toward each class of group member (and by each class of group member toward subjects) were calculated for each behavioral category over four-month blocks comprising the subjects' first two years of life. The "stabilization point" for each behavior was operationally defined as the first four-month period in which the proportion of total initiates for that behavior did not differ significantly from the proportion calculated for that category *during any succeeding four-month period*, as determined by Fisher's Exact Test ($p < .01$).

Figure 8 presents stability points for each category of initiates within each relationship for male and female subjects, while Figure 9 presents comparable stability points for behaviors directed toward male and female infants by each class of group member. The degree and direction of change for each category prior to reaching stability is also illustrated in the two figures. Careful examination and comparison of the data illustrated in these figures inevitably lead to at least four major conclusions.

First, there existed a wide range of variability with respect to distributions of stability points across all categories of initiates toward a given class of social partner by infants, and vice versa. For some sets of interactions, e.g., male infant initiates toward fathers or toward other adult males, the chronological points of stability were the same for all behaviors, e.g., 5–8 months. For other sets of interactions, e.g., male infant initiates toward mothers or toward other adult females, different categories stabilized at different chronological points. Consequently, the point at which *all* categories of initiates toward a given class of social partner had become stable also varied across the different relationships that male and female infants formed with members of their social group.

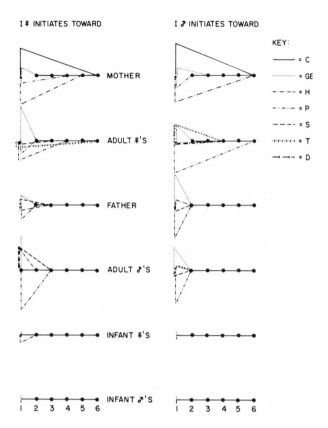

FIG. 8. Stabilization points for initiates by female infants (left half) and male infants (right half) toward each class of group member. Each line represents a separate category; see key for code. Stability occurs at the point where category line meets the horizontal axis. Direction of change is indicated by whether line drops to the horizontal (a decrease) or rises to the horizontal (an increase). Magnitude of change indicated by vertical distance from point 1. Points 1,2,3,4,5, and 6 refer to 1–4, 5–8, 9–12, 13–16, 17–20, and 21–24 months of age, respectively.

A related point finding was that specific categories of initiates by male and female infants stabilized at widely varying points across relationships, depending on the category examined. For example, groom-explore initiates by male infants stabilized at 1–4 months in interactions with male and female peers, at 5–8 months in interactions with fathers and other adults of both sexes, and at 9–12 months for interactions with mothers. Play initiates by male infants stabilized at 1–4 months for interactions with male and female peers, at 5–8 months for interactions with mothers, fathers, and other adult females, but were still increasing proportionally at 21–24 months for interactions with other adult males. Similar findings existed for initiations by other group members toward male and female infants. Thus, there was no "standard" chronological point at which specific categories of initiates tended to stabilize independent of the set of partners involved. Instead, the point of stabilization for a given category of initiates was dependent on the particular relationship examined.

A third point is that there existed a wide range of sex differences in patterns of stabilization for initiates by male and female infants, as well as for initiates directed toward these infants. For example, sex differences between infants in distributions of stabilization points for initiates toward male peers were nonexistent for all categories, those for initiates toward mothers were moderate, while those for initiates toward adult females existed for virtually every category examined.

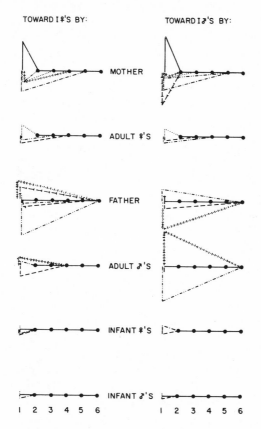

FIG. 9. Stability points for initiates by each class of group member toward female (left half) and male (right half) infants. Legend coding same as in Figure 8.

Finally, even a casual comparison of Figure 8 with Figure 9 reveals that for some of the relationships, the points at which the proportions of specific categories stabilized for infant initiates coincided exactly with the stabilization points for the same categories initiated toward the infants by those very same group members. In other words, there was symmetry with respect to stabilization points for each category of initiates by both partners in the relationship. This was largely the case for relationships between infants of both sexes. For other relationships, e.g., those between male infants and their fathers, the point at which a given category of initiate by the infant stabilized tended to be quite different from the point at which the same category of initiate by the partner stabilized, i.e., the relationship was asymmetric with respect to stabilization points.

The various findings presented thus far indicate that infant monkeys reared in nuclear-family environments develop relationships with various group members that initially are characterized by different overall frequencies of initiations and involve different distributions for various categories of behavior, depending on the particular relationship examined. Furthermore, as the infants grow older, these relationships change to different degrees, and at varying rates, again depending on the particular relationship under examination. On the basis of the present data, it would appear to be a mistake to characterize a general pattern of social development by young rhesus monkeys based solely on examination of a single type of social relationship, e.g., that with mother or that with peers. Clearly, such characterizations are highly dependent on the particular class of social relationship examined, at least with respect to the present data set.

Variability of Relationships across Social Environments

An important question that logically follows from the above conclusions is to what degree the above findings regarding particular social relationships generalize to rhesus monkey infants reared in other social environments. In other words, do monkeys raised in large pens lacking internal cage restrictions, or on a provisioned island, or in a forest area in India, develop similar relationships with their mothers, with peers, etc., as did those reared in highly artificial laboratory "nuclear families"? This question will be briefly examined by comparing data gathered on two sets of infants reared in groups of similar social composition but residing in different physical environments.

One set of infants was raised in a group containing their mothers and fathers housed in a nuclear-family apparatus identical to those described previously. The second set of infants was likewise raised in a group with mothers and fathers, but all these monkeys were housed in a 2.5 × 2.5 × 2 m pen, with no internal housing restrictions. The adults in this pen group had unrestricted physical access to all other adults and all other infants, whereas in the nuclear-family environment each adult could only interact physically with its mate and with any infant that happened to enter its living cage. On the other hand, nuclear-family infants had a play area where they could avoid interactions with any adults, including their parents, whereas pen-reared infants were always within the potential reach of every adult male and female in the group.

Data were collected on these two groups of subjects using the same scoring system and observation schedule as was employed for the data presented in the previous sections. For the purpose of simplicity, only data collected for each infant when it was 20 to 26 weeks of age will be presented in the analysis that follows, although the major points to be made are characteristic of the entire longitudinal data set.

Comparison of the distribution of total initiates by infants toward various group members (and vice versa) in the two environments revealed that overall frequencies of mother–infant interactions were slightly higher in the pen than the nuclear family. This result was largely due to higher levels of mother-directed initiates by pen infants; frequencies of initiates by mothers toward infants did not differ between the two environments. On the other hand, huge differences between pen- and nuclear-family reared infants were found with respect to frequencies of interactions with other infants and with other male and female adults (because of the small n's involved, male and female infants were lumped into a single comparison class, as were fathers and other adult males). Nuclear-family infants had much higher frequencies of initiates, both toward and from peers, whereas pen-living infants had much higher levels of initiates both toward and from other adult females and other adult males.

Examination of frequency distributions for categories of initiates toward (and from) each class of social stimuli reveals pen–nuclear family differences that reflect the magnitude of the above differences. Figure 10 presents these distributions for categories of infant initiates toward mothers, and by mothers toward infants, in the nuclear-family and pen environments. The figure also presents the distribution of response patterns to each of these initiates. It is apparent that, proportionally speaking, the patterns of initiates by infants toward mothers, and by mothers toward infants, were virtually identical in the two living environments. Moreover, the distributions of maternal response to each category of infant initiates, and of infant responses to initiates by mothers, were highly similar in both situations. Thus, at least as indexed by the above measures, the variability in mother–infant relationships across the two living environments was exceedingly small.

Figures 11, 12, and 13 present comparable distributions of initiates

MOTHER-INFANT RELATIONSHIPS

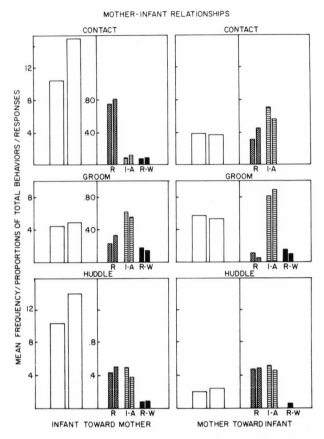

FIG. 10. Frequencies of selected categories of initiates, and associated proportions of response patterns by targets, for initiates by infants toward mothers (left half) and by mothers toward infants (right half). Left bar of each pair represents nuclear family levels; right bar represents pen levels. Code for response patterns is R = reciprocate, I-A = ignore or passively accept, R-W = reject or withdraw, and F = fear–disturbance reaction.

and associated response patterns that characterized the interactions of infants with peers, other adult females, and adult males in the nuclear-family and pen environments, respectively. In contrast to nuclear-family reared infants, pen infants' relationships with peers were more likely to involve huddling behaviors than play activity. Moreover, these infants exhibited virtually no sexual posturing or threats in peer interactions, whereas the nuclear-family infants displayed peer interaction patterns highly consistent with those described in the previous sample. Similarly, there were major differences between nuclear-family and pen-reared infants in patterns of interactions with adult males and other adult females. Thus, in contrast to the findings regarding mother–infant relationships, there existed considerable variability across the two environments with respect to relationships between infants and other members of their social group, even though the social composition of the two groups was identical with respect to number and age–sex distribution of members.

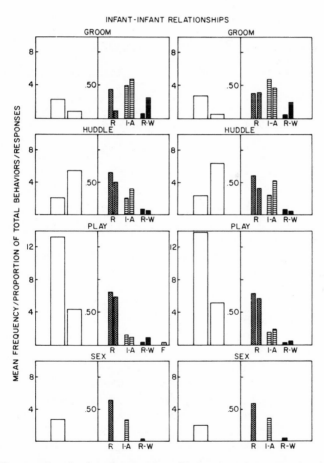

FIG. 11. Frequencies of selected categories of initiates and associated proportions of responses by targets for initiates, by infants toward peers (left half) and by peers towards infants (right half). Legend coding same as in Figure 10.

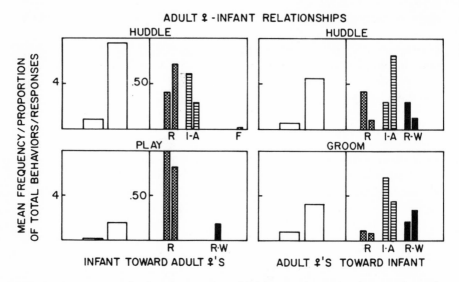

FIG. 12. Frequencies of selected categories of initiates and associated proportions of responses, for initiates by infants towards other adult females (left half) and by other adult females toward infants (right half). Legend coding same as in Figure 10.

DISCUSSION

The data presented in this chapter were collected in order to describe the social network of rhesus monkey infants reared in laboratory environments that contained parents, peers, and other adults. When reared in such settings these monkey infants rapidly established different types of relationships, as characterized by the frequencies and forms of the component behavior interchanges, with different members of their social group. These various relationships changed over the next two years, but they changed to different degrees at different rates and in different directions, depending on the specific relationship examined. Moreover, there was differential variability across social-living environments in the behavioral basis of different classes of social relationships, e.g., those involving mothers or those involving peers. It is difficult to escape the conclusion that the dynamics of social development in these group-living rhesus monkey infants were far from simple.

Certain cautions should be expressed with respect to the potential implications and generality of these findings. First, the particular dependent measures used in these studies represented relatively gross indices of interactions, in that they involved only frequencies of initiates and (in the cross-sectional data) first order (lag-1) response patterns.

More complicated derived measures that might have presented more complete descriptions of the emerging relationships, e.g., calculations of lengths of interactive bouts or use of higher-order lag analyses, were not employed. Second, the proportional distributions that were presented represented overall group levels, rather than proportions for individual subjects. Third, the social environments in which the infants were reared were clearly artificial, with no direct counterpart to be found within the rhesus monkey's wide range of natural habitats. Finally, the comparisons presented between nuclear-family and pen-reared infants were cross-sectional rather than longitudinal in nature.

Nevertheless, the findings that rhesus monkey infants display differential development of various social relationships are interesting in several respects. First, they demonstrate quite clearly that the relationships developed by infants with mothers are hardly representative of the relationships that are established with other members of their social group. These latter relationships can be distinguished in terms of characteristic interaction patterns within the first few months of life; they subsequently change at different rates and in different directions

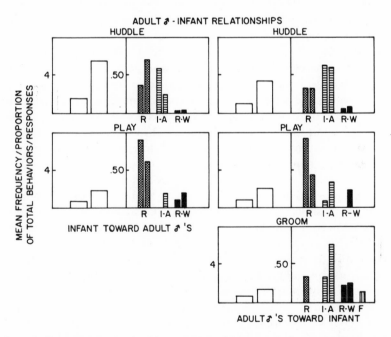

FIG. 13. Frequencies of selected categories of initiates and associated proportions of responses, for initiates by infants toward adult males (left half) and by adult males toward infants (right half). Legend coding same as Figure 10.

and are probably more variable across different environments than are the relationships established with mothers. At the very least, such findings indicate that infants respond selectively to different aspects of their social environment from very early in life. Taking these data at face value, one might hypothesize that different individuals in an infant's social network might well fulfill different roles in the process of socialization. For example, mothers might serve primarily as caretakers, peers might serve as individuals with whom emerging social behavior patterns can be practiced and perfected, while other adults might serve both as social models and as "enforcers" of group "rules." If so, it is conceivable that the infant's capability to establish such different relationships may be, at least in part, the product of its evolutionary history.

The finding that interactions between infants and various classes of conspecifics differed across the nuclear-family and pen environments, even though the age–sex compositions of the two groups were comparable, is also suggestive in several respects.

First, the data clearly show that differences in mother–infant relationships in the two environments were quite small relative to differences in other social relationships formed by the infants. It can be argued that infants have certain caretaking requirements that must be provided for to insure their survival, no matter what environment they are raised in. It may well be that monkey mothers have evolved to interact with offspring in ways that satisfy such caretaking requirements independent of other elements in the environment; hence, one would expect variability in maternal behavior, at least in the infant's initial months of life, to be relatively small across different environments. In this respect, the present findings are consistent with those of previous studies, e.g., Suomi (1976). If the function of other social relationships is to shape the infant's emerging repertoire toward group norms, one would then expect infants to be responsive to variability in the social stimulation they receive from others in the group. The present data support such a prediction. If those findings generalize to other environments and/or to other species, one might well expect to find different "roles" provided for infants by group members that are representative of the particular social structure of the group under study.

The finding that different interaction patterns characterize different social relationships suggests that future experimental attempts to shape the social behavior of individuals by manipulating the social environment might well consider identifying those relationships in which the particular behavior patterns of interest are most prominent. For example, if one is interested in modifying contact behavior, he or she should concentrate on mother–infant interactions; if the interest lies in play behaviors, peer relationships would seem most ripe for modification.

Similar strategies might be profitably applied to attempts to identify cognitive and/or physiological concomitants of the development of particular behavior patterns by young primates.

Finally, what are the implications of these findings for understanding the social network of the human infant? One is clearly on dangerous ground when entertaining direct analogies between specific monkey findings and human social developmental phenomena, particularly given the cautions previously aired. At the very least there are substantial differences in the emerging behavioral repertoires and cognitive capabilities of human and monkey infants, as well as substantial differences between those in their respective social worlds. Nevertheless, investigators of human social ontogeny might well keep in mind the enormous complexity that can exist in monkey social networks when formulating strategies for study of the development of social relationships in human infants. The message is that simplistic models that attempt to deal with highly complex phenomena of this nature may well lead to inadequate and/or inaccurate understanding of the developmental processes involved.

ACKNOWLEDGMENTS

Much of this chapter was written while the author was a Visiting Scientist at the Zentrum für interdisziplinäre Forschung, Universität Bielefeld, Bielefeld, West Germany. The longitudinal data were collected by C. D. Eisele and S. G. Chapman and the cross-sectional data by L. Golopol. Special thanks are expressed to C. Fulland for final preparation of the manuscript.

REFERENCES

Chamove, A. S., Rosenblum, L. A., & Harlow, H. F. Monkeys (*Macaca mulatta*) raised only with peers: A pilot study. *Animal Behaviour*, 1973, *21*, 316–325.

Dienske, H., & Metz, H. A. J. Mother–infant body contact in macaques. A time interval analysis. *Biology of Behaviour*, 1977, *2*, 3–37.

Hansen, E. W. The development of maternal and infant behavior in the rhesus monkey. *Behaviour*, 1966, *27*, 107–149.

Harlow, H. F. Age-mate or peer affectional system. In D. S. Lehrman, R. A. Hinde, & E. Shaw (Eds.), *Advances in the study of behavior*, (Vol. 2). New York: Academic Press, 1969.

Harlow, H. F., Gluck, J. P., & Suomi, S. J. Generalization of behavioral data between nonhuman and human animals. *American Psychologist*, 1972, *27*, 709–716.

Harlow, M. K. Nuclear family apparatus. *Behavior Research Methods and Instrumentation*, 1971, *3*, 301–304.

Hinde, R. A. On describing relationships. *Journal of Child Psychology and Psychiatry,* 1976a, *17,* 1–19.

Hinde, R. A. Use of similarities and differences in comparative psychology. In G. Serban & A. Kling (Eds.), *Animal models of human psychobiology.* New York: Plenum, 1976b.

Hinde, R. A., & Spencer-Booth, Y. The behaviour of socially living monkeys in their first two and a half years. *Animal Behaviour,* 1967, *15,* 169–196.

Hinde, R.A., & White, L. E. Dynamics of a relationship: Rhesus mother–infant ventro – ventro contact. *Journal of Comparative and Physiological Psychology,* 1974, *86,* 8–23.

Kaufmann, J. H. Behavior of infant rhesus monkeys and their mothers in a free ranging band. *Zoologica,* 1966, *51,* 17–28.

Lindburg, D. G. The rhesus monkey in North India: An ecological and behavioral study. In L. A. Rosenblum (Ed.), *Primate behavior* (Vol. 2). New York: Academic Press, 1973.

Redican, W. K. Adult male–infant relations in captive rhesus monkeys. In D. Chivers (Ed.), *Proceedings of the Sixth International Congress of Primatology,* Vol. 1: Behaviour. New York: Academic Press, 1978.

Ruppenthal, G. C., Harlow, M. K., Eisele, C. D., Harlow, H. F., & Suomi, S. J. Development of peer interactions of monkeys reared in a nuclear-family environment. *Child Development,* 1974, *45,* 670–682.

Sameroff, A. J. Early influences on development: Fact or fancy? *Merrill-Palmer Quarterly,* 1975, *21,* 267–294.

Suomi, S. J. Mechanisms underlying social developments: A reexamination of mother–infant interactions in monkeys. In A. Pick (Ed.), *Minnesota symposium on child development* (Vol. 10). Minneapolis: University of Minnesota Press, 1976.

Suomi, S. J. Adult male–infant interactions among monkeys living in nuclear families. *Journal of Child Development,* 1977, *48,* 1255–1270.

12

Young Children's Concepts of Social Relations: Social Functions and Social Objects

Carolyn Pope Edwards and Michael Lewis

As a consequence of the growing interest in social development, there has been a recent increase in concern for considering the social network of young children, both from the perspective of what children and infants actually do as well as what they believe. Although most emphasis has been placed on the mother–child relationship, it has recently become clear that even during infancy, children enthusiastically interact with a variety of people in their environments. Moreover, children's initiations and responses to the different people—for example, to mothers, fathers, strange adults, or brothers or sisters, and younger, older and same-age peers—become patterned early in life (see, for example, Lewis, Young, Brooks, & Michalson, 1975). Clearly, almost all young children form lasting relationships with people besides their primary caretakers and make distinctions between people, which has the consequence of allowing them to vary their behavior toward a wide array of people, both those who are familiar as well as those who are strangers. Unfortunately, not much is known about the overall organization of these social relationships of young children. There are at least two different

Carolyn Pope Edwards • School of Education, University of Massachusetts, Amherst, Massachusetts 01003. Michael Lewis • The Infant Laboratory, Institute for the Study of Exceptional Children, Educational Testing Service, Princeton, New Jersey 08541. The research reported in this paper was conducted while Carolyn Edwards was a postdoctoral fellow at the Educational Testing Service. The research was funded by a grant for postdoctoral training from the Public Health Service to ETS.

ways of understanding that organization. The first way is from a systems perspective, that is, analyzing the structure and operation of the networks in which the children are involved. The second way is from the children's perspective, that is, finding out about children's representational schemas of the social world; schemas that we hold guide the children's own action and enable them to predict the behavior of others. The first mode of analysis would fall in the subject matter of network theory and the second that of what has come to be called social cognition. For discussion of these two modes, see Lewis and Rosenblum (1975); Lewis and Weinraub (1976); Weinraub, Brooks, and Lewis (1977).

Whichever approach is used, it is necessary to create meaningful dimensions of analysis. Lewis and Feiring (1979b) have articulated the concept of a social matrix for the developing infant that contains two dimensions: social objects (people) and social functions (classes of behavior, what people do). In the world of the young child, these two dimensions may be highly related, at least for some social objects and functions, or may be unrelated. The dimension of social objects may be usefully ordered by means of a small set of mutually independent factors. There are three factors that Lewis and Feiring (1979b) believe will prove essential in understanding the young child's social behavior with the diversity of people that are typically encountered. These three are gender, age, and familiarity. They have in common a critical feature, namely, their connection with overt, readily apprehended, perceptual cues. Unlike such abstract classifications as socioeconomic class, occupation, religion, or value orientations, they can be used by the young child to sort people just through looking. This is an essential feature given young children's cognitive tendencies for the concrete. Moreover, not only are all three factors overt and concrete, but also, as argued by Lewis and Feiring (1979b), the three can be used to make useful social distinctions. In fact, they are the basis for the very social distinctions that are first made by children and that are of foremost importance to them, that is, between mother and father (gender), between parents and siblings and grandparents (age), between family members and strangers (familiarity), to name a few.

"Age" as an Organizing Schema

Of the three factors, gender and familiarity have received most research attention as critical variables in early social interaction and concept development. The age factor is surely the least understood. We know relatively little about the operation of age relations in the child's real-life social system (a subject for network analysis), and we know only slightly more about how young children use concepts of "age" to classify the social world, predict the behavior of others, and as a guiding schema for their own action (questions from the domain of social cognition). This chapter focuses on the issue of the relationship of age to social function and centers on social cognition. In reviewing what is known about the young child's age concepts the following questions may be addressed:

1. *Meaning of language concerning age.* What is the nature of the young child's understanding of words concerning age and age groups? What is the developmental course by which these complex concepts are acquired?
2. *Age-group classification.* How and when do children begin to use age-associated appearance cues to sort people into groups or classes? When can they rank order people along an age dimension and make reasonable guesses concerning a person's age in years?
3. *Concepts of age relations expressed in behavior.* When do children use age-cues to initiate differential behavior to the people around them? Does the differential behavior suggest expectations based on age-cues concerning others' behavior?
4. *Concept of age roles.* When do children begin to associate social functions with social relations defined by age-criteria? When are they able to verbally express concepts of age roles?

Because all of these questions concern the young child's concepts of self, others, and social relations, they can be said to fall into the domain of social cognition (Lewis & Brooks, 1975; Youniss, 1975).

Very little attention has been directed to the process by which children develop the ability to use words concerning age, in contrast to the great amounts of work that has been done on the acquisition of concepts of gender and gender-identity (for the latter, see Emmerich, Goldman, Kirsh, & Sharabany, 1977; Kohlberg, 1966; Thompson, 1975). However, the two processes undoubtedly have much in common. For example, children around two years in age begin to apply age-relevant labels to self and others ("grownup," "child," "baby," etc.), just as they begin to use gender-relevant categories ("boy," "girl," etc.). In fact, most of the labels that children learn to identify people by gender equally involve distinctions according to age group. At about the same time that children begin to acquire age-group labels, they also begin to answer, "I'm two," or "I'm three," to the frequently asked question, "How old are you?" That is, they learn to label themselves according to what they will much later understand to be the interval scale of chronological age. Not until the school years will they understand that scale fully and realize the social groups—"baby," "child," "grownup"—are based on numerical ages. In order to understand the relationship between numerical ages and age groups, children must move beyond simple labeling toward a comprehension of what kind of characteristic "age" really is. Specifically, just as they must construct the knowledge for themselves that gender is a necessarily stable attribute of the individual that is determined by fixed physical characteristics present at birth, so they must learn that age is an attribute that necessarily changes with the individual and is related to predictable physical changes from birth to death. Both gender and age concepts have a cognitive basis in the child's development of concrete operational thought because they require abilities to understand what attributes of people are conserved or changed by the passage of time.

Around age two, then, children first apply age-group labels to self and others. This is the beginning of the development of a system for classifying the human world into age groups. Brooks and Lewis (in press) have found that children as young as sixteen months produce the label "baby" to photographs of infants and the word "daddy" or "mommy" to photos of strange adults as well as their own parents. The labels, "child" or "girl" or "boy," for photos of children, seem to appear later. Recent research shows that by age three-and-a-half, children have acquired the ability to sort and classify photos of people of all ages (including themselves). This sorting behavior is remarkably consistent from child to child in terms of category boundaries (Edwards & Lewis, 1978). In a study using photos of faces of people aged one to seventy, children 3.5 to 5 years of age demonstrated that they could readily distinguish "children" from "adults" or "grownups" (no category of "teenagers" seems to be prominent in the category systems of preschoolers). Within those two major categories they could distinguish "little children" from "big children" and "parents" (younger adults) from "grandparents" (old adults). The boundary between little and big children was placed around age 5, the boundary between children and grownups around age 13, and the boundary between parents and grandparents around age 40, for both male and female social objects. Although children under five are thus able to use age-cues based on appearance to classify people into social groups, they by and large cannot assign absolute ages or even rank order people in terms of older/younger. The ability to rank order people appears around age 5–6, and the ability to assign absolute ages with reasonable accuracy quite a bit later, around age 8–10 (Britton & Britton, 1969; Kogan, Stephens, & Shelton, 1961; Looft, 1971; Kratochwill & Goldman, 1973).

An alternative approach to studying children's developing concepts of age groups is through their differential behavior to strange and familiar people who vary in age. This approach has not been much used, yet studies show that selective behavior to people of different ages appears early in life, perhaps earlier than differential behavior to males versus females. Even during infancy, children show more positive approach behavior to strange peers than to strange adults (Lenssen, 1975; Lewis & Brooks, 1975). With midgets, who have the facial features of adults but the physical size of children, their social behavior is different still; it is surprise, not wary nor friendly as shown to adults and children (Brooks & Lewis, 1976). By age 3–4, children's behavior to people of varying ages is thoroughly differentiated. Studies of East African children in homestead settings (Edwards & Whiting, 1976; Whiting & Edwards, 1977) indicate that much of the behavior initiated to people several years older than the self can be classified as "dependent" (including seeking help, attention, information, proximity, or concrete resources). The bulk of behavior to infants or people several years younger than the self can be classified as "nurturant," "prosocial," or "dominant" (including giving help, comfort or concrete resources, giving commands, and correcting social behavior). Finally, most of the behavior to children close in age to the self can be called "sociable," "playful," or "aggressive" (including chasing, rough and tumble play, talking with, teasing and insulting, etc.). These patterns of differentiated behavior probably begin to emerge during later infancy, as suggested by studies of English and American infants and toddlers observed interacting with their siblings and parents (Dunn & Kendrick, this volume; Lamb, 1978). The existence of differentiated behavior provides a natural way to study children's implicit age categories, by finding out exactly what variations in real age of social objects elicit selective behaviors.

By age 3–4, as noted above, children classify the human world into age groups and behave quite differently to adults and children older, younger, and the same age as themselves. Such behavior indicates that they have gone beyond classifying the world into age groups to developing expectations about what behavior makes most sense or is most appropriate with each group. Such expectations would constitute part of emerging concepts of age *roles*, that is, ideas about proper performance of given social functions, by persons of one age group toward another. Emmerich (1959), in a classic study of children's concepts of age roles, found that preschool–aged children could discriminate parent and child roles on a power dimension. The study showed that the children tended to assign high power functions (such as depriving, controlling, blaming) to male and female parent figures more than to boy and girl figures. The children also showed a tendency to assign low power functions (such as demanding, conforming, asking) to child rather than parent figures, but not to such a clear extent. Emmerich suggested that the preschoolers were more aware of the presence of power in parent roles than its absence in child roles. However, the study did not answer what functions, if not power, preschoolers might perceive as especially present in child roles. Nor did it investigate how children might think about the social roles of children of different age groups.

Conceptual Relationships between Social Objects and Social Functions

Given that age groups (or what we adults know to be age groups) are readily discriminable by very young children, the question is whether those age groups provide a classification scheme or framework that children actually use to think about appropriate behavior toward others. If so, then we would learn something new about young children's social concepts, more specifically, about how children organize the world and relate the domain of social objects to the domain of social functions. Investigating this domain is a task we believe to be worthwhile in the study of social development.

The present study is intended to learn more about young children's concepts of age roles for a broad range of social groups. The study investigates roles by asking children to match particular social behaviors, or functions, with the appropriate social objects, or persons. The domain of social objects that the children considered is composed of males and females of the five age groups found to be salient to them in our earlier study (Edwards & Lewis, 1978): younger children, peers, older children, and young and old adults. The domain of social functions consists of selected types of positive behavior: dependency (seeking help and information), sociability (companionable play), and nurturance (sharing food). These functions are frequently initiated behaviors by preschool children to others; they are differentially found in interaction with persons older, same age, or younger (Whiting & Edwards, 1977). Thus, the study investigates how young children relate the domain of social objects to the domain of social functions using social objects and functions prominent during the preschool years.

In order to investigate the question, two studies were performed with preschool-aged children. The first used symbolic representations of different age groups (dolls) and the second used photographic representations. In both studies, the children chose which social object they would want to interact for a specified kind of social action. More precisely, given themselves as initiators, and given particular types of initiations, the children were asked to choose appropriate "targets," or social objects to receive those initiations, targets that varied in represented age but not in sex. The initiations had to do with the giving and receiving of nurturance and sociability, that is, with positive and nonaggressive interaction.

Study 1: Dolls

The first study was conducted at two day-care centers in the greater Princeton area, with 24 black and 24 white children aged 3.6 to 5.9 years. Half of the children were girls and half were boys (balanced with respect to ethnic background and age). The children came from working- and lower-middle-class backgrounds.

Each child was told a series of stories involving a set of doll-house figures. There were black and white dolls (as well as a black and a white tester) for the two ethnic groups of children. Each child was first told that one small-sized girl (or boy) doll represented the child herself and that the rest of the dolls represented "friends." The "friend" dolls included four pairs of male and female figures, to stand for adult, older child, peer, and infant age groups. The child was asked to demonstrate that she could identify the "man" and "woman" (adult dolls), the "big boy and girl" (older child dolls), the "boy and girl three (four/five) years old just like you" (peer dolls, exactly the size of the self doll), and the "baby boy and girl" (infant dolls). The dolls standing for each group were different in size and no child had trouble learning the categories.

The stories that were told to the children involved four social functions or behaviors. In turn the self doll was portrayed as (1) getting hurt and wanting someone to *help* her, (2) finding an unfamiliar toy and wanting someone to *show* her how to use it, (3) having extra food and wanting to *give* or share it with someone, and (4) growing tired of being alone and wanting someone with whom to *play*. The stories thus involved (1) the seeking of help and (2) information, (3) the giving of resources, and (4) companionable play. Each story was acted out for the child, and then the child was asked to complete the story by going to the person whom she wanted to ask to help, to show, etc. (the dolls were arranged in a row in random order). After selecting one choice, the child was asked to select a second choice, and so on, to obtain a complete rank ordering of preference. However, in order to reduce the number of choices with which a child had to deal at one time, the child first went through the set of stories (functions) using only the dolls representing her own sex group, and then went through them again using the opposite-sex dolls.

The mean rank orders of the children's choices for male and female social objects on each function are shown in Figure 1. The figure was

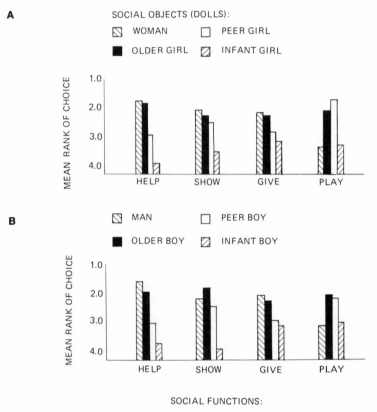

FIG. 1. Day-care-center findings. Preference (mean rank of choice) for dolls representing four age groups, for four social functions. (Data pooled on girl and boy subjects, $n = 48$.)

constructed by combining girls' and boys' responses, since there were few differences as a function of the respondents' sex. There are two striking results apparent in the figure. The first is the clear-cut nature of the pattern of relationships found. The second is the similarity of the pattern of the children's responses to male (Fig. 1B) and female (Fig. 1A) social objects.

One way to examine the patterns is to note which social objects scored higher and which lower on each function. This highlights the similarities and differences of the children's responses to different functions. For example (generalizing across Figure 1) the two stories that elicited the most different responses were help and play. With respect to seeking help, the ordering principle for choosing was straightforward: the older the social object, the more highly preferred. However, when selecting someone with whom to play, the older social object was not necessarily better. Rather, the children tended to choose adults and infants last, after peers and older children, whom they preferred about equally. When seeking someone to show them how to use the unfamiliar toy, the children preferred three social objects to about the same degree— namely, the adults, older children, and peers—and chose definitely last the infant social objects. On the story involving the giving of food, the children showed the least differentiation of preference of social objects. In fact, during testing it was noticed that most children simply started with whatever doll was nearest and then went down the row giving to each doll in turn, something that they did not do on any other story. Overall, the older social objects did tend to be given food before the younger ones, but this was not as differentiated as on the help function.

As a statistical test of the differentiation of social objects within each social function, the repeated measures F-test was used. For each function separately, two-way F-tests were performed using age (four levels) and sex (two levels) of social objects as independent variables. That is, the statistical test measured whether children's choice patterns were significantly related to either represented age or sex of the social objects that they were choosing among. For three of the social functions (help, give, and play), sex of social object did not significantly affect the children's choices. The children's patterns of choosing were not significantly different, whether they were choosing among male or among female social objects. On the show function, sex of social object was a significant predictor of choice patterns [F (1,47) = 8.52, p = .005]. Figure 1 indicates that for male social objects, older boys were the most chosen and adult men were second; whereas for female social objects, adult women were most chosen, older girls second. As shall be described below, this difference did not replicate in the second study and may not be of importance. Age of social object was a very strong predictor of choice patterns for all four social functions. The magnitude of the effect was greatest for the help function [F (3,47) = 77.24, p < .001], second for the show function [F (3,47) = 33.14, p < .001], third for the play function [F (3,47) = 27.05, p < .001], and least by far but still highly significant for the give function [F (3,47) = 9.27, p < .001].

Another way in which to examine the patterns in Figure 1 is to note, for each social object, which social functions were selected relatively early or "high" in the rank order and which relatively late or "low." This method highlights the differences and similarities between social objects. Adult dolls generally received high rank orders on three functions, help, show, and give, but the lowest mean rank order of all social objects on the play function. Infants received low rank orders generally, were not chosen much, across all functions. However, they were chosen relatively more on play and give functions than on help and show. Same-aged peer social objects were chosen relatively most on the play function, next most on show, give, and relatively least on the help function. Finally, the dolls representing older children provided interesting findings in that they received high rank orders across all social functions. They were on average selected first or second by the children on every one of the four functions. On the help and give functions, they were chosen almost as highly as were adult social objects. On the play function, they were chosen almost as highly as were peer objects. On the show function, they received the highest average rank of all age groups.

As a statistical test of differentiation of social functions within each social object, F-tests were again used. For each age of social object separately, two-way F-tests were again used. For each age of social object separately, two-way F-tests were performed using sex of social object (two levels) and function (four levels) as repeated measures independent variables. The tests measured whether the children's responses to a particular represented age level of social object (e.g., the infant) were significantly affected either by which social function was involved or the sex of social objects that they were choosing among. For the adult social objects, social function was a highly significant predictor of the children's choices [$F\ (3,141) = 37.86, p < .001$]. For the older child social objects, in contrast, social function approached but did not attain statistical significance [$F\ (3,141) = 2.54, p < .10$]. For the peer objects, social function was again highly significant [$F(3,141) = 22.13, p < .001$], as it was for infant objects [$F(3,141) = 14.64, p < .001$]. Thus, the findings indicate that response to the different social objects was extremely differentiated across functions for all but the older child social objects, who were rather indiscriminately highly chosen on all stories, as described above. Sex of social object was not a significant predictor as a main effect for any social object. However, for infants, there was a significant interaction between sex and function [$F(3,141) = 3,14, p < .05$]. The show and help functions changed relative positions for male and female infant objects; so also did give and play functions (see Figure 1). This interaction did not replicate in the second study.

Study 2: Photographs

The second study of object × function relationships were conducted at a private nursery school near Princeton. The sample included 25 girls and 25 boys aged 3.7 to 5.1 years. All of the children came from white middle- or upper-middle-class families. Photographic representations of the different age groups were used to see whether the earlier findings would hold using an alternative methodology.

The children were again asked to complete stories by selecting appropriate objects for particular types of social interaction. The stories were illustrated for children in picture books, one set for girls and one set for boys, identical except for gender of the main character. During the test session the main character was designated to be the child being tested, and this character was portrayed in the same four situations described above for help, show, give, and play functions. In addition, a fifth situation was portrayed in which the child became lost on her way to a store and wanted to ask someone directions to *find* the way. The child was asked to complete each story by selecting from among three randomly arranged photographs the one that she would ask to help, to show, etc. The photos were not labeled in any way for the child, but they represented a choice of different age groups. After making one selection, the child was asked to make another choice, to obtain a rank ordering of preferences. As in the previous study, the children performed the tasks first for same-sex social objects (photos), then for opposite-sex social objects.

The photographs used were color head and shoulder shots of people who varied in chronological age. The photos were taken face on from a fixed distance, and therefore the head size of the people in the pictures did vary somewhat as a function of actual size. Five sets of photos of males and females were constructed, each containing the following age groups: (1) *younger child* (actually aged 18–24 months); (2) *peer* (actually aged 4 years); (3)*older child*(7–8 years); (4) *parent-generation adult* (25–30 years); and (5) *grandparent-generation adult* (50–80 years). As mentioned earlier, these ages were selected on the basis of the results of the classification task briefly described earlier (Edwards & Lewis, 1978). In each set of photos, the faces were matched as closely as possible for emotional expression (degree of smiling), head position, hair color, and facial complexion. Each set of photos was used an equal number of times with each function; that is, order of presentation of photo sets was varied across children to control for possible peculiarities of particular photographs.

In order to reduce the complexity of the choosing task presented to the children, the following procedure was followed. Each child was presented with only three rather than five photos on a trial. One group of 20 children saw photos representing *younger child, peer,* and *older child* age groups only. A second group of 20 children saw the *peer, older child,* and *parent-generation adult* photos. A third group of 10 children saw *peer, older child,* and *grandparent-generation adult* photos.

The results of this study (Figure 2) generally confirm the day-care-

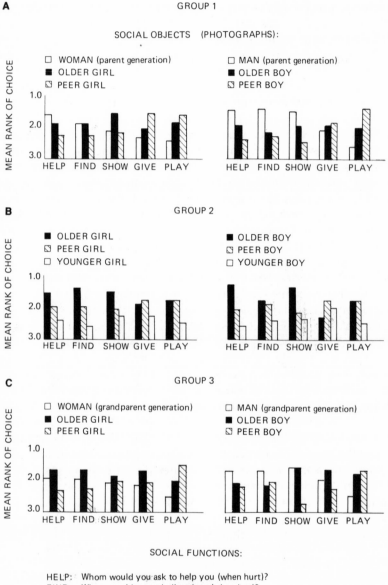

A   GROUP 1

SOCIAL OBJECTS   (PHOTOGRAPHS):

☐ WOMAN (parent generation)   ☐ MAN (parent generation)
■ OLDER GIRL   ■ OLDER BOY
◩ PEER GIRL   ◩ PEER BOY

MEAN RANK OF CHOICE

HELP FIND SHOW GIVE PLAY   HELP FIND SHOW GIVE PLAY

B   GROUP 2

■ OLDER GIRL   ■ OLDER BOY
◩ PEER GIRL   ◩ PEER BOY
☐ YOUNGER GIRL   ☐ YOUNGER BOY

MEAN RANK OF CHOICE

HELP FIND SHOW GIVE PLAY   HELP FIND SHOW GIVE PLAY

C   GROUP 3

☐ WOMAN (grandparent generation)   ☐ MAN (grandparent generation)
■ OLDER GIRL   ■ OLDER BOY
◩ PEER GIRL   ◩ PEER BOY

MEAN RANK OF CHOICE

HELP FIND SHOW GIVE PLAY   HELP FIND SHOW GIVE PLAY

SOCIAL FUNCTIONS:

HELP: Whom would you ask to help you (when hurt)?
FIND: Whom would you ask directions (when lost)?
SHOW: Whom would you ask to show you how to use a toy (which you found)?
GIVE: To whom would you give extra food?
PLAY: Whom would you ask to play with you (when alone)?

Fig. 2. Nursery-school findings. Preference (mean rank of choice) for photographs of faces representing five age groups, for five social functions. (Data pooled on girl and boy subjects, *n*'s = 20 group 1, 20 group 2, 10 group 3.)

center findings. The figure was constructed by combining the responses of girls and boys. As before, patterns of responses to male and female social objects were highly similar.[1]

On two of the dependency functions, namely, getting help when hurt and getting help in finding the way, the following age rule generally describes the pattern of results: the older the social object, the more highly chosen. However, on the third dependency function, asking to be shown how to use a toy, that rule describes the data for male social objects only. For female social objects, the older child social objects were preferred to both sets of adult objects (parent- and grandparent-generation). The relevant findings for the help and show functions thus agree in large measure with those for the day-care study (Figure 1). The findings for the play functions are also fairly similar. Again, the peers tended to receive the highest rank orders and the older children next highest, with the adults and younger child social objects ranking far behind. Finally, the giving of food was the function on which children showed the least systematic or interpretable differentiation of social objects. This resulted from the fact that, as in the earlier study, many children declined to "choose." Rather, they simply pointed to the nearest photo and then went down the row to give to each in turn.

Examining the functions selected for each age group of social object, additional conclusions emerge (still generalizing across male and female social objects). Parent- and grandparent-generation adults are treated very similarly by the children. They are highly chosen on the dependency functions (help, show, find) but less to give to or play with. Peers, as before, received their highest rank orders on the play function. They are also fairly preferred on the give function (a discrepancy with the earlier study), but they are low ranked on the dependency functions. Younger child social objects are selected almost as frequently as other social objects on the give function, but as with the infant social objects in the previous study, they are ranked last on play and dependency functions, distinctly behind older child and peer social objects. Finally, the older child social objects are again extremely highly preferred overall. In the fifteen histograms displayed in Figure 2, the older child figures are first or second chosen in all but two.

The patterns for male and female social objects were again quite similar. Most discrepancy occurred on the give function (see Figure 2B, C), but this discrepancy is probably not meaningful since in general no systematic patterns seemed to underlie the children's choosing on this

---

[1] F-tests were not performed to test the magnitude or choice differentiation within social objects and functions as they were with the day-care sample. The nursery children were divided into groups of 20, 20, and 10 subjects and it was felt that these n's were too small for the tests to be performed validly.

function. On the help, find, and show functions, there were tendencies for the older girl social objects to outrank woman objects, but for man objects to outrank older boys (see Figure 2A, C). These findings are in some sense a reverse of the findings in the day-care study, where it was the older boy social objects who were exceptionally highly preferred on the show story. It is difficult to know what to make of these findings. Certainly it is interesting that for both samples the difference between male and female patterns occurred for older child social objects. The older child was an important object to the children, highly chosen on all stories. The gender of this social object may somehow be significant for the children in a complex way that interacts with the social function involved, and perhaps the social class of the children themselves (since the working-class day-care and middle-class nursery-school children showed opposite results). Further work will have to be done to clarify this problem.

The results across both studies indicate a strong social object–social function interaction with some functions more relevant for some objects. In particular, older people are preferred for dependency functions centering around help-giving. Interestingly, not all help-giving was so ordered. When help involved a teaching function, as in showing the child how something worked, older peers were chosen. In terms of play the combined sample results are most clear; peers, either older or same age, are preferred, certainly over adults (either parents or grandparents) and younger children. Giving showed the least consistency across samples but in general appeared to be equally distributed across all the social objects. In summary, then, adults are preferred for dependency needs, older peers for teaching, older peers and peers for playing, and all social objects equally for giving. Thus, by three years the matrix of social objects–social functions appears highly articulated.

The Effect of Family Structure, Sibling Order, Age, and Sex on the Formation of Age Roles

Thus far we have described the age roles emerging from the common structure of the children's responses. Yet, we might suppose that age-role concepts would be affected by individual children's personal experiences. The question of how age roles might differ according to family and demographic characteristics of children was examined using the large day-care sample. The mean ranks for all four social objects on all four social functions were compared for children who differed in sex, chronological age, and racial group. In addition, children of different sibling orders were compared (mean number of children in the sample families was 1.8, 52% of the children were only children).

Finally, children who lived with two adult caretakers were compared with children who lived with one adult (19 children lived with mother and father and two lived with grandmother and grandfather; 25 lived with mother only and two lived with grandmother only).

Chronologically older children in the sample differed from younger ones in choosing the adult female less on the food-sharing story [$t(46)$ = −2.60, $p < .05$]. Further, on the story involving choosing a playmate, they selected the male adult doll less [$t(46)$ = −2.90, $p < .05$] and the older boy more [$t(46)$ = 2.05 $p < .05$] than did younger children.[2] Girls differed from boys in several instances. They chose the infant boy more to play with [$t(46)$ = −2.52, $p < .05$] and to help them [$t(46)$ = −3.55, $p < .001$]. They also chose the peer girl more, to show them how to use the unfamiliar toy [$t(46)$ = −2.67, $p < .01$]. Boys ranked higher the older boy doll, on the stories involving giving food [$t(46)$ = 2.22, $p < .05$] and companionable play [$t(46)$ = 2.05, $p < .05$]. Black and white children differed significantly on the two dependency stories (show and help). Black children chose the infant girl more to help [$t(46)$ = 3.27, $p < .01$] and show [$t(46)$ = 2.46, $p < .05$] and the infant boy more to show [$t(46)$ = 2.21, $p < .05$]. They also chose the adult female more, to give food to [$t(46)$ = 2.02, $p < .05$]. White children chose the peer girl [$t(46)$ = −2.67, $p < .01$] and the older boy more [$t(46)$ = −2.18, $p < .05$] on the show function. Thus, the difference between older and younger children involved a shift in preference from adult to child social objects. Such a difference might represent part of the general shift in social orientation from adults to children that is believed to occur during the preschool years. The difference between girls and boys involved a greater tendency for the girls to select the baby and peer social objects and the boys to select the older boy figure. The sex difference thus involved choices of child social objects only, not choices surrounding adults. Girls had a tendency to more highly select the youngest social objects (babies and peers), on certain functions, while boys seemed to have a tendency to select the same-sex older child figure more. This sex difference fits with our earlier study (Edwards & Lewis, 1978), in which it was found that preschool boys were significantly more likely than girls to classify themselves as "big children." The two sets of findings suggest that during the preschool years, boys have a tendency to want to conceive of themselves as, and to associate themselves with, "big" children in the age group one up from their own, whereas girls are more likely to conceive of themselves, and want to be with, "little" children in the approximately under-five age group. Finally, the differences between the

---

[2] All tests of significance reported are based on two-tailed tests.

two ethnic (racial) groups occurred primarily on the two dependency functions, helping and showing. On these functions, black children more highly selected infant social objects while white children more highly selected others of the child figures. Like girls, black children may be especially oriented to infants, perhaps as a result of the high value that their cultural group has traditionally placed on the having of children. However, there may be another, more correct explanation for these ethnic differences. The problem with the explanation is that it does not indicate why the ethnic group differences occurred on the dependency stories rather than on the functions where it might more reasonably have been expected, namely, nurturance and sociable play— more appropriate social behaviors with infant social objects.

Very few significant findings emerged concerning sibling order, probably due to the fact that so many of the children were only children and therefore comparisons were difficult to make. Only children did not differ significantly from children with siblings. However, an interesting difference did appear between children from one and two adult homes. This difference had to do with the degree to which the adult social objects were chosen differentially across functions. The help and play functions were the most contrasting and therefore were used to measure degree of differentiation. The mean rank for the social object on the help function was subtracted from the mean rank on the play function; the greater this number, the more differentially the adult social object was treated from the one story to the other. For the girls in the day-care sample, living with one rather than two adult caretakers predicted greater differentiation, with respect to both adult female and male social objects $[t(22) = 3.40, p < .01; t(22) = 2.44, p < .05]$. For boys, the trends were in the same direction but to a considerably lesser magnitude $[t(22) = 1.74, p < .10; t(22) = .74, p$ nonsignificant].

It is reasonable to suppose that these differences between children from one and two adult homes may be based in realities of how caretakers actually do behave. Single caretakers, busy and under stress, may be more task-oriented and less playful with their children, causing the children to see them more as objects of dependency, less as potential objects of play. If this is indeed the correct explanation for the findings, it would follow that girls would show the effect more than boys. The single caretakers were female in all cases, and daughters would be expected to be more highly identified with them and therefore more sensitive to parental roles in their families. Also, it would follow that both girls and boys would show the effect more for adult female than for adult male social objects (see *t*-scores reported above), since the single caretakers were in fact female. Overall, the adult female social object did *not* receive greater differentiation scores than did the adult male social object; the difference had only to do with the degree to which the differentiation was systematically related to the household variable of number of caretakers.

Social Cognition and Social Relationships

Young children think about age in a concrete, static, preoperational way. They link the concept of age with a concrete characteristic, "bigness," rather than the correct, abstract one, years of life. Nevertheless, they readily use physical cues about age (including size, face, and hair) to classify people into social groups, and their resultant categories have great significance for them in helping them to predict and initiate social interaction around specific functions. In fact, children learn during infancy to associate particular social functions with particular age groups. "Age roles" or functions first emerge on the behavioral level when the child behaves differentially to other infants, children, and adults. Then, during the preschool years, children begin to label and classify others in a systematic way and to discuss what kinds of behavior are appropriate for infants, little and big children, "parents" (young and middle-aged adults), and "grandparents" (old adults).

The studies that we have described show that there is a great deal of shared knowledge among preschool children about what kinds of social behaviors it makes sense to do with different age groups. Each social object (infant or younger child, same age peer, older child, parent-aged adult, grandparent-aged adult) showed a distinctive profile of high and low preference across the social functions studied. Moreover, these profiles were highly similar for male and female social objects of the same age group. The profiles for same-aged peers and parent-aged adults were perhaps not surprising, given what we know about children's relationships with two much studied sets of social partners, namely, schoolmates and parents. The preschoolers saw peers primarily as objects for companionable play and parent-aged adults primarily as objects of dependency (seeking help and information).

The findings for the other three age groups were perhaps more unexpected since we know little about children's concepts of, or behavioral interaction with, those kinds of social partners. The profiles of social functions for grandparent-aged adults turned out to be very similar to those for parent-aged adults. That is, grandparent–aged photographs were highly selected on the dependency stories but not on the companionable play story. The results suggest that preschool children associate the same kinds of functions with both age groups of adults, at least in the situation where they are choosing not between adults but between one of those two types of adults versus children. The infant social objects (study one) and young, toddler-aged ones (study two) received low scores on all social functions. That is, they were not highly chosen on any function, though they did relatively best on the nurturance (food-sharing) story. The latter finding was expected, because observational studies of family life in a variety of communities worldwide have found infants to invite or "elicit" nurturance from all ages of persons who interact with them (Whiting & Whiting, 1975). A further finding was that the infant social objects were avoided significantly more in the first study by boy and white subjects than by girl and black subjects. These differences may have been the result of culture- and gender–related values and goals. In general, the extent of the avoidance or low preference related to the infant and toddler social objects seemed surprising. In African communities, behavioral observations have found children aged two and under to receive relatively high levels of nurturant and sociable initiations from the preschool aged children in their homesteads (Whiting & Edwards, 1977). However, in those African households, there were relatively few same age peers available as playmates for children. Therefore, our findings in the present study may, on the one hand, reflect cultural values (our low evaluation of persons younger than the self as "interesting" persons with whom to spend time). On the other hand, they may possibly reflect a more universal preference for peers and older children, as opposed to infants and younger children, when a choice is available to the preschool child.

A seeming preference for older children was, in fact, one of the most clear-cut and outstanding findings of our study. Both samples of children, middle and working class, showed a pattern of ranking highly the older child social objects on all social functions. Adults in advanced societies such as our own do not usually think of 7–8 year old children as especially likely caretakers or companions for young children, but mothers in many technologically simple societies certainly do (Whiting & Whiting, 1975). Preadolescent children serve as child nurses for their younger siblings in many cultures in which adult women play a major role in the subsistence labor and therefore require daily help in running their households. The findings of our study indicate that even in a culture in which child nurses are not the custom, preschool aged children have a tendency to view older, preadolescent children as appropriate sources of help and information, as well as desirable objects of companionable play. Perhaps our society should make a greater effort to bring these two adjacent age groups together, in school or child-care settings (see Lewis & Rosenblum, 1975; Lewis et al., 1975). Children of adjacent age groups might benefit from teaching and learning from one another in important ways, ways different from the benefits of exchange between children of the same group or children of very distant age groups (e.g., infants and adolescents).

Finding out more about the conceptual systems of preschool children may help us to better design their social environments and to facilitate their forming social networks to their own best advantage.

Besides these general findings concerning the relationships of social objects and functions in the conceptual systems of the preschoolers, there were also results showing individual differences in the children's concepts. Girls' concepts of age roles differed from boys' in their greater choosing of the male infant doll on help and play functions and the peer girl on the show function. Boys showed a greater choosing of the older boy doll on play and give functions. These sex differences may relate, as discussed earlier, to a strong wish on the part of preschool boys to be "big," whereas preschool girls more readily classify themselves as "little," part of the group of children under about age five. The boys' "wish" to be big probably derives from their rather concrete idea of what it means to be a boy rather than a girl. It is well-known that children first become aware during the preschool years of adult sex differences in the areas of size and strength. Because of their cognitive tendencies to fasten onto the concrete, they attach great importance to these size and strength differences and use them as first defining characteristics for male versus female (Kohlberg, 1966). Thus, gender as well as age differentiations are linked to physical size in the minds of young children. This presents young boys a special problem, because while they are "little" in terms of age group, they are "big" in terms of gender group. Perhaps boys attempt to resolve this confusion by classifying themselves as "big children" and seeking to associate themselves with the boys in the age group one up from their own. Girls, more able to be objective and classify themselves as "little" in terms of age, may also more readily associate with "little" children such as infants and toddlers. If this explanation is correct, it would suggest a partially cognitive origin for the greater behavioral orientation to, and nurturance with, infants by girls than by boys (e.g., see Berman, Monda, & Myerscough, 1977; Whiting & Edwards, 1973, 1977).

A further interesting difference that was found between children concerned their household structures. Children who lived with one female caretaker (mother or grandmother) associated social functions with the adult social objects in a way different from children who lived with both parents or with grandmother and grandfather. The former children made the adult social objects (especially the female one) to be relatively more of a helper and less of a playmate. That is, while all of the children tended to choose the adult dolls *before* child dolls on the help story and *after* them on the play story, the children from one-adult homes exaggerated this tendency relative to other children. The findings clearly indicate that our methodology is sensitive to the life histories of individual children. Although we were not able to discern differences related to sibling order, this may have been because so many of the children were only children and it was difficult to get leverage on the sibling set of variables. Future work will investigate in greater depth the relationship between life history and children's conceptual systems concerning social objects and functions.

A final note concerns developmental differences, that is, differences related to the age of the children. The older children in the sample (the older fours and fives) chose the male adult relatively less and the older boy relatively more on the play function than did younger children. They were also less likely to offer food to the adult female social object. These differences fit the picture of a general shift in social orientation from adults to children during the preschool years. However, the small number of age differences found suggests that the age role concepts uncovered by our methodology are well-established in children by age three-and-a-half years. The social functions investigated were clear-cut ones that are prominent in the behavior of preschool children, and the social objects studied represented age groups that had been found to be salient to the children. Perhaps not surprisingly, therefore, the children agreed to a substantial extent about which social functions were appropriate for each social object. The children clearly demonstrated that age-group differentiations have important social meanings for them. Their concepts of age groups provide them with a general and useful framework to structure social functions and to guide their everyday social interaction.

Social Functions–Social Objects

The view that the young child and mother (perhaps fathers as well) constitute the only as well as the most important social relationship has become increasingly disfavored and in its place a more complex social network has been suggested (Weinraub, Brooks, & Lewis, 1977). One of the most important features of this social network has been the belief that there are multiple social objects that occupy meaningful space in the young organism's life and that there are multiple functions that the organism needs to attend to. Moreover, Lewis and Feiring (in this volume) have stressed the importance of the matrix that may be described between objects and functions. This matrix is not constant but remains throughout the lifetime in a state of change with the addition and loss of both objects and functions. Moreover, this matrix should be affected by a host of factors, including, among others, the values of the culture as well as the structure of the family.

The data from the present two studies complement each other and clearly supply support for the notion of a highly articulated matrix in the young child. This matrix reveals object-function relationships that support the notion of differential cells within the matrix. In this particular case adults are best for caring for dependency needs, older peers for learning and teaching, and peers (as well as older peers) for play. These findings, concerning the dependency and play functions, find support in the work of others looking at one- to three-year-old children (Lewis *et al.*, 1975; Mueller, this volume; Mueller & Lucas, 1975).

The findings that there are both a large set of functions (or needs) and a large set of objects that can satisfy these needs allows us to go beyond the simple notion of a limited social experience in early childhood and direct our attention to how best to match social functions with social objects.

ACKNOWLEDGMENTS

The authors wish to thank the directors, teachers, and children of the Child Care Research Center, the Frog Hollow Nursery School, the Better Beginnings Day Care Center, and the Lawrence Day Care Center for their whole-hearted help and cooperation.

REFERENCES

Berman, P. W., Monda, L. C., & Myerscough, R.P. Sex differences in young children's responses to an infant. *Child Development*, 1977, *48*, 711–715.

Britton, J., & Britton, J. H. Discrimination of age by preschool children. *Journal of Gerontology*, 1969, *24*, 457–460.

Brooks, J., & Lewis, M. Person perception and verbal labeling: The development of social labels. Paper presented at both the Society for Research in Child Development meetings, Denver, April, 1975, and the Eastern Psychological Association meetings, New York, April, 1975.

Brooks, J., & Lewis, M. Infants' responses to strangers: Midget, adult and child. *Child Development*, 1976, *47*, 323–332.

Brooks, J., & Lewis, M. Early social knowledge. The development of knowledge about others. In H. McGurk (Ed.), *Childhood social development*. London: Methuen, in press.

Dunn, J., & Kendrick, C. Interaction between young siblings in the context of family relationships. In M. Lewis & L. Rosenblum (Eds.), *The child and its family: The genesis of behavior*(Vol. II). New York: Plenum, 1979.

Edwards, C. P., & Lewis, M. Preschool children's classification of people aged one to seventy into age groups. Unpublished manuscript, University of Massachusetts, Amherst, 1978.

Edwards, C. P., & Whiting, B. B. Dependency in dyadic context: New meaning for an old construct. Paper presented at the annual meeting of the Eastern Psychological Association meetings, New York, April, 1976.

Emmerich, W. Young children's discrimination of parent and child roles. *Child Development*, 1959, *30*, 403–419.

Emmerich, W., Goldman, K. S., Kirsh, B., & Sharabany, R. Evidence for a transitional phase in the development of gender constancy. *Child Development*, 1977, *48*, 930–936.

Kogan, N., Stephens, J. W., & Shelton, F. C. Age differences: A developmental study of discriminability and affective response. *Journal of Abnormal and Social Psychology*, 1961, *62*, 221–230.

Kohlberg, L. A cognitive-developmental analysis of children's sex-role concepts and attitudes. In E. E. Maccoby (Ed.), *The development of sex differences*. Stanford, California: Stanford University Press, 1966.

Kratochwill, T. R., & Goldman, J. A. Developmental changes in children's judgments of age. *Developmental Psychology*, 1973, *9*, 358–362.

Lamb, M. Interaction between eighteen-month-olds and their preschool-aged siblings. *Child Development*, 1978, *49*, 51–59.

Lenssen, B. G. Infants' reactions to peer-strangers. Paper presented at the annual meeting of the Society for Research in Child Development, Denver, April, 1975.

Lewis, M., & Brooks, J. Self, other, and fear: Infants' reactions to people. In M. Lewis & L. Rosenblum (Eds.), *The origins of fear: The origins of behavior* (Vol. II). New York: Wiley, 1974, 195–227.

Lewis, M., & Brooks, J. Infants' social perception: A constructivist view. In L. Cohen & P. Salapatek (Eds.), *Infant perception: From sensation to cognition* (Vol. II). New York: Academic Press, 1975, 101–143.

Lewis, M., & Feiring, C. The child's social world. In R. M. Lerner & G. D. Spanier (Eds.), *Contributions of the child to marital quality and family interaction through the life-span*. New York: Academic Press, 1979a.

Lewis, M., & Feiring, C. The child's social network: Social object, social functions, and their relationship. In M. Lewis & L. Rosenblum (Eds.), *The child and its family: The genesis of behavior* (Vol. 2). New York: Plenum, 1979b.

Lewis, M., & Rosenblum, L. (Eds.). *Friendship and peer relations: The origins of behavior* (Vol. IV). New York: Wiley, 1975.

Lewis, M., & Weinraub, M. The father's role in the infant's social network. In M. Lamb (Ed.), *The role of the father in child development*. New York: Wiley, 1976, 157–184.

Lewis, M., Young, G., Brooks, J., & Michalson, L. The beginning of friendship. In M. Lewis & L. Rosenblum (Eds.), *Friendship and peer relations: The origins of behavior* (Vol. IV). New York: Wiley, 1975, 27–66.

Looft, W. R. Children's judgments of age. *Child Development*, 1971, *42*, 1282–1284.

Mueller, E. (Toddlers + toys) = (an autonomous social system). In M. Lewis & L. Rosenblum (Eds.), *The child and its family: The genesis of behavior* (Vol. 2). New York: Plenum, 1979.

Mueller, E., & Lucas, T. A developmental analysis of peer interaction among toddlers. In M. Lewis & L. Rosenblum (Eds.), *Friendship and peer relations: The origins of behavior* (Vol. IV). New York: Wiley, 1975, 223–258.

Thompson, S. K. Gender labels and early sex role development. *Child Development*, 1975, *46*, 339–347.

Weinraub, M., Brooks, J., & Lewis, M. The social network: A reconsideration of the concept of attachment. *Human Development*, 1977, *20*, 31–47.

Whiting, B. B., & Edwards, C. P. A cross-cultural analysis of sex differences in the behavior of children aged 3–11. *Journal of Social Psychology*, 1973, *91*, 171–188.

Whiting, B. B., & Edwards, C. P. (Eds.). *The effect of age, sex, and modernity on the behavior of mothers and children*. Report to the Ford Foundation, December, 1977.

Whiting, B. B., & Whiting, J. W. M. *Children of six cultures: A psychocultural analysis*. Cambridge, Mass.: Harvard University Press, 1975.

Youniss, J. Another perspective on social cognition. In A.D. Pick (Ed.), *Minnesota symposium on child psychology* (Vol. 4). Minneapolis: University of Minnesota Press, 1975.

13

The Changing American Family and Its Implications for Infant Social Development: The Sample Case of Maternal Employment

Michael E. Lamb, Lindsay Chase-Lansdale, and Margaret Tresch Owen

Within the last decade, major changes have occurred in the way psychologists view psychosocial development in infancy. Prominent among these are conceptual advances bringing the realization that infants play an active role in their socialization, and an acknowledgment that the infant's social world is a multidimensional one, comprising relationships with mother, father, sibling(s), and, to an increasing extent, peers.

Consensus regarding the view that infants are not passively socialized has emerged following a series of theoretical papers (e.g., Bell, 1971, 1974; Bell & Harper, 1977; Rheingold, 1969) and the publication of a number of research reports illustrating both how congenital characteristics affect the types of interaction to which infants are exposed (e.g., Thomas & Chess, 1977), and how babies modulate bouts of interaction (Schaffer, 1977). Some of the relevant data were presented in an earlier volume in this series (Lewis & Rosenblum, 1974).

Michael E. Lamb, Lindsay Chase-Lansdale, and Margaret Tresch Owen • Center for Human Growth and Development and Department of Psychology, University of Michigan, Ann Arbor, Michigan 48109.

Opinion has jelled more slowly around the view that the infant's social world is vastly more complex than traditional conceptualizations proposed (Ainsworth, 1969; Maccoby & Masters, 1970). Yet, although there is still disagreement about the claim that the infant's social world is multidimensional, and although there is no unanimity regarding the relative formative significance of the infant's relationships with its mother, father, and sibling(s), there is an emergent consensus that the social world of the young infant is complex indeed. We believe, and many would surely concur, that progress toward understanding the role of early experience in personality development is dependent on appreciating the different yet interdependent influences of the mother–, father–, and sibling–child relationships. For the most part, however, our aim here is not to rearticulate an argument that has been documented and defended elsewhere. Rather, we want to urge that psychologists look closely at the models being proposed today before they become unquestioned tenets like many of the notions of yesteryear.

Three simple questions are all we need ask in reevaluating models of psychosocial development. First, how do psychologists describe the roles played by mothers, fathers, and siblings in sociopersonality development in infancy? Second, how adequately do these conceptualizations depict the social experiences of most young infants in our culture? Finally, if the models are deficient, in what ways might they be improved?

The Essence of the Models: The Nuclear Family

Since Freud's seminal contributions (e.g., 1949; see Ainsworth, 1969, for a review) psychologists have not lacked theories concerning the character and significance of the mother–infant relationship. Although there are major differences among the most popular theories, all principals agreed until recently that the mother–infant relationship was perhaps the single most important factor in psychosocial development.

To our minds, the most fruitful conceptualization of the nature and importance of the mother–infant relationship has been provided by Bowlby (1958, 1969) and Ainsworth (1969, 1972). These theorists have proposed that infants are equipped with a biological predisposition to emit socially significant behaviors whose common characteristic is their utility in promoting proximity to or contact with adults. Adults, attachment theorists hold, are biologically predisposed to respond solicitously to the signals of young infants. The net effect of the baby's and the parent's behavior, thus is to guarantee adult–infant contact and protection of the infant. Infants develop attachments to those who have responded to them most frequently, reliably, and appropriately.

Once attachments have formed, infants use their attachment figures as "secure bases" from which to launch forays into the social and nonsocial environment. Central to the model developed later in this chapter is the proposition that the infant's ability and willingness to interact with the environment is largely a function of the quality of adult–infant attachments. Infants whose attachment figures have been sensitively and contingently responsive appear to have faith in the reliability and predictability of the latter persons. Such babies are called securely attached infants.

The quality of caretaker–infant attachment may influence the child's social development in two ways. First, securely attached infants are more willing to interact with others than those who are insecurely attached. This increases the likelihood that they will have enriching experiences with others. Second, securely attached infants may expand their trust in the reliability and predictability of their caretakers into a generalized trust of people (cf. Erikson, 1950). These two sequelae have been viewed by many as the major developmentally formative aspects of early psychosocial development.

We have argued that the above formulation has to be broadened in two respects (Lamb, 1976, 1978c; Lamb & Stevenson, 1978). First, there is evidence that most infants form attachments not only to their mothers, but to their fathers as well. As far as we know, the same mechanisms govern the formation of attachments to mothers and fathers, so that these data do not necessarily alter the basic postulates of the ethological attachment model. The second change we have urged involves a more substantial amendment to the model, though we believe that it can be viewed as an addition to, rather than a fundamental reworking of, Bowlby's and Ainsworth's position. Essentially, we believe that parents are important in the infant's life not only because they serve as sources of security, but also because they are the participants in most of the baby's social interactions. The *contents* of its experiences with them are surely of formative significance. It is here that the contributions of mothers and fathers may diverge, inasmuch as their behavior is a function of the societally prescribed sex roles that have become aspects of their personality. Mothers and fathers thus serve as models of the ways males and females behave. Females interact largely within a caretaking role, and their play tends to be rather conventional. Males, by contrast, are seldom party to caretaking interactions, and are associated largely with playful interactions, within which males tend to behave vigorously, spontaneously, and somewhat unpredictably (Lamb, 1977a). From very early, furthermore, mothers and fathers encourage their infants to pay especial attention to the same-sex parent. There is suggestive evidence that this facilitates the acquisition of gender-appropriate behavior (Lamb, 1977b).

However differently mothers and fathers behave toward their infants, though, they are both adults, potential caretakers, and sources of security. This assures a large element of similarity in their styles of interaction and in the processes of influence with which they are likely to be associated. Siblings are rather different. They are seldom the focus of dependent or proximity-seeking behaviors (Edwards & Whiting, 1976; Lamb, 1978a) and on all classical criteria one would have to assume that infants are not attached to their siblings. Furthermore, unlike parents, preschool-aged siblings (at least in the West) are expected neither to initiate frequent interaction with nor to socialize with their infant brothers and sisters. As a result, direct interaction (involving bouts in which preschoolers and infant siblings focus their social behaviors on one another in a mutually contingent fashion) occurs rather infrequently. Despite this, we believe that infants may learn a great deal from their siblings. Most obviously, preschool-aged siblings facilitate toy play and provide models of ways in which objects in the environment can be utilized (Lamb, 1978a; Rubenstein & Howes, 1976). Imitation of behavioral roles may also be important (Sutton-Smith & Rosenberg, 1970) since children appear to be the major influences on the acquisition and modulation of sex-appropriate and aggressive behavior (cf. Hartup, 1976). In humans, as in rhesus monkeys, it seems that the adult and peer interactional systems comprise relatively independent sources of influence on the development of infants and toddlers (Lamb, 1978b; Suomi & Harlow, 1975, 1978; Suomi, 1979).

How Veridical Is the Formulation?

With some exceptions, we believe that the above model may provide a useful framework for research on the social development of infants raised in intact nuclear families within which caretaking and breadwinning roles are traditionally allocated. The model is deficient, however, when applied to cases in which the child's mother seeks extrafamilial employment and so is not a full-time caretaker, and it is surely inadequate when applied to single-parent families. Are these significant deficiencies in a theory of contemporary psychosocial development? Unfortunately, there is good reason to believe that they are.

The Changing "Ecology of Childhood"

Urie Bronfenbrenner, our latter-day Paul Revere, quickened the pulse of social scientists a half-dozen years ago with his Cassandra tale of imminent social collapse (e.g., Bronfenbrenner, 1975). His message was simple: the major social institution involved in childrearing, the family, was under stress. In one respect, Bronfenbrenner's mission was remarkably successful, for in the last few years the lonely refrain of one psychologist has been replaced by a cacophony of social scientists singing in discordant harmony. The traditional family, they all agree, is in danger of joining the extended family as a thing of the past.

Clearly, the social ecology of childhood has changed, and the changes have been dramatic. Two sociological developments have elicited most comment: the rising rate of divorce, which has markedly increased the number of children being raised in single-parent families, and the increase in the number of working mothers. The statistics alone are impressive. Eighteen percent of the children (0–18 years) in the country live in single-parent families. No longer are marriages being sustained for the sake of younger children; 15% of the children under six, and 13% of those under three live in single-parent households. Traditional societal and judicial prejudices ensure that the majority of the children in single-parent families are being raised solely by their mothers.

In part, the ranks of working mothers have been swollen by the number who have been forced to work in order to surmount the economic straits imposed by single-parenthood. Thus, 67% of single mothers with school-age children, 54% of those with preschoolers, and 45% of those with children under three work. The preponderance of those who work (> 80%) have to work full-time. This is not the whole story, however. While the rates remain lower than for single mothers, an increasing number of married mothers are seeking employment outside the home; 51% of those with school-age children, 33% of those with children under 6, and 30% of those with infants and toddlers, are active and permanent members of the labor force.

More impressive than these statistics, moreover, are the accelerating rates of change. Within the last generation, both the proportion of children in single-parent families, and the proportion of children whose mothers work have doubled. If present trends continue, we are likely to witness some of these rates (especially those relating to the under-threes) doubling again within the 1980s.

These figures have been cited so frequently within the last few years that they no longer elicit the incredulous gasps that first greeted them. We present them again, albeit briefly, because we believe that social scientists have failed to address themselves to the central questions these statistics raise. The computation of statistics such as these should be the task of demographers, not psychologists. It is our responsibility to determine what consequences these social changes are likely to have, and in this respect the performance of developmental psychologists has been less than inspirational. In the main, they have simply reiterated the assumption that the effects must be harmful. None have heeded Bronfenbrenner's plea for description and assessment of the ways in which demographic trends are translated into individually significant changes in the socialization process.

It is, we believe, unreasonably parochial to propose that any deviation from the traditional context of socialization must have "harmful" consequences for young children, and it is premature to evaluate the consequences of social changes before making any explicit attempt to elucidate the processes whereby their impact on individuals will be mediated. Our goal in the present paper is to provide a partial remedy for this deficiency. We have chosen to deal exclusively with the effects of maternal employment upon the nexus of relationships surrounding the infant because space constraints prevent us from undertaking a more exhaustive analysis. We would rather do justice to the complexity of issues involved in assessing how maternal employment may affect infants in intact families than provide a panoramic but shallow view of all the ways in which changes in the context of child-rearing impact individuals.

DECIDING WHETHER AND WHEN TO WORK

Previous considerations of the effects of maternal employment on young children have addressed the question, Of what are children being deprived? We suggest that it would be more fruitful to assess what the experiences of the children really are. Concern with this issue leads rapidly to a realization that the children of working mothers are exposed to any of a remarkably heterogeneous array of experiences. The couple's attitudes regarding maternal employment, their attitudes regarding child development, "macro" societal factors that reinforce or enforce their decisions and behaviors, and the characteristics of the child all influence the types of interaction the parents have with their infants and the types of care provided by others. In this section we will discuss each of these considerations with a view to elucidating their probable effects on infant social development. We shall relate our analysis to the process variables of the "nuclear family model" outlined in the preceding section: Our aim is to account for individual variation along these dimensions. Broadly speaking, the nuclear family model proposes that there are two major dimensions of parental behavior that have long-term implications for the child's development. First, each parent's behavioral *sensitivity* is the key determinant of the quality or security of the attachment relationship each will establish with the infant. In our view, at least four types of maternal attitude relating to employment affect the sensitivity of a mother to her baby's signals: self-esteem and self-fulfillment, commitment to the infant, perceived effectance, and guilt. Their roles will be discussed extensively in the pages that follow. Second, the content of the interaction between each parent and his/her infant is *typed* in accordance with the parent's *sex*, thus assuring the infant of easily distinguishable models of masculine and feminine behavior. The parents' subsequent efforts to ensure maximum salience of the same-sex parent may play a crucial role in the establishment of appropriate gender identity.

In our attempt to specify how the maternal employment decision influences the child, consequently, we will focus on sensitivity and the content of social interactions. We should emphasize, furthermore, our conviction that a decision process like the one we describe occurs in the majority of American families today, regardless of whether the woman chooses to be full-time caretaker and housekeeper or decides to work outside the home as well. In both cases, maternal and paternal attitudes about career and family roles affect the nature of the infant's formative experiences and relationships.

The Parents' Attitudes about Maternal Employment

For increasing numbers of women, self-esteem and feelings of self-fulfillment are based on satisfactory performance within a chosen career as well as fulfillment of the demands of traditional femininity.[1] Regardless of the traditionality of one's attitudes, however, individuals certainly differ in the degree to which parenthood is personally valued. We believe that high evaluation of parenthood implies that parenthood is sought for internal rather than external reasons. Thus, parenthood is less valued by those who have children "because it is expected" (since they are acting in response to external societal pressures) than by those who have internalized a need to become and succeed as parents in order to feel fulfilled. It is important to recognize that evaluation of parenthood and evaluation of work vary independently of one another.

Differences in the individual's commitment to traditional and nontraditional goals, and differences in the value of parenthood obviously influence decisions about maternal employment. So too do a number of other factors. However much a woman perceives herself as nontraditional, though, the onset of pregnancy and the preparation for parent-

---

[1] Unfortunately, we know relatively little about the determinants of nontraditional gender orientations. We presume that they develop over the many years of socialization and that they are affected by the nature of the woman's experiences in the world prior to pregnancy and parenthood.

hood have a profoundly traditional effect on most couples (Cowan, Cowan, Coie, & Coie, 1977; Lamb, 1978d). Nurturant maternal behavior is so integral a part of the societal definition of femininity that the pregnant woman cannot avoid the converging societal expectations and pressures to become a full-time mother. In addition, uncertainty about the anticipated role leads women to seek traditional models who offer examples of the "safest" appropriate behavior (Perloff & Lamb, 1978). One consequence is a reevaluation of the woman's relationship with her own mother, leading to a more empathic understanding of the role and responsibilities of motherhood (Arbeit, 1975).

Together these factors ensure that most women face a difficult decision about how to combine maternal and employment roles. Although nontraditional aspirations are likely to be strongest among professional women whose prestigious occupations lead them to derive substantial self-esteem from their career-performance, we believe that a conscious and often difficult decision must be made by most childless young women in America today. Popular and professional debates have placed the issues in the public eye, while the technology of contraception has been developed to such a degree that pregnancies are increasingly likely to be planned rather than fortuitous. As a result, parenthood is likely to occur by choice, and it is likely to be the center of far-reaching family decisions.

Whether a woman with nontraditional motivations will return to work has much to do with her husband's attitudes as well as her own. Most obviously, a mother is more likely to resume employment if her husband is supportive of her career aspirations. In addition, his attitudes and behavior will influence how well the family is able to adjust to the wife's attempts to combine employment and maternal roles, and how satisfied the mother feels with her performance of the maternal role. A husband who shares his wife's nontraditional attitudes is more likely to help with housekeeping and child-rearing, whereas a husband who disapproves of his wife's decision to work is unlikely to assist in these regards (Hoffman, 1977). As a result, his wife may be forced to fill homemaker, maternal, and professional roles without her husband's assistance. Indeed, some degree of paternal resentment is likely, given the evidence that men tend to have more traditional attitudes about women's roles than women themselves do (e.g., Araji, 1977). Couples who share traditional values are unlikely to find the decision for the wife to remain at home a difficult one. Their crisis is likely to come if the wife is forced to work for other reasons.

Marital conflict concerning role expectations will affect not only what decision is made, but also how the working mother subsequently evaluates her decision. When both parents believe that the wife's need to fulfill career aspirations is important, the woman is less likely to feel that her decision was prejudicial to the baby than is a woman whose unsupportive husband subtly or unsubtly communicates his belief that her decision was selfish, inappropriate, and maternally negligent. The fact that maternal employment has only become widespread within the last few years ensures that most working mothers feel some apprehension about their decision; an unsupportive husband, however, can change doubtful anxiety into agonizing guilt. Guilt about one's nontraditional aspirations is the first of the mediating variables we plan to discuss.

Guilt, defined here very specifically as concern about whether one's life-style is fair to one's infant, is perhaps the most commonly discussed construct in the maternal employment literature (e.g., Hoffman, 1974), and it is the only one of our mediating variables that is likely to occur only among working women. The degree of guilt experienced by a working mother will be positively related to the difficulty of the decision to work, and the extent to which the parents' role is perceived as important. Individual guilt will be exacerbated by the unsupportive attitudes of husbands and peers, and by the feeling that one's performance as a mother is ineffective. Although guilt should function to focus the mother's attention on the infant when mother and baby are together, we believe that the net effect will be counterproductive. Women who feel guilty about "abandoning" their infants are likely to overcompensate when they are with their babies, overstimulating them and dominating interactions to such an extent that the infants' role in social interaction is compromised. In addition, guilt-ridden women are likely to overinterpret infant cues. Both of these strategies will render mothers insensitive to infant signals, and this will make it difficult for secure attachment relationships to develop.

A second mediating variable, self-esteem, is related to the traditionality of a woman's orientation as well as the degree to which she values parenthood. *Self-esteem* involves meeting the requirements of and succeeding in the personal goals to which one aspires, that is, it results from the experience of self-actualization. For a traditional woman, high self-esteem may be obtained and maintained by being successful in the roles of wife, mother, and homemaker. The nontraditional woman, meanwhile, is unlikely to feel fulfilled unless she pursues the career of her choice as well as her family roles. This makes the maintenance of self-esteem more complex for the nontraditional mother. The urge to maintain her career not only speeds her return to work, but also colors the nature of mother–infant interaction prior to as well as consequent to the resumption of work. If re-employment is delayed too long, most women may miss the activities and the social contacts that employment brought. In addition, professional women may be concerned that their absence from work will harm their professional reputation. In both cases self-esteem may be placed at risk. Our prediction, that low self-esteem reduces parental sensitivity, is predicated on the assumption that a woman who feels fulfilled is freed from self-destructive introspection and is able to focus empathically on the needs and emotions of others. Consequently, we suggest that the quality of interaction between a nontraditional mother and her infant may actually improve following the woman's return to work. Similarly, one would expect low self-esteem and thus reduced sensitivity among nontraditional women whose decision to stay home is determined by unsupportive husbands and peers.

The nontraditionally motivated woman who feels unfulfilled because her career is being jeopardized by full-time motherhood is also likely to resent her infant and its insistent demands on her. *Resentment* is inimical to the sensitive empathic monitoring of infant signals and the execution of appropriate and contingent responses that are critically important in the formation of secure attachment.

Macro-Societal Factors

The attitudes and aspirations of the woman and her husband have to be viewed in the context of the society in which they live. Macro-societal factors such as peer-group attitudes and the financial viability of the family affect the implementation of attitudes toward work as well as the manner in which these are evaluated. As noted earlier and elsewhere (Perloff & Lamb, 1978; Lamb, 1978d), there remain societal expectations that a pregnant woman should withdraw from work and become a full-time housewife and mother. The nontraditional woman will find defense of her decision to continue a career easiest when her immediate reference group consists of individuals who share her goals and motivations, and who have, like herself, returned to work after a brief maternity leave or else plan to do so. Such a woman is comforted by the fact that her friends have made compatible decisions, are translating those decisions into child-bearing and -rearing practices, and provide evidence that these decisions are damaging to neither infants nor their marriages. They also identify what problems to expect, and what resources are available for their resolution. By contrast, in the absence of peer-group backing, a woman may find herself isolated from friends at a time when their support is maximally necessary. This situation is likely to exacerbate guilt about seeking employment because the societal expectations are made especially salient to the individual via her peers. For the woman who decides not to work, of course, peer-group attitudes are also salient. Nontraditional friends may lead the woman to feel unfulfilled or resentful of her baby, especially when the decision not to work was a difficult one.

Second, economic considerations are increasingly salient in contemporary America. For a large number of women today, the major decision is not whether to work, but whether to accept a lower standard of living. Many women feel compelled to work regardless of their attitudes, because of their families' economic precariousness. The effects are likely to be similar regardless of the woman's attitudes. Without economic constraints traditional women may feel so guilty that they would not work. Nontraditional women, meanwhile, have yet another justification for their decision. They may be comforted by the knowledge that their decision was essentially altruistic ("the family needs the money") rather than selfish ("I must fulfill myself").

Implicit Theories of Child Development

Individual and consensual attitudes toward maternal employment comprise a complex set of related considerations affecting the woman's decision and her evaluation of it. Another important component of the decision process concerns the parents' attitudes about their role in child development.

Two extreme positions define the continuum along which parents can be arrayed. At one extreme are those who believe that development is governed by a maturational timetable, and that it proceeds largely independent of variations in environmental stimulation and parental input. Adherence to this belief involves a perception of the parents' roles as relatively unimportant, apart from providing basic caretaking and affection. Nontraditional motivations can be fulfilled without extensive guilt by those whose implicit theory is maturational. The decisions about whether to work, when to resume work, how much to work, and what sorts of substitute care to arrange are all much easier.

At the other extreme, there are those who believe that the social and nonsocial environments (both of which are composed of or chosen by the parents) mold development from infancy onward. Infants need to be frequently stimulated and showered with opportunities for playful, affectionate interaction if they are to attain psychological health. Environmentalist parents believe in the importance of stimulation but do not necessarily believe that they must be the ones who provide it, since what is crucial is the proper arrangement of the environment. Either decision about maternal employment may thus be compatible with the environmentalist view.

The midpoint between these two extreme implicit theories of child development represents a combination of the two viewpoints, an interactionist theory. Parents who are "interactionists" believe that infant development is a result of both the infant's maturation and the parents' influences. These parents will be appreciative of individual differences and will shape their interactions accordingly. While they believe that their influence as parents is important, they also maintain a certain flexibility toward their infant's own propensities. An interactionist may believe in principle that persons other than parents can provide the necessary experiences. She or he may doubt, however, that another person could be as highly motivated to monitor the infant's abilities and propensities. This sensitive monitoring is viewed as essential if experiences are to be timed in accordance with individual and developmental differences in order to optimize their impact. Such persons are faced with an especially difficult decision if their attitudes are nontraditional, since their working may limit their participation in interactions that they view as critically important. Many are likely to postpone career plans in deference to the baby's perceived needs, and however much they miss their work, some may avoid a decline in self-esteem since they believe that what they are doing is important.

The woman's implicit theory of child development and the extent to which she values parenthood together exert a major impact on maternal sensitivity. The highest sensitivity will occur in a person whose implicit theory is interactionist and for whom parenthood is highly valued. Such a person may believe that the parents play a crucial role in ensuring that the infant's experiences are appropriate for its individual needs, propensities, and stage of growth. One might expect somewhat lower sensitivity on the part of the environmentalist whose belief in experience disregards individual differences among infants and developmental changes in infant needs. Such parents may be overzealous in their attempts to shape the infant to meet their own needs and goals. For example, an extreme environmentalist who wishes to return quickly to work may try to force the baby into a schedule that is convenient to her work schedule. This mother would be the maturationist who sees the environment and her particular behavior toward the infant as unimportant to development.

Sensitivity can be high regardless of the mother's work status and regardless of the traditionality of her attitudes and life-style. The non-traditionally oriented mother may display her commitment either by choosing to stay home with the infant (which may or may not lower her self-esteem), or by carefully timing the return to work to mesh with the baby's stage of development, being especially careful in the choice of substitute care arrangements, and monitoring the infant's adaptation to the family's work situation. A highly committed mother is likely to think seriously about the possible implications of her working decision for the infant, and will thus closely monitor its adjustment to the arrangements, and monitoring the infant's adaptation to the family's work situation. A highly committed mother is likely to think seriously about the possible implications of her working decision for the infant, and will thus closely monitor its adjustment to the arrangements made for its care and be especially involved with and attentive to the infant when they are together.

A nonworking mother who values parenthood highly and who is an interactionist would be careful to ensure that housekeeping tasks and community activities do not compromise the best interests of the infant. She would aim to be accessible, cooperative, and sensitive (cf. Ainsworth, Blehar, Waters, and Wall, 1978). An interactionist view, then, appears destined to maximize maternal sensitivity, regardless of maternal employment status.

Characteristics of the Infant

Individual and societal attitudes about career satisfactions and motherhood and implicit theories of development affect the decision process prior to the baby's birth. In many cases, we suspect, a tentative decision about maternal employment has been reached, based on these considerations, prior to parturition. Nevertheless, expectations are invariably unrealistic, and a reevaluation of the decision early in the child's life is almost inevitable. At this stage, a fourth set of variables impact the decision process, the child's characteristics.

Most obviously, the decision to work is transformed from consideration of the fate of hypothetical organism to a decision about a demanding, personally appealing individual. Most parents are elated with their infants, develop strong affectionate bonds very rapidly, and are at pains to discern individual differences in the appearance of their infants. The emotional commitment to the baby may make it difficult for some women (especially those who subscribe to an interactionist view of developmental determination) to follow through on their decision to work. On the other hand, bonding may facilitate the wife's employment in cases where the father is especially and unexpectedly moved by the experience of parenthood, and becomes willing to adjust his own life-style and career-trajectory to assist in caretaking.

All infants, of course, are not equivalently healthy or attractive, and the parents' desire to care for their infant may be sorely strained. Sick, premature, and otherwise unattractive infants, as well as those whose temperament is difficult, are particularly likely to elicit ambivalent emotions in their parents. Parke and Sawin (1975) and Corter, Trehub, Boudykis, Ford, Celhoffer, and Minde (1977) have shown that reliable assessment of attractiveness can be achieved by parents and nurses in the neonatal period, and that infants receive less attention from people who view them as unattractive. We have shown (Frodi, Lamb, Leavitt, Donovan, Neff, & Sherry, 1978) that the cries and facial characteristics of premature infants are perceived as more aversive than those of full-term infants. Indeed, simply describing a stimulus baby as "premature" led parents to perceive it as more aversive than the same baby described as normal (Frodi, Lamb, Leavitt, & Donovan, 1978). This may explain why Cohen (1977) found that the mothers of the smallest premature babies (i.e., those *most* in need of intensive solicitous care) chose to work more frequently than the mothers of larger babies. The smaller prematures may have been especially unappealing to their mothers, who thereupon sought escape in employment.

Finally, temperamental differences may also be salient. Difficult infants are notable for emotional lability, irritability, arrhythmicity, and inconsolability (Thomas & Chess, 1977; Carey, 1970). Experimental evidence indicates that mothers who perceive their babies' temperaments as difficult fail to respond to changes in infant signals; they have come to regard infant cues as signals not requiring immediate attention, and they are physiologically and behaviorally less sensitive (Donovan & Leavitt, 1977; Donovan, Leavitt, & Balling, 1978). Parents report less sympathy for crying babies labeled as "difficult" than for "normal" infants (Frodi, Lamb, Leavitt, & Donovan, 1978).

These characteristics of difficult infants are likely to make their caretakers feel frustrated, as well as relatively helpless and ineffective (Eichler, Winickoff, Grossman, Anzalone, & Gofseyeff, 1977). The frustration, we suspect, decreases the relative value of caretaking vis-à-vis working, while perceived ineffectiveness may lead a woman to feel that she is not accomplishing anything and thus might as well return to work. By contrast, the mothers of easy babies may regard their experiences as particularly rewarding, and they may interpret their infants' responsiveness and positive emotional state as reflections of the babies' appreciation of their ministrations. This could assure the traditional woman that her decision not to work was appropriate and that mothering is fulfilling, while it could lead a woman with nontraditional motivations to believe that her baby is sufficiently robust emotionally to be left with others. (Indeed, the sociable easy baby will likely appear to interact with others.) It is clear that the women's implicit theories of development as well as the traditionality of their attitudes will determine which of these interpretations is favored.

The crucial mediating variable in this case is what we shall refer to as *perceived effectance*. Perceived effectance refers to a mother's belief that her caretaking is competent and effective, that their interactions are enjoyed by the infant, and that they positively affect its development. Perceived effectance is a complex mediating variable that must be considered in relation to the other variables we have described. Most obviously, perceived effectance will be maximally salient to highly committed interactionists. There are surely a multitude of factors influencing perceived effectance, but perhaps the most salient are the infant's temperament and the caretaker's skill. The mother of an "easy" baby will feel that she is indeed a competent caretaker, for she is able to quiet her baby easily, can see that it enjoys being bathed or fed by her and that it is apparently contented with its lot, since its moods are generally positive and predictable. Grandparents, peers, and husband will respect the woman's skills, thereby reinforcing her self-esteem. By contrast, the mother of a difficult baby may rapidly become disillusioned by her apparent inability to soothe the baby, to predict its rhythms, or to make life for her or the baby pleasurable. She has, in her mind, failed as a caretaker and thus as a mother.

Perceived effectance does not predict whether or not the mother will decide to seek paid employment or remain at home. The nonworking mother who perceives herself to be effective is likely to be content with her decision, in the same way that an effective working mother feels that her decision was not detrimental to the baby or their relationship. By contrast, the ineffective nontraditional woman who chose full-time motherhood may feel doubly unfulfilled (having sacrificed the satisfaction obtained from her job only to find herself incompetent as a mother).

Clearly, perceived effectance has personal meaning very similar to that which we attribute to self-esteem. Its effect on maternal sensitivity is likely to be similar. The effective mother will delight in her success as a parent, and is likely to be open to the infant's needs. The ineffective mother, by contrast, is likely to feel incompetent, frustrated, and—to the extent that she admits failure in her attempts to be an effective parent—is likely to become insensitive. Since the working mother has regular escapes from interactions that depress her self-esteem, her interactional style may be less affected by perceived ineffectance than that of the traditional nonworking mother would be. We should emphasize, furthermore, that the self-ascription of incompetence may be quite inappropriate since the "fault" often lies in the infant rather than in the mother.

Summary

As we have stressed repeatedly, we believe that it is essential to consider each of the above mediating variables when predicting how sensitive a mother will be and thus what sort of attachment she is likely to foster. All contribute in multiplicative fashion. It is clear that the most sensitive mother is one who feels that her aspirations (whether traditional or nontraditional) are *fulfilled*, who *values parenthood*, who as an interactionist, is *committed* to her infant's development, who perceives herself as an *effective* caretaker, and who does *not* feel *guilty* about her employment status nor *resentful* of her infant's dependency. The most sensitive mother is not necessarily the traditional nonworking mother. Likewise, working and nonworking mothers do not comprise homogeneous groups of insensitive (working) and sensitive (nonworking) parents. Consider, by way of illustration, two families in which there is a breadwinner father and a full-time caretaking mother. One woman has traditional motivations while the other is nontraditionally oriented. Assume that the traditional mother has thought less about the relevance of her role in the infant's development so that her commitment is to society's prescriptions rather than to her infant. By contrast, our nontraditional mother may have chosen to postpone her career plans temporarily in the belief that her input is crucial to the infant's healthy development. She is likely to be more sensitive to her infant, and the mother–infant relationship is likely to be more rewarding than that between this traditional woman and her infant.

EMPLOYMENT CONSIDERATIONS AND ALTERNATIVE CARE ARRANGEMENTS

In any comprehensive evaluation of the effects of maternal employment on young children, we need to consider the characteristics of family relationships, the characteristics of the substitute caretaking environments and the caretaker–infant relationships, and the potential for interaction with other children.

Our primary goal in this paper has been to explore the way in which the infant's experiences within its family are affected by its mother's decision about the pursuit of career and family goals. Our analyses would be incomplete, however, if we failed to discuss the alternative care arrangements necessitated by a decision to return to work soon after parturition. Our discussion will be brief, though, for we simply want to demonstrate that some of the factors that determine whether a mother will work, and what sort of relationship baby and mother will establish, also influence the seriousness of the search for an alternative caretaker. We will *not* consider in any detail the dimensions along which substitute caretaking environments can be differentiated, nor the ways in which the substitute arrangement may directly or indirectly affect personality development. These topics deserve a more searching analysis than we have the space to provide here.

The crucial elements in caretaker choice are the parents' implicit theory of child development, their evaluation of parenthood, and the infant's characteristics. Clearly, if the parents feel that a stable, consistent, sensitive caretaker is important, they are likely to choose a babysitter whose personality and experience with children is carefully evaluated. Others may seek the same characteristics in a caretaker, yet also believe that experience with other children is necessary and so they may seek a sensitive family day-care mother. By contrast, if the parents are maturationalists, to whom parenthood is less important, the choice of caretakers will likely be based on personal and practical considerations. On solution might involve hiring a housekeeper who cares for both house and baby. Among less affluent families, meanwhile, the convenience of the location may affect the choice of a substitute caretaker more than the quality of the care does.

Sociable, engaging, and "easy" infants, we suspect, are more likely to have their best interests considered and served by parents eager to ensure that their infants continue to receive the best possible care. Unattractive and difficult infants, by contrast, are likely to receive short shrift, not simply from less sensitive and involved parents (cf. Donovan et al., 1978; Sawin & Parke, 1975) but from caretakers selected less carefully because their parents believe that anyone could do as well as they.

Once decisions regarding child-care arrangements have been implemented, parents will differ in the extent to which they monitor the quality of the care provided. This has implications not only for the extent to which they ensure optimal care, but also for the extent to which the baby's two realms of experience are integrated with one another. Committed parents and the parents of attractive easy infants are especially likely to inquire about the baby's experiences during the day so that they can tailor their interaction in the evening appropriately. In addition, committed sensitive parents will attempt to remain in close contact with alternative caretakers, exchanging information about recent achievements, experiences, mood changes, and so on. These contacts should minimize the extent to which the baby's world is confusingly bifurcated.

The similarity of the caretaker's and the parents' styles of interaction, care, and discipline must have a major bearing on the extent to which the infant's best interests are served by the family's career orientations. Compared with the mothers for whom they substitute, family day-care providers are likely to be older, to have more experience with children, to be more traditional in orientation, and to be less educated (Emlen &

Perry, 1975), but the types of experiences each provides are highly idiosyncratic (Saunders & Keister, 1972).

Finally, realistic evaluation of the quality of substitute care may not be achieved by working women who feel guilty about their decision. Two types of distortions are most likely: the perception of minor variation in the child's behavior as an index of infant response to abandonment, and the unrealistic perception of the substitute caretaker as especially competent, convincing the mother that the decision was in the infant's best interests.

Any adequate assessment of the effects of maternal employment must pay attention to the content and characteristics of the infant's experiences with persons who are not family members, although we will not develop this argument here. We simply want to demonstrate that the parameters of our decision model have implications for the substitute care aspects of the infant's experiences as well. We are pitifully lacking in information about the nature of substitute caretakers' behavior and characteristics, largely because research on maternal employment effects has been guided by the assumption that substitute care *must* be inferior simply because the infant is being deprived of its biological mother's care.

FATHERS, MOTHERS, AND MATERNAL EMPLOYMENT

The four central considerations that we have described affect the nature of the infant's formative relationships with several socializing agents (e.g., father, sibling, extrafamilial caretaker), not simply its mother. It is obviously the case, however, that the most interesting and complex interactions among these factors concern mothers, and that is why we have devoted most of our attention to the mother–infant relationship. At this point, we wish to consider variations in the paternal role within the families of working and nonworking mothers, but will for the most part defer discussion of the influences on paternal sensitivity (see Lamb & Easterbrooks, in preparation).

One obvious area of impact is on the degree of involvement of fathers in child-rearing. Although time-budget studies do not confirm the finding, and although the studies all refer to older children rather than infants, there is fairly consistent evidence that the husbands of working women tend to be more involved with, and closer to, their children (e.g., Hoffman, 1977; Robinson, 1977; Winnett, Fuchs, Moffatt, & Nerviano, 1977). We suspect that paternal involvement will not be much altered when the father does not empathize with his wife's career aspirations or when he tolerates her employment because it is financially necessary, yet feels that his breadwinning role is implicitly threatened and criticized. In fact, the man who disapproves of his wife's career commitment may view his wife's "abandonment" of the baby as justification for his own avoidance of close involvement with the infant. By contrast, paternal involvement may be dramatically and positively affected when the two parents applaud the woman's commitment to her career, and when both believe in the importance of the parents' contribution to child development. Women who have less traditional attitudes about female roles will, we presume, have less traditional attitudes about masculine roles. Thus, both parents may seek involvement in their children's care and development.

Perhaps more important than amount of interaction, however, is the quality of interaction. Our prediction is that the quality of father–infant relationships will be good when the man concerned values parenthood highly and is committed to the interactionist ethic, regardless of the employment status of his wife. Strain seems predictable, though, when the woman has low regard for her effectiveness as a parent for she may resent the relationship between father and children and interpret their closeness as a negative reflection on her role performance. Whatever resolution the couple choose in such circumstances, the children seem likely to lose. If the father withdraws from the children in order to remove the perceived threat to his wife, the children are deprived of a psychologically important relationship. Unlike Pedersen (1975), we do not perceive this as a benign resolution, particularly as there is every reason to believe that the mother will still feel anxious about her role performance. Overcompensating maternal behavior is likely to be even more marked, furthermore, when the husband is unwilling or unable to compromise his relationship with the children.

Maternal Employment and the Content of Mother– and Father–Infant Interactions

The nuclear-family of social development proposes that the mother's interactions with her infant center around caretaking activities and conventional play, whereas the father is minimally involved in caretaking, and engages in physically stimulating and idiosyncratic types of play. These distinctly sex-typed interactional styles are likely to be less apparent in the families of working mothers.

In traditional families, it is not unreasonable for the woman who has been at home with the baby all day to define the evenings as "father's playtime." In the families of working women, however, the husband's attitude about maternal employment may be the key determinant of what sorts of interaction will occur. If the husband shares his wife's nontraditional aspirations, he is more likely to assume some of the housekeeping and child-care responsibilities, reducing his relative availability for carefree play, and increasing her relative availability for interaction with the child outside caretaking contexts. This will reduce the extent to which the mother is identified as "caretaker" and father as "playmate" in the families of working women. On the other hand, if the father does not share his wife's nontraditional (aspirations or when both are traditional and her employment is an undesirable economic necessity), he is unlikely to help much with child care or housekeeping tasks. His wife will have little time for the children outside caretaking interactions, and the traditional maternal and paternal roles will prevail. Motherhood is probably not very rewarding for most of these women.

In traditional families, mother–infant interaction seems centrally related to stereotypically feminine activities whereas father–infant interaction portrays for the infant "masculine roles in action." To the extent that this scenario is likely to be affected by maternal employment we of course wish to know how serious the consequences are likely to be. Women who are not sole caretakers may be more likely than traditional mothers to engage in the types of idiosyncratic play typically associated with fathers. On superficial examination, this suggests that infants in these families may have difficulty distinguishing male and female modes of behavior and consequently that the processes of gender identity and sex-role adoption may be affected deleteriously. We suspect that harmful consequences are unlikely. First, there is no reason to believe that the gender identity of working women is in any way less feminine than that of full-time homemakers. While they may present *nontraditional* models they are still sex-appropriate models. Second, early gender identity appears to depend not on the child spontaneously choosing to identify with the same-sex parent, but upon the same-sex parent becoming more salient in the infant's life, whereupon the latter identifies with its most salient parent. There is no evidence to suggest that this process will be affected by maternal employment, though the results of a current study should clarify this issue.

In sum, then, the nature of the father's role is unlikely to be affected in dramatic fashion by maternal employment. The father's contribution to child development appears to depend on relative differences between maternal and paternal roles within the family, and these relative differences can exist even if the absolute degrees of involvement of the two in child-care roles are not as divergent as in traditional families. One predictable consequence, however, may be that the amount of time between fathers and children increases. This may take over threshold level some men who might otherwise be psychologically absent from their children's lives.

MATERNAL EMPLOYMENT AND THE SIBLING'S ROLE

We have described in this chapter the elements of the employment dilemma faced by families around the time of the first child's birth. As such, the decision model we have presented does not lend itself to analysis of the effects of maternal employment on the nature and importance of the sibling–infant relationship. The sibling's role in dual career families deserves an explicit consideration, however, and it is to this topic that we now turn our attention.

Most obviously, the amount of interaction between an infant and its sibling is likely to change under all alternative care arrangements other than when a sitter or housekeeper is responsible only for the children of one family. When family day care is the arrangement selected, both children can choose among a variety of playmates other than their own siblings, and thus the children are less likely to interact with one another (Lamb, 1978b). The total amount of interaction the infant has with other children is likely to be as much as or more than the amount that would occur if only the sibling was available, and the net effect may be beneficial for the infant. The mixed age group represented in the family day-care arrangement permits the infant to participate in three types of child–child relationships. With age-mates it can interact in an egalitarian fashion: neither child dominates the other. The presence of older children ensures that it is also able to observe and learn socially and cognitively competent behaviors from several children (the sibling included) slightly older than the infant itself. Finally, if there are younger children present, the infant is party to nonegalitarian relationships in which it is dominant. In other words, the social environment in a family day-care home may provide the infant with a richer variety of significant relationships than it would experience in the nuclear-family setting. Providing the arrangement is stable, furthermore, there is every reason to expect both that affectively salient relationships will develop and that the type of interaction will become richer as familiarity increases (Mueller & Vandell, 1979). The individual sibling's role may be diminished, but its function is not compromised.

This may not be true when the children are enrolled in a day-care center rather than an individualized caretaking situation. Although some centers may provide more intensive adult–infant interaction than family day care does, there is a tendency toward structured age-segregation. This facilitates the provision of stimulating activities and protects the younger children from potentially harmful domination by older children. Unfortunately, it also deprives the youngsters of the opportunity to learn from observation of the more competent older children or from supervisory or nurturant interactions with younger children. Konner (1975) has been especially emphatic in his assertion that it is through interaction in mixed-age groups, rather than in the same-age peer group, that children have their greatest impact on the socialization of one another.

The sibling's role is also affected in quite another way by maternal employment. When the older child has been in substitute care itself, the birth of an infant has a far less dramatic impact on the child simply because there is not so powerful a threat to its own central position in the social world. While the parents may indeed by preoccupied with care and admiration of the new infant, the world in which the older child spends much of its day does not suddenly "reject" the child. Indeed, the child may receive additional attention from people excited about the sibling's birth! The fact that the infant's birth does not trigger a marked withdrawal of attention by the only salient adults in the child's life surely reduces the extent of sibling rivalry. This is turn maximizes the likelihood that the children will form a positive and formatively significant relationship. In other words, maternal employment may indirectly ensure more affectively satisfying sibling relationships than would typically occur.

CONCLUSION

The demographic data reviewed earlier suggest that the mothers of young infants are increasingly likely in contemporary America to seek employment outside their homes. In light of these societal changes, our goal in the present chapter has been to describe how the nexus of relationships involving the infant may be affected by maternal employment. Our strategy has been to identify the formatively salient characterisitcs of mother–infant relationships in traditional nuclear families and then assess the manner in which these relationships can be affected by maternal employment.

We have presumed that it is the quality of the mother–child interaction when the two are together that is important, not merely the amount of time they are together, and our aim has been to determine how the infant's development will be affected by its mother's employment. In analyzing the process surrounding employment decisions, we have identified several mediating variables that transform the mother's attitudes into components of interpersonal relations and thus affect the infant's development. Following Ainsworth's recounting of the determinants of secure attachment, the key factor is whether or not the sensitivity of the woman will be affected. We propose that all the major components of the employment decision process are in fact likely to affect maternal sensitivity.

Maternal employment may also affect the types of interaction that come to characterize the mother–infant relationship and distinguish it from the father–infant relationship. Available data about role allocation in the families of working mothers suggest that fairly traditional roles usually prevail. Even when there is a more equitable distribution of caretaking and play times with the infant, this seems unlikely to have deleterious effects on the process of gender-identity acquisition. Provided the child identifies with the same-sex parent we can see no reason why the nontraditional character of the model's behavior should be disadvantageous in comtemporary society. Like the other predictions made in this chapter, of course, we hope that this statement will invite attempts to assess it. It has been our aim throughout to formulate a model that is conceptually reasonable, explicitly falsifiable or verifiable, and heuristically provocative.

Our central conclusion stands in stark contrast to that which has guided the largely tendentious and disapproving discussions of maternal employment in the past. We believe that whether or not a woman decides to work outside the home is in itself of little consequence. What is important is why she made the decision, how she feels about the decision once it has been made and acted upon, what substitute care arrangements are made, and the husband's role in and opinion about the decision.

REFERENCES

Ainsworth, M. D. S. Object relations, dependency, and attachment: A theoretical review of the infant mother relationship. *Child Development*, 1969, 40, 969–1025.

Ainsworth, M. D. S. Attachment and dependency: A comparison. In J. L. Gewirtz (Ed.), *Attachment and dependency*. Washington, D.C.: Winston, 1972.

Ainsworth M. D., Blehar, M. C., Waters, E. C., & Wall, S. N. *The strange situation: Observing pattern of behavior*. Hillsdale, N.J.: Lawrence Erlbaum Associates, 1978.

Araji, S. K. Husbands' and wives' attitude–behavior congruence on family roles. *Journal of Marriage and the Family*, 1977, 39, 309–320.

Arbeit, S. A. A study of women during their first pregnancy. Unpublished doctoral dissertation, Yale University, 1975.

Bell, R. Q. Stimulus control of parent or caretaker behavior by offspring. *Developmental Psychology*, 1971, 4, 63–72.

Bell, R. Q. Contributions of human infants to caregiving and social interaction. In M. Lewis & L. Rosenblum (Eds.), *The effect of the infant on its caregiver*. New York: Wiley, 1974.

Bell, R. Q., & Harper, L. V. *Child effects on adults*. Hillsdale, N. J.: Lawrence Erlbaum Associates, 1977.

Bowlby, J. The nature of the child's tie to his mother. *International Journal of Psychoanalysis*, 1958, 39, 350–373.

Bowlby, J. *Attachment and loss* (Vol. 1). *Attachment*. New York: Basic Books, 1969.

Bronfenbrenner, U. The next generation of Americans. Paper presented at the American Association of Advertising Agencies, Dorado, Puerto Rico, March, 1975.

Carey, W. B. A simplified method for measuring infant temperament. *Journal of Pediatrics*, 1970, *77*, 188–194.

Cohen, S. E. Caregiver–child interaction and competence in pre-term children. Paper presented at the Biennial Meeting of the Society for Research in Child Development, New Orleans, March, 1977.

Corter, C., Trehub, S., Boukydis, C., Ford, L., Celhoffer, L., & Minde, K. Nurses' judgments of the attractiveness of premature infants. Unpublished manuscript, University of Toronto, 1977.

Cowan, C., Cowan, A. P., Coie, L., & Coie, J. Becoming a family: The impact of a first child's birth on the couple's relationships. In L. Newman & W. Miller (Eds.), *The first child and family formation*. Chapel Hill: University of North Carolina Press, 1977.

Donovan, W., & Leavitt, L. Early cognitive development and its relation to maternal physiologic and behavioral responsiveness. Paper presented to the Society for Research in Child Development, New Orleans, 1977.

Donovan, W. L., Leavitt, L. A., & Balling, J. D. Maternal physiological responses to infant signals. *Psychophysiology*, 1978, *15*, 68–74.

Edwards, C. P., & Whiting, B. B. Dependency in dyadic context: New meaning for an old construct. Paper presented to the Eastern Psychological Association, New York, April, 1976.

Eichler, L. S., Winickoff, S. A., Grossman, F. K., Anzalone, M. K., & Gofseyeff, M. H. Adaptation to pregnancy, birth, and early parenting: A preliminary view. Paper presented to the American Psychological Association, San Francisco, Calif., August, 1977.

Emlen, A. C., & Perry, J. B. Child care arrangements. In L. W. Hoffman & I. Nye (Eds.), *Working mothers*. San Francisco: Jossey-Bass, 1975.

Erikson, E. *Childhood and society*. New York: Norton, 1950.

Freud, S. *An outline of psychoanalysis*. New York: Norton, 1949.

Frodi, A. M., Lamb, M. E., Leavitt, L. A., & Donovan, W. L. Father's and mothers' responses to infant smiles and cries. *Infant Behavior and Development*, 1978, *1*, 187–198.

Frodi, A. M., Lamb, M. E., Leavitt, L. A., Donovan, W. L., Neff, C., & Sherry, D. Fathers' and mothers' responses to the faces and cries of normal and premature infants. *Developmental Psychology*, 1978, *14*, 490–498.

Hartup, W. W. Peer interaction and the behavioral development of the individual child. In E. Schopler and R. J. Reichler (Eds.), *Psychopathology and child development*. New York: Plenum, 1976.

Hoffman, L. W. Effects of maternal employment on the child—A review of the research. *Developmental Psychology*, 1974, *10*, 204–228.

Hoffman, L. W. Effects of the first child on the woman's role. In W. Miller & L. Newman (Eds.), *The first child and family formation*. Chapel Hill: North Carolina Press, 1977.

Konner, M. Relations among infants and juveniles in comparative perspective. In M. Lewis & L. A. Rosenblum (Eds.), *Friendship and peer relations*. New York: Wiley, 1975.

Lamb, M. E. The role of the father: An overview. In M. E. Lamb (Ed.), *The role of the father in child development*. New York: Wiley, 1976.

Lamb, M. E. Father–infant and mother–infant interaction in the first year of life. *Child Development*, 1977a, *48*, 167–181.

Lamb, M. E. The development of parental preferences in the first two years of life. *Sex Roles*, 1977b, *3*, 495–497.

Lamb, M. E. Interactions between 18-month-olds and their preschool-aged siblings. *Child Development*, 1978a, *49*, 51–59.

Lamb, M. E. The effects of the social context on dyadic social interaction. In M. E. Lamb,

S. J. Suomi, & G. R. Stephenson (Eds.), *Social interaction analysis: Methodological issues*. Madison: University of Wisconsin Press, 1978b.

Lamb, M. E. The father's role in the infant's social world. In J. H. Stevens & M. Mathews (Eds.), *Mother/child, father/child relationships*. Washington: National Association for the Education of Young Children, 1978c.

Lamb, M. E. The influence of the child on marital quality and family interaction during the prenatal, paranatal and infancy periods. In R. M. Lerner & G. B. Spanier (Eds.), *Child influences on marital and family interaction: A life-span perspective*. New York: Academic, 1978d.

Lamb, M. E., & Easterbrooks, M. A. Individual differences in parental sensitivity to infants: Some thoughts about origins, components, and consequences. In M. E. Lamb & L. R. Sherrod (Eds.), *Infant social cognition*. Hillsdale, N.J.: Lawrence Erlbaum Associates, in preparation.

Lamb, M. E., & Stevenson, M. B. Father–infant relationships: Their nature and importance. *Youth & Society*, 1978, *9*, 277–298.

Lewis, M., & Rosenblum, L. A. (Eds.). *The effect of the infant on its caregiver*. New York: Wiley, 1974.

Maccoby, E., & Masters, J. C. Attachment and dependency. In P. H. Mussen (Ed.), *Carmichael's manual of child psychology* (Vol. 2) 3d ed. New York: Wiley, 1970.

Mueller, E., & Vandell, D. Infant–infant interaction. In J. Osofsky (Ed.), *Handbook of infant development*. New York: Wiley, 1979.

Parke, R. D., & Sawin, D. B. Infant characteristics and behavior as elicitors of maternal and paternal responsivity in the newborn period. Paper presented to the Society for Research in Child Development, Denver, April, 1975.

Pedersen, F. A. Mother, father, and infant as an interactive system. Paper presented to the American Psychological Association, Chicago, September 1975.

Perloff, R. M., & Lamb, M. E. The development of gender roles: An integrative life-span perspective. Unpublished manuscript, University of Michigan, 1978.

Rheingold, H. L. The social and socializing infant. In D. A. Goslin (Ed.), *Socialization theory and research*. Chicago: Rand McNally & Co., 1969.

Robinson, J. P. *How Americans use time: A sociological perspective*. New York: Praeger, 1977.

Rubenstein, J., & Howes, C. The effects of peers on toddler interaction with mother and toys. *Child Development*, 1976, *47*, 597–605.

Saunders, M. M., & Keister, M. E. Family day care: Some observations. Unpublished manuscript, University of North Carolina at Greensboro, 1972.

Sawin, D. B., & Parke, R. D. Infant characteristics and behavior as elicitors of maternal and paternal responsibility in the newborn period. Paper presented to the Society for Research in Child Development. Denver, April, 1975.

Schaffer, H. R. (Ed.). *Studies in mother–infant interaction*. New York: Academic, 1977.

Suomi, S. J., & Harlow, H. F. The role and reason of peer relationships in rhesus monkeys. In M. Lewis & L. A. Rosenblum (Eds.), *Friendship and peer relations*. New York: Wiley, 1975.

Suomi, S. J., & Harlow, H. F. Early experience and social development in rhesus monkeys. In M. E. Lamb (Ed.), *Social and personality development*. New York: Holt, Rinehart, & Winston, 1978.

Sutton-Smith, B., & Rosenberg, B. G. *The sibling*. New York: Holt, Rinehart, & Winston, 1970.

Thomas, A., & Chess, S. *Temperament and development*. New York: Brunner/Mazel, 1977.

Winett, R. A., Fuchs, W. L., Moffatt, S. A., & Nerviano, V. J. A cross-sectional study of children and their families in different child care environments: Some data and conclusions. *Journal of Community Psychology*, 1977, *5*, 149–150.

Author Index

Italic numbers indicate pages where complete reference citations are given.

Abely, P., 115, *123*
Adamson, L., 31, 33, *42*
Ainsworth, M. D. S., 16, 25, 53, 55, 63, *64*, 268-269, 279, 288, *289*
Alexander, J., 47, *65*
Allen, V. L., 136, *140*
Als, H., 31, 33, 35, *42*, 49, *66*, 69, 81, *87*
Ames, L. B., 111, *124*
Amsterdam, B., 108, 111-112, 116, *123*
Anderson, B. J., 50, 59, *64*, *66*, 81, *88*
Anderson, J. W., 190, *192*
Anthony, E. J., 192
Antonis, B., 51, *66*
Anzalone, M. K., 280, *290*
Araji, S. K., 274, *289*
Arbeit, S. A., 274, *289*
Arlman-Rupp, A., 68, 84, *88*
Ashby, R., 41, *42*

Baldwin, J. M., 192
Bales, R., 183, *193*
Balling, J. D., 280, *290*
Barry, W. A., 59, *64*

Baum, C., 115, *125*
Becker, J. M. T., 162, *167*
Becker, W. C., 92, *104*
Beckman, L. J., 139, *140*
Bee, H. L., 68, 92, *104*
Beebe, B., 151, *168*
Bell, K. F., *125*
Bell, R. Q., 87, *104*, 267, *289*
Bell, S. M., 55, 63, *64*, 86, 104, 115
Belmont, L., 133-135, *140*
Bem, S. L., 137, *140*
Bennett, S. L., 151, *168*
Berger, P. K., 133, *140*
Berman, P. W., 263, *265*
Bernstein, B., 68, *87*
Berscheid, E., 129, *140*, *142*
Bertenthal, B. I., 113-114, 116, *123*
Bever, T. G., 121, *125*
Bieber, I., 137, *140*
Bieber, T. B., *140*
Bielert, C., 213, *217*
Bigner, J. J., 138, *140*
Biller, H. B., 49, *64*, 82, *87*

Bing, E., 92, 104, *105*
Blackman, L. H., 59, *65*
Blake, J., 127, 139, *140*
Blatz, W. E., 133, *140*
Blehar, M. C., 279, *289*
Bleier, M. R., 182, 190, *193*
Bloom, K., 67, *87*
Borgatta, E., 183, *193*
Bott, E. A., 133, *140*
Boudykis, C., 279, *290*
Bowen, M., 97, *105*
Bower, T. B. R., 30, *42*
Bowlby, J., 1, 16, *25*, 268-269, *289*
Boyle, M., 115, *125*
Brazelton, T. B., 29, 31, 33, 35, 40, *42*, 49, 62, *66*, 69, 81, *87*, 151, 162, *167*, 188, *193*
Breland, H. M., 135, *140*
Brenner, J., 157, *168*, 174, 177, 181, 187-188, *193*
Bretherton, I., 53, *64*
Brim, O. G., 138, *140*
Brittain, C. V., 133, *141*
Britton, J., 248, *265*

293

Subject Index